Walk Like A Cow

© Brendan Ryan 2020

This book is copyright. Apart from any fair dealing for the purposes of study and research, criticism, review, or as otherwise permitted under the Copyright Act, no part may be reproduced in any manner without first gaining written permission from the author.

Cover image: Alison Girvan

(Ocean Beach, west coast of Tasmania, near Strahan)

Walleah Press
1/4 Floreat Crescent
Trevallyn
Tasmania 7250 Australia
ralph.wessman@walleahpress.com.au

ISBN: 978-1-877010-98-9

Walk Like A Cow

A Memoir

Brendan Ryan

2020

Acknowledgements

The following chapters have been previously published in literary journals.

1. Centre of the world, in *Footy Town: Stories of Australia's game,* ed. Daffey P. Harms, J, Malarkey Publications, 2013
2. Ash Wednesday: a memorial, in *Heat 22,* Giramondo, 2010
3. Walk like a cow, in *Heat 9. New Series,* Giramondo, 2005
4. John Forbes in Carlton, in *Southerly; The lives of others* 78.2, February 2019
5. The killers, in *Southerly; Violence,* The Long Paddock, 2019

This memoir could not have been written without the support and cooperation of a number of people, most notably, my parents, Frank and Mary Ryan, for their memories, stories and long chats about the farm, their lives and our family. Thanks also to other family members who have read earlier versions of the memoir and provided invaluable encouragement. The memoir has been a number of years in gestation and draft form and thanks are due to the following people who have read chapters and provided comments: the late Max Richards (1937-2016), who read a number of chapters as essays and gave invaluable support and encouragement for me to continue with this project, Kate Ryan for her close reading and editorial feedback, Don Watson, Barry Gillard, the editors of various literary journals where some chapters were previously published, Ralph Wessman at Walleah Press for his friendship and willingness to take on another project, and my family Alison Girvan, Lucinda and Ruby for their patience, encouragement and good humour at various stages of the book.

The following poems from previously published collections are included in the manuscript:

1. Morning after, *Why I am not a farmer*, Five Islands Press, 2000
2. I know, I know, *A paddock in his head*, Five Islands Press, 2007
3. Catholic daydreams, *A paddock in His Head*, Five Islands Press, 2007
4. Mother and daughter, *Travelling through the family*, Hunter Publishers, 2012
5. Man on the gate, *Travelling through the family*, Hunter Publishers, 2012
6. Farm boys, *A paddock in his head*, Five Islands Press, 2007
7. Cows in India, *Small town soundtrack*, Hunter Publishers, 2015
8. Milk fever, *Why I am not a farmer*, Five Islands Press, 2000
9. Blister country, *Travelling through the family*, Hunter Publishers, 2012

Other books by Brendan Ryan

Poetry

Why I am not a farmer
A paddock in his head
A tight circle
Travelling through the family
Small town soundtrack
The lowlands of Moyne

Contents

1.	Memory line	1
2.	Dark stars	5
3.	Chased by a tea towel	8
4.	The killers	12
5.	Two rooms	18
6.	Places we went	36
7.	Down to the river	47
8.	The lost world of the walk-through	50
9.	Four women	55
10.	Shadow figures	70
11.	Skull stumps	76
12.	Cows and bulls on the loose	81
13.	The boy in the shadow of the bus	84
14.	Inflated by memory	89
15.	Centre of the world	108
16.	Ash Wednesday; a memorial	118
17.	Farm boys	139
18.	The boundaries of a fruit picker	142
19.	Paringi	147
20.	Killing Beefy	154
21.	Baptised	158
22.	Like walking down a paddock	161
23.	Learning to write, learning to read	166
24.	Toads	176
25.	Songs of longing and drama	191
26.	Walk like a cow	195

27.	Cows in India	205
28.	The open-cut mine	211
29.	A paddock	219
30.	John Forbes in Carlton	227
31.	A town called malice	236
32.	Afterword	241

For my parents

Memory line

I am six years old and walking along the gravel drive that loops around our back yard and past the dairy where the tanker driver collects the milk each day. I walk past the wood heap with chocks of wood scattered beneath the shelter of a fusty cypress tree. Wide logs with axe marks scoring their centres lay facing the day. There are 'chips', our word for kindling, surrounding the logs. The chips are wet and their pale woody colour is darkening from days of rain. I walk on past two forty-four gallon drums lying on their sides. The cattle dogs, Rover and Joe, are chained to iron droppers beside the drums. Their chains rattle on the drums when they come out to greet me. It is a sound of metal scraping on metal that I am familiar with. They can only waddle so far before the length of chain pulls them up sharp. I walk on past the corrugated iron roof of the chook shed. I look at the roof line of the shed which is five feet high and I guess my height against it. I remind myself that when I am as tall as the chook shed, I will be a big boy. I will be grown up. I walk on past coils of fencing wire on the ground; one of the many stashing places on the farm for wire, machinery parts and lengths of poly pipe that resemble snakes part-covered with grass. Next to the coils of wire is a long cylindrical petrol tank that my father and older brother, Mick, use for filling up our lime yellow Valiant station wagon. They pump the petrol by a hand pump into the tank of the car, inevitably spilling petrol on their clothes. The sweet smell of petrol is ever-present when I walk past the tank. Its metal is painted silver with the top showing signs of corrosion. My brothers and sisters and I sit on the warm metal in the afternoon, feel the heat of the sun on our legs and arms. Sometimes I press my cheeks against the metal to inhale the petrol smells. Sometimes we play a game to see who can slide down the tank the slowest and not land on the ground. Sometimes we just sit on the tank to watch the paddocks.

I walk past the grassy teardrop-shaped roundabout that the tanker driver loops around to collect the day's milk. My brothers and sometimes a sister play football on this roundabout well into the dark. At one end of the roundabout is a telephone pole with a cable support anchored at a 45 degree angle into the ground. The triangular space between the pole and the cable support is our goal line. While the cows are being milked at night, we play marathon games; staining our trousers, scraping knees, throwing each other to the ground. We don't need a paddock to test our football skills; the smaller the space, the more skilful we become at ducking and weaving or aiming at the goal from tight angles. Somebody runs into the telephone pole. Somebody runs into the cable. The smell of mud on our palms is similar to the smell of the cow yard; a smell of home that is never far from us.

Across from the roundabout is the machinery shed with its half-moons of dried mud from the tractor wheels at its entrance. Rough-cut poles and sheets of corrugated iron hold the shed together. In strong winds, the sheets of iron lift and groan, creating a jarring music which seems to affect my day. The moan of iron, the squeal of chooks, the caw of crows; the wind is always upsetting things on the farm. The shed is a crowded space with enough room for a Massey Ferguson tractor, benches for tools and a mezzanine platform used for storing superphosphate bags, sacks of crushed oats, machinery parts and more coils of fencing wire. Dad's nuts, bolts and tools are stored in old ammunition boxes. Lengths of pipe stand in a corner beside spades, bars, thistle hoes and rakes. There is an order to the stacking of tools; an order that was begun but forgotten by the need to find a shifter in a hurry. To find the right sized washer is to embark on a mission through dust and grease smells. Smells that I love. I have never been handy with tools and when I am in the machinery shed I am driven by the mystery of not knowing what I might chance upon. Yet when I have nothing to do, I like to spend time in the shed mucking around with a rust-coloured vice – sharpening a mower blade, loosening an elbow join on a galvanized pipe. If anything needs fixing, I remind myself, it might be worth sitting it in the vice and winding the handle tight.

I walk on past the shed to the black cast-iron burner. Each day Mum shoves newspapers, biscuit wrappers and scraps of paper into it. These are the years before recycling. Whenever it is full, the burner is set alight and the toxic smells spiral skyward. A blackened lid keeps the fire contained and a small opening at its base allows us to see how the fire is going. Nearby are the clothes lines Mum uses to hang out the washing. A hills hoist cops the brunt of smoke from the burner. The space around the burner is where my parents often meet on their way to jobs through the day – Dad coming out of the machinery shed, Mum carrying a basket of washing to a clothes line. I listen to them talk about money, shopping, a neighbour or a cousin. Sometimes they talk and turn away when they see myself or one of my brothers and sisters approaching. It is at the burner that I talk to my parents about wanting to leave school in Year eleven, and later on, my idea of moving to Melbourne. It seems to be a place to catch them off-guard and a place where they surprise me with their views on what a girl should do if she becomes pregnant. It's a space where they talk in a different tone to how the priest talks at Mass. Sometimes I listen to them and find out what they don't talk about. A circle of ash keeps the mown grass from the burner. A short distance away is the place where we kill our sheep.

There are memory lines scattered around our house. Some created by myself, some worn down by my brothers and sisters, some followed by dogs. Each line takes me to where I need to go and sometimes where I don't want to. I have been making these lines up all my life. They are reliable as a memory or what I choose my memories to be. I carry a memory with me, like a bullet in a pocket, of what it is like to be six and of being allowed to walk down the paddock alone.

I know, I know

The horizon by the back roads which lead to it
and when we start selling mushrooms in May
our neighbours up the road will follow

My brothers and I know which bull we can't trust
we play sock footy down the hall
as the radio gives the day's footy scores
from Bessiebelle

each night our house is hugged
by the wind
each night our paddocks are interrupted
by lights from the neighbour's dairy
today everything hangs askew

I lay back on the super bags
listening
to dogs dragging their chains
over half-buried bones

Mum walks out into the paddock
hurls tea leaves down the drain
we empty the toilet bucket into

some days I lay under the house
listening to the scrape
of chairs on lino

some days are rosaries that never end

Dark stars

Living on a farm, I was exposed to the intimacy of weather and the closeness of farm animals. Being one of ten children also ensured that my upbringing was different to my friends at school who lived in the suburbs of Warrnambool or in the paved streets of small country towns. Before we renovated our house, I queued up under the stars for the lone outside toilet with my brothers and sisters. The toilet was a thunderbox with spiders and it was a boy's job to empty the tin drum of raw sewage that was positioned beneath the wooden toilet into a drain in a nearby paddock throughout the week. I went to bed listening to rain thrash the tin roof of our farmhouse. I woke to the sound of cows pulling at grass a short distance from my bedroom window. The smell of cowshit was ever-present on the farm; it greeted me as a memory colouring the air whenever I stepped out of a car on my return to the farm from being away. And yet, I imagine that many of the things that I did on the farm with my brothers and sisters were similar to the preoccupations of children in the suburbs. The main difference being that we had plenty of space – four hundred acres to walk in, drive tractors around in and to stare at. When we weren't working on the farm, each of us was looking for ways to pass the time. Time became a second skin that we wore around the farm. Time itched and scratched at us when there was work to be done. Other times it hung like a great cloak around our shoulders weighing us down with its endless routine. Our parents were too busy to take us anywhere such as shopping or going to the beach. We were a family bound by the fences of our farm and the imaginations we worked at; looking to the clouds, the deep blues of summer and the trails of dust from a stranger's car coming down the road.

Night skies on the farm were luminous and breathtaking. The Milky Way blazed overhead stretching across our paddocks and south towards Naringal. Pin pricks of light were scattered across black skies. On cool nights after tea I stood on the gravel lane beside the house and looked up to Orion and other constellations, amazed by the ferocity of their glow, comforted by the regularity of their position. They were cities in the sky, gatherings of celestial light giving shape to the dark that appeared to surround me. However, the lights of other farm houses two or three kilometres away reminded me that I wasn't completely isolated. There were other life forms out there. When the quiet outside the house was disturbed by the sound of cows pulling at grass, the heavy plod of their hooves, or a snort or two, I was reassured. Yet when the cows weren't near the house the darkness clung to me even after my eyes had adjusted to it. I'd imagine presences; shapes or shadows appearing from beneath the cypress trees that towered around the house. I turned around to the glow of the kitchen, its yellow walls, smell the smoke from the fire place and think about this place I called home. I walked back inside to the warmth of voices and laughter, Lassie the cross-breed that looked like a Labrador but was the size of a Daschund sniffing under chairs for food scraps. Yet despite the comfort of our kitchen, the cold darkness of the country night was always out there. It lived in my dreams, had taken on the form of mountains chasing me across paddocks and had been the depthless black I dropped into during those falling dreams. I kept it at bay with the company of my brothers and sisters and later I learnt to accept it as that space between two periods of changing light – dawn and dusk. A space illumined by stars, depthless in its uncertainty.

Sometimes after tea, when I needed some quiet, I sat outside on our front verandah, watching the stars and considering the day. Sometimes my breath was caught by a meteor dropping at an angle across the sky. During summer, crickets and cicadas chirped and sang on the lawn around me. The darkness became a presence I could walk through with ease. My brothers and I kicked a footy until it became dark, or rode motorbikes and push bikes up Vickers Road. Cars rarely passed our farmhouse and if they did, we knew about them. Winter nights were the worst with the wind and rain keeping us inside. I looked out my bedroom window to the darkness that seemed palpable, close and continuous. I looked for that spray of light, those dark stars pulsating like a galaxy taken fright.

Chased by a tea towel

Mum remembers years by the child who was born that year or who she was carrying. With one set of twins and eight children born roughly every two years, twenty years of her life were accounted for by giving birth and bringing up a new child. Part of the deal with having a large family is that Mum and Dad often confused the names of children they were trying to speak to. Dad might ask Brendan, Dennis, Kieran, Michael *get that load of wood from the wheelbarrow*. Annette, Theresa, *here give me that bottle, I'll open it for you*. Mostly the confusion made each of us shake our heads and smile; sometimes it annoyed us. Speaking up for yourself in a large family was always paramount, even more so when you were confused with a younger brother. For the record, here is the family roll call.
AnnetteTheresaMichaelBrendanKathrynDennisDavidPhillipKieranRebecca.
The names ran into each other and so, to an outsider, the distinctions were blurred. But each of us knew the differences, the characters and moods of each sibling. Ten children – it was virtually a footy team.

I was born on December 4, 1963. Mum sanctified each of us with a birth song played on air at 3YB in Warrnambool after we were born. My birth song was The Wild Colonial Boy. An extra child meant an extra mouth to feed and for Dad to maintain his work regimen to bring in the money. After twelve months I started to have febrile convulsions. The first time that I took a fit, Mum didn't know what was happening as I writhed and went red on the floor. She called a neighbour who helped her take me to a local doctor's clinic and then to the Warrnambool Base hospital. Apparently I had stopped breathing for a minute until my temperature calmed down. I would continue taking convulsions intermittently over the next four years. There was a visit by train to a Melbourne specialist when I was four. I can still remember the nervousness and sense of something larger than myself I felt boarding the train at the now closed Panmure train station; the station master extending his red flag, the slowly approaching engine, shadows of cypress trees darkening the platform, one or two other people also waiting and of sitting in a seat, my legs barely touching the floor with Mum on the long journey to the city. I took penicillin daily – a thick, white, sour-tasting syrup until the convulsions stopped when I was five. I have a faint recollection of having a fit when I was sitting in the back seat of our old blue EK Holden. My arms were shaking up and down and I started to lose focus on who was around me. Apart from medication, Mum's other cure was to place me in a cool bath and sponge my forehead to try and bring my temperature down.

I was a middle child in a family of ten. This meant that I was always looking for attention from either of my parents or my siblings. Creating an identity within a family of ten has always been a fraught and lengthy experience. A sense of competition always existed amongst my brothers and sisters as to who a person could be. There could only be one painter, one singer, and one teacher. Each of my siblings at some stage seemed to be defined by their opposition to or similarity to another sibling. While Mick was working on the farm I decided that I didn't want to be a farmer. Annie studied at teacher's college in Ballarat to be a primary school teacher. Theresa married a farmer and so she worked on the farm. I learnt to be a writer by writing about the family around me, and of where I wanted to be – miles away from country people, but in my head, close to the paddocks of the farm. I could never be entirely satisfied because I was always seeking something else that the country couldn't provide. Creating my own version of the country was a way of finding the place that I wanted to be in.

Our family stayed home and sometimes the games we played got out of control. This was always going to be the case with a growing family of six, seven or ten children. There were the typical childhood games: hopscotch on the concrete path in the back yard, tennis on the gravel driveway; a red swing set with a white wooden seat in the front garden, singing concerts for our parents after a bath. What altered my experience of these games was that I imagined they would simply continue on and on. My life on the farm was enclosed by paddocks and a gravel road. Dad was busy ploughing or fixing broken fences and Mum was running between five lines of washing. We dressed up in men's and women's clothes from a black suitcase or rode our bikes around the house until there was mud or dust coating the weatherboards. There was no social media.

However, we could rarely remain outside for long and soon we were running through the house, screaming and shouting; something we were repeatedly told not to do on account of waking the baby. There always seemed to be a baby sleeping in the white bassinette in Mum and Dad's darkened bedroom. If the baby started crying, Mum would shout and chase us outside with a tea towel or wooden stick she used for lifting the washing into the manual washing machine. Outside and running for our lives, the games would change. We played hide and seek in 'the prickly bush' – a large, squat shrub that seemed to expand each year Mum and Dad forgot to prune it. Other hiding places were under a towering Callistemon tree outside their bedroom, or under a tank stand beside the house where dogs dragged their bones and old tennis balls and rags were thrown. Under the tank stand with the cool of the white Mt Gambier Stone bricks around me, I listened for the thud of my brothers and sister's footsteps. It was another world of earthy smells under the tank stand, even more so, under the house where I could crawl beneath the floorboards and listen to Mum's footsteps bouncing between the laundry and the kitchen. I kept a look out for snakes and lizards, but all I found were tennis balls, rags, scraps of plastic and a stillness so different to being inside the house.

Sometimes the games we played became more heightened through our sense of competition and rivalry. Dares were common, if only to relieve the slow drag of school holidays. Before the old weatherboard farmhouse was renovated there was a wooden verandah looking west onto Vickers Road. An old brown upright piano that had belonged to the Vickers family was left on one side of the verandah. Nobody in our family could play and so the piano became something to tinker on, run our fingers along the keys before we moved off into the next adventure. The lower cupboard section of the piano had been damaged and taken away. It was a space small enough for a child to crouch down under the piano keys, and so, it became a perfect hiding place in hide and seek games. However, one afternoon seemed to drag on and our games developed an edge. Somebody had an idea to bash up the piano. Once the call was given, my brothers and sisters and I rushed into the machinery shed, grabbed a hammer and an axe from the woodheap and returned to destroy the piano. We had destroyed other things on the farm, usually our own creations – cubby houses, old buckets, toys and billy carts. There was excitement in the frenzy of wrecking something, an energy that transported us beyond ourselves. We took to the piano with our axe and hammers, laughing at the crash of the soundboard, keys and strings inside. It didn't take long for Mick, Jack and I to push the piano over. After it lay in a crumpled mess sprawled across the verandah – wires and hammers scattered like body parts, we ran inside to tell Mum. Mum always got told of our latest adventure and when she came to see what we had done to the piano, she wasn't smiling. Her face went red and she lost her temper, shouting at us to 'Get out! Get Out!' She chased us with a tea towel down the hallway of the house, shouting at us, as if we were animals who had managed to slip inside.

The killers

One of the essential jobs that we had to do on the farm was to kill a sheep so that our family could have some meat to eat. We ate most parts of the sheep; lamb chops, ribs and liver. Mum boiled the bones into a broth and pan fried the liver for our breakfasts. The liver was a prized delicacy carried into the kitchen, still warm and slippery from the freshly slaughtered sheep. Killing the sheep was a job that involved a certain amount of drama; rousing up my brothers and sisters to help catch the sheep or killers as we called them, the heightened moments of trying to grab one and then the slaughter itself. Once our cattle dogs sensed that a sheep was going to be caught they danced around in circles, wagging their tails, looking to Dad for directions before he shooed them towards the sheep paddock a short distance from our house.

The five or six sheep that we kept sensed that something was about to happen as each of us climbed through the cyclone wire fence and into their paddock. Immediately they ran to the far corner of the paddock to escape our shouts. Joe and Rover, our cross-bred Border Collies, nipped at their hooves while Dad shouted directions to them to drive the sheep into a holding corner next to the pigsty. My brothers and sisters and I formed a line closing in on the sheep. Each of us had a space to guard. We stepped forward slowly with arms outstretched watching their eyes for any sudden movement or change of direction. My heart was racing and it was always a competition amongst my brothers and sisters to see who could grab the killer. Once Dad gave the direction to pounce, each of us lunged forward, our fingers clawing at the fleece as the sheep dived, leapt and squirmed out of our reach. The sheep knew no boundaries and they ran over the backs of their own or one of us to escape what they feared. Once I saw a ram head-butt Dad and give him a blood nose; an act that set him roaring. When the killer was finally caught, it was dragged between Dad's knees up to the paddock gate, all the while the dogs biting its hind legs. The other sheep ran back to the far paddock corner, bunched up and scared of what might happen to them. While the chosen sheep was dragged through the open gateway, the fear in its eyes seemed to darken them. We all stood back, catching our breaths and watching while Dad dragged the sheep towards the killing spot near our clothes line, a patch of dirt stained with the blood of other sheep, flung the killer down on its side and then asked for the knife.

The job of killing the sheep was over in less than a minute but the experience has remained with me. Some things are hard to forget. At first, Dad killed the sheep while my elder brother Mick and I watched and learnt about taking responsibility for what we were eating. But killing a sheep was also an act of demonstrating that I was up to the job, a job I became better at, and thought less about, the more that I did it. It was simply something that needed to be done if we were going to have something to eat. I knelt on the sheep's stomach and neck, my weight keeping the sheep still, while Dad looked on. I took the knife and ran it back and forward along a sharpening stone. The sound of a knife being sharpened on the stone quietened us all. The metallic scraping of the blade, the wriggling of the sheep under my weight, the dogs circling for something to nip at. It was a moment of focus. Once the knife was sharpened and warmed in hot water, the next job was to prise apart the lice-riddled folds of wool, cut the neck and lean my weight onto the sheep to steady the death tremors. To make sure it was properly dead, the sheep's neck had to be broken by pulling its head back against my knee until the neck bones cracked, the eyeballs rolled back and the gagging ceased. Sometimes nerves kicked in and the sheep thrashed its legs after its throat had been cut. It was an odd sight, similar to the chooks running around in circles after their heads had been chopped off with an axe. I stood up, looking down at the bloody gash in the sheep's neck and knew that something had set me apart from my younger brothers and sisters. They would have to look up to me.

After the sheep's neck had been cut, the next part of the job was to skin the sheep; a job that Dad was more skilled in. The first part of skinning the sheep was to cut the fleece free below the neck and pull the wool back so that Dad could push his fist down over the sheep's stomach and separate the wool from the skin. Little nicks were made with the knife along the skin folds as he went so that ultimately he could push his fist down along the sheep's stomach and then pull the wool from the body. The skin was still warm and a certain amount of strength was needed to push and gouge the fleece from the skin. With the fleece removed and the head and hooves severed, the sheep's carcass could be carried over to a cypress tree where a chain and pulley was rigged up to lift the body off the ground.

While the killing and skinning were being carried out, smaller jobs were given to Mick and I, sometimes my brothers Jack and David if they were around. Our sisters had disappeared inside by this stage, and while it was unpleasant work, it was necessary. One job that we had to do was to carry the sheep's head by the ear down to a nearby drain where the cattle dogs could feed on it while the sheep was being disemboweled. It was a weird sensation to carry the head of the sheep away from the body that only moments before had been a sheep feeding in a paddock. Once the head was thrown into the drain, the cattle dogs would pad forward, sniffing at this new treat. Dad and Mick carried the carcass over to the killing tree – a cypress tree with its lower branches cut back to allow a carcass to hang and sway. A curving butcher's bar was inserted between the two hind legs of the sheep and a metal chain was hooked around the bar. Dad or Mick and I pulled on the chain which lifted the sheep into the air. After we had lifted the sheep to a height that made it easy for Dad to cut its stomach open, the chain was anchored to a tree limb and Dad set about his business.

The intestines, organs and stomach flopped out after the sheep had been sliced down the middle. The sky blue intestines swirled around the liver in the dirt and the first thing Dad did was to cut away the liver and pass it to myself or Mick to then carry it inside on the red-dotted chopping board for mum. The brown liver was still warm and it swirled and slid on the chopping board as we ran inside shouting, 'Mum. Mum. I got the liver!' Mum rushed to the back screen door, shooing away flies and ushered us inside to drop the liver into the sink where she washed it, laid it on a plate covered by a tea towel and placed it in the fridge. The next morning we could have fried liver for breakfast.

My next job was to drag the stomach and intestines down toward the drain where the dogs could continue their feast. This was a heavy job and even with two of us dragging the sheep's guts away, Mick and I had to stop for breaks to try to get a better grip on the slippery stomach and gizzards of the sheep. Looking down at the sheep's stomach and intestines made me wonder how a sheep could carry such weight around inside their bodies. Often there would be pieces of organ or intestines left behind on our journey to the drain; scraps that the dogs and cats could later clean up. Together, we hurled the stomach into the drain and stood back to watch the dogs paw at the intestines. The water from the drain flowed into Mt Emu Creek, a distance of two paddocks away. In summer, the drain was mainly dry and the dogs could chew on the stomach and intestines undisturbed and leave what was left to the circling crows. There was always a bucket of warm water nearby to wash our hands when we returned and to clean the knives. Inevitably, blood would be spilled on our clothes and boots. But that was sheep's blood; blood that could be covered with cowshit from milking later in the day. I wiped the blood from my hands on my trousers and watched Dad, waiting for him to parcel out the next job.

After the sheep had been gutted and cleaned, a pointed stick was wedged in the stomach to keep the sides apart and to allow air to circulate. The last thing that we wanted was off-meat. A white sheep bag was then fitted over the carcass to protect it from flies. The sheep bag was blood-stained and kept in the machinery shed away from the house. Depending upon the weather, the carcass would often be left for a day or two before Dad would pull it down and cut it up. The sight of the sheep swaying in the sheep bag under the cypress tree used to give me the chills, especially at dusk when the body hung there like a human body. The following morning revealed what we had done the day before. A sheep had been transformed into a hunk of meat swaying in a white bag under a cypress tree. Such were the equations of farming. When the sheep was ready to be cut up, Dad cut it down the middle of its spine with a hack saw. Half of the sheep was carried over his shoulder to the chopping block – a round slice of a tree trunk just outside our back screen door. The surface of the chopping block was scored with knife cuts and stained with sheep's blood. It was also the place where chooks' heads were severed, rabbits skinned and gutted and where my brothers and sisters played King of the Castle. Dad hacked the sheep into smaller pieces that could be slid into freezer bags to be kept in our Deep Freeze. Some of the sheep's bones would be brought into the kitchen for Mum to make bone soup.

Once the sheep had been cut up and put away, the next job was to deal with the sheep skin. Immediately after the kill, the skin was slung over the two metre high chicken wire fence of our chook run and left to dry out before it was sold to the 'sheep man' for $1.00 a skin in Warrnambool. When the skins were fresh, scraps of fat and blood trails were left on them and the wet skins always attracted crows and magpies to circle and pick over them. Usually the birds flew off when we walked out and shouted or clapped our hands at them. The 'sheep man' was a company in Warrnambool who tanned and dyed the skins. Occasionally a man from the company drove around farms to pick up skins, but we usually bundled two or three sheep skins into a bag and drove them into Warrnambool on shopping days. The smell of the skins from the back section of our station wagon was over-powering, but it was a farm smell we only had to put up with for twenty minutes. Once a month we killed a sheep, sometimes more often during school holidays when there were more regular mouths to feed. Like many of the jobs that we did on the farm, it was a job that seemed necessary at the time.

Being introduced to violence through farm work at an early age possibly helped me to see the world in a clear-eyed way. The division between life and death could be brief or arbitrary. I saw calves come into the world and with an axe I took feeble calves out of this world. Sometimes cows had calves in the paddocks that were too small to rear or were born with twisted or broken legs. Often the solution was to bring these sickly calves to the cowyard, fetch the axe and knock the calf on the head with the blunt end of the axe. It was a job that I didn't enjoy doing as I swung the axe between my legs at the head of the calf. The thud of the axe on the calf's head brought death quickly to it and the next job was to drag the dead calf down to the bull paddock drain for the crows and dogs to eat. Not that violence is necessary on a dairy farm. It is more that sometimes it became a quick-fix solution to problems that we were too isolated to fix. I was always sympathetic to the suffering of animals and winced whenever Dad whacked the cows in the dairy with a length of poly pipe. In time, I also whacked the cows on their backs with poly pipe when things were not going my way. The things we did on the farm were not defined by violence or the rough treatment of animals. They were the jobs that we had to do. Dirt, dust, cowshit and blood were daily parts of our lives, as were the starlit skies, the knowledge we acquired and the place I created for myself amongst ten children on a dairy farm in the Western District.

Two rooms

Recently I returned to the farmhouse that I grew up in. It was unnerving as I opened the back screen door and stepped into the hallway of the house. Wherever I looked my mind created a memory; of what had been there before, my association with a particular space while I was being dislocated from the house by its silence. No more shouts or jibes from my brothers and sisters. No longer did Mum walk across my field of vision carrying a basket of washing. I felt like an intruder with an inside knowledge of the rooms that was no longer relevant. I felt like a robber.

I walked into the rooms looking at what had become of the house that had shaped my past. I flushed the toilet, noticed bugs and dead flies scattered over the kitchen lino tiles. The fire-place where I had spent so many nights talking to Mum and Dad or sat turning side-on to watch TV, it was boarded up. Perhaps it is better to close a door on the past. Yet when I walked into one of the front bedrooms, 1973 came flooding back to me – of summer light, listening to Elvis on the record player, three single beds with a brown wardrobe lined up against pale lemon walls. The house was like a photo activating the good memories. I would need time on my own to understand those other ones. I took some photos and tried to understand how the life I had lived here before was no more. There were few traces of the family and the person I had been. Just the shell of a house bringing up memories; the good, the bad and the others that I had to rely on.

The kitchen was the life-force of the house. It was where we hung out as a family, where we watched TV and where we kept warm. A pale sliding door retained the heat from the fire-place and kept the cold night outside. Whenever someone stepped out of the kitchen to go to the toilet, which was off the back hallway, the temperature would drop by five degrees. The warmth of the kitchen enclosed us and kept the backs of legs warm whenever someone stood in front of the fire. Although each of the five bedrooms was equipped with a small bar heater and a larger electric heater was located in the lounge, the bedrooms were paddock-cold.

The kitchen was unassuming and a large aluminum window faced east allowing a view of the cows filing away from the dairy each morning and night. If I concentrated I could identify the two pine trees standing sentinel near the boundary of our back paddock. The trees represented the outer reaches of the farm and a type of boundary that I learned to stare against. From an early age I had acquired the knack of looking long distance over the paddocks, checking on cows, a heifer that might have escaped or whether the cows needed shifting from the paddock of rape. It was a way of looking that Dad had unconsciously given to us by the gaps in his talk when he would look away from us and down the paddock to the cows. It was almost a dreaming look, or a day-dream look, of attention being focused elsewhere. The view from the kitchen window was also a way of measuring time. When the cows were plodding up the track it was time for Mum to drive us to the bus stop. Alternatively, when the cows were leaving the dairy at night, it was time for Mum to put the tea on and for the children to begin setting the table. I learned a lot by what I saw from the kitchen window. It was a way of opening up spaces, of peering up at the vastness of the sky. In the early years on the farm, a row of old cypress trees bordered our backyard. The spread of their branches concealed much of the view of the dairy and paddocks. Yet the gaps between the trees allowed me to watch the cows walking up the track. A compromised view perhaps, but one that I enlarged through the repetition of watching the dairy each day.

Over time the yellow kitchen walls were dulled by smoke from the fire-place. A coloured cloth map of Ireland was nailed into the wall above the chair where Dad sat at the head of the table. A calendar advertising a local machinery business was nailed underneath the map while Mum's Magellan calendar with its religious reproductions was nailed to the wall beside the pantry cupboard. The cupboard was an old meat safe that Mum and Dad had brought out with them from their first house together in Crossley. A spice rack that I made in Year 10 woodwork was nailed to the side of the pantry cupboard which was also painted lime green. A red laminex table with silver edges was the table ten children and two adults attempted to sit around. Five kids could squeeze onto a red cushioned stool and there was an assortment of chairs pushed in at any space around the table. Invariably one or two of us had to sit in the door way to the lounge to eat, and when Dad's back was playing up, he stood up and ate his tea from the top of the fridge.

Meal times were loud, sometimes chaotic, with people talking over the top of each other; brothers punching each other's shoulders, giving dead legs and sometimes Dad thumped his fist on the table for quiet so that he could watch the ABC news. Minor accidents such as spilt meals were common and any mess was quickly licked up by a cat or dog. With so many bodies in the kitchen, children getting up to fetch cutlery, Mum serving meals to the table or Dad coming in from the dairy to stand in front of the fire to warm up, someone was bound to be knocked over. One accident I remember was when I poured boiling hot water down Jack's back as he sat at the table. It may have been to pour on my Weet Bix. It may have been to top up the tea pot. I remember stumbling toward the table and the boiling water cascading down his shirt back. He leapt up out of the chair with a scream and quickly the shirt was ripped from his back. Cold water was splashed onto his blotchy steaming skin. I couldn't believe what I had done and I blushed at the shouts from Mum and others. More cold water was poured down his back and he made a quick recovery. This was the same brother I had stabbed with a pocket knife when we were feeding out hay to the cows on a wet and windy day. And yet, Jack could be unpredictable at times. When he was younger, he rode dragsters up Vickers Road and left signature skids and burnouts for Dad to read. Later this love transferred into trail bikes and scramble bikes. Often he would mono around the house waving to anybody who was near. One day he was unhappy with something I said to him and so he simply picked up a lump of wood and rammed it into my face. He never bore grudges against anyone.

In the 1970s, country television was limited to two TV channels- the ABC and BTV6. BTV6 was based in Ballarat and was a broadcast channel for the commercial television channels from Melbourne. Some Melbourne TV shows were relayed through BTV6 such as *Get Smart, World Wide Wrestling, I Dream of Genie* but others such as *Lost in Space* were lost to country viewers. Variety TV shows were common such as *The Mike Walsh Show* and *Saturday Night Live* with Mike Williamson and Mary Hardy. Mary Hardy had relatives in Koroit and so Mum and Dad, ever loyal to family connections, enjoyed watching her madcap humour on the show on Saturday nights. Ballarat also had its own variety show with *Six Tonight* hosted by Fred Farghar. The Ballarat variety show set was more basic than the Melbourne variety shows while some of the guests such as Jane Scali, Dennis Walter and Issy Dye appeared on each of the variety shows. Mum watched *The Mike Walsh Show* over lunch and she always sat down to watch when Cliff Portwood came on. His big hair, deep voice and unbuttoned shirts had Mum sitting on her chair, smiling and entranced. She bought his records and everybody in the kitchen had to be quiet whenever he was singing. Often, Dad and later Mick and I came in from the farm for lunch and sat down to watch the *Mike Walsh Show* with her. The visiting guests and regulars on the show such as John Michael Howson were in stark contrast to our jobs of bringing in cows and calves, straining fencing wire or ramming a post in a new fence line. Mike Walsh and his guests represented the other world; the city and tidy, neat clothes. We ate our sausages for lunch in shit-splattered Yakka pants while Mum sipped her tea with a smile on her face.

To organize meals for the family and to keep ten children occupied and busy, various rules and rituals were created. With so many children to choose from, often Mum chose whoever was near for setting the table, washing and wiping the dishes, or collecting wood for the open fire. There were demarcations made between boys' jobs and girls' jobs with the boys tending to do more of the milking and farm work while Annie, Theresa and Kathryn worked inside. Theresa seemed to enjoy working in the kitchen and so she often helped Mum out with cooking and preparing meals. Annie was either in her room doing homework or reading – something she loved to do so much that she would walk down the paddock to a favourite tree to sit and read, and in doing so, miss out on any jobs that were needed. If a child hadn't been chosen for a job, each of us competed with each other by buzzing for the easiest job. If we had been asked to set the table for tea, someone would buzz 'butter n that!' This job involved getting the butter from the fridge, placing salt and pepper, and tomato sauce or pickles in the centre of the table. Someone else might call out, 'knives and forks', and so place them around the table, while the hardest job was squatting down to count and retrieve the plates from the corner cupboard and lay them out. Washing and wiping the dishes in the sink needed to be done soon after tea so that children could get ready for bed. There was no dishwasher, and so the dishes piled up like Japanese temples around the pots and pans. For many years, Mum preferred velvet soap and Jex soap pads to wash up with. The steel wool soap pads become smaller and smaller the more they were used and the grey hairs often congealed into a small bun from use. While Annie or Theresa might wash up, Kathryn, Mick or I might wipe. Tea towels were flicked at each other's legs while we waited for a plate to be washed. Sometimes it took nearly an hour to wash up, but if Mum was washing, a lot of things could be talked about in that time.

The meals that we ate were reasonably consistent. Steaks from cows we had killed were polished off at breakfast, dinner and tea. Lamb chops, roasts, stews, tuna and sausage casserole were all cooked on the small electric oven wedged between the lime green saucepan cupboard and the fridge. Potatoes, pumpkin, peas, beans and cabbage were boiled and usually mashed. These were standard meals of the country in the 1970s. Occasionally, Dad would cook chips from potatoes but the treat that we looked forward to were the cream cakes Mum brought home in a cardboard box after a Wednesday shopping day. The cakes were devoured in minutes and apart from Mum's scones there would be no more cakes until the following Wednesday.

Fresh milk was collected from the vat at the dairy each morning. Someone would slip into their rubber boots and rush over to the dairy with the large white milk jug. Unlike today, the milk vats of the 1970s were not totally encased in stainless steel. Back then, the lid of the vat was rested at an angle so that any one of us could dip the jug into the swirling rectangle of milk. During winter and spring when the cows had calved and their butterfat content was high, there would be cream on top of the milk. We spread the cream over sliced bread and jam while drinking up to four glasses of milk each day.

Every now and then, the fridge required defrosting which involved taking all the food and containers out of the fridge, placing them on the table while Mum washed out the fridge and slowly let it defrost. A plastic container sat on the bottom shelf of the fridge to collect the ice and drips of water as the fridge melted. Sometimes I could hear the thump and crack of the ice from my bedroom at night. It was an otherworldly sound that seemed to fit in with the crashing of wind and groans of roofing iron being reluctantly lifted. The table would become a reproduction of our lives and what we were eating that week. There would be vegetables, lettuces, jugs of milk, bowls of beetroot and tomato, congealed chops on a plate, a Neapolitan ice cream container, cans of condensed milk and eggs. Mum draped table cloths over the lot to protect the food from the flies. The next morning, my brothers and sisters and I came down for breakfast, pushed the dishes and containers into the middle of the table and ate our cereal around the mess without talking.

Throughout the noise of each day and calm of the nights, the Grandfather clock ticked on. It was an heirloom that belonged to Dad's father, Pop, and after it was restored the bronze dial never stopped swinging. It had a white square face, Roman numerals, ornate mahogany swirls on its head and it sat on the wooden mantle piece above the fire. Beside the clock were the knick-knacks that accumulate in a farmhouse: a curled remembrance card for a local boy who had died young, ear tags for cows, pins and rubber bands, rosary beads, hair clips and empty glasses of water. The clock was the highest object in this daily tableau of our lives and so time assumed its importance. We looked to the clock at 3:30 to think about getting the cows in for afternoon milking. We looked to the clock for school bus times, afternoon tea time, bed time and leaving for the footy time. The ticking of the clock could be heard from our bedrooms. I woke on freezing mornings to the sound of the clock which was often the first sound of day thawing night and introducing the prospect of school. It was the music my mother padded to at night or in the morning as she put the kettle on. Some nights I sat with her in front of the fire looking up at the clock as she talked about her family or what was coming up in the next week. There was a consistency to the clock and to the rhythms of our talk that never wavered.

The copper and brown brick surround of the fireplace fascinated me and I stared into the ridges and grooves of the masonry while listening to Mum or Dad talk. I loved the combination of heat and the music of their talk. Mum's voice rose as she took offence to something Dad had said while his voice was flatter in tone and its short rhythms. Dad usually smiled and agreed. He didn't want to argue in front of us kids while Mum was always determined to correct his cracks at self-pity or the plans for the farm he had devised without consulting her. I looked into the fire at the red cities crumbling, the flare-ups from a piece of paper or Alfoil. One log crumbled and another was heaped on top of it. So much of our lives revolved around repetition and rituals. I stared into the crumbling cities in the fire and almost felt sorry for the parts of wood that had to fall. I listened to my parents' talk and felt the heat around my eyes. It was a warmth I kept returning to.

One of the requirements of being a Catholic has been to pray regularly. The most common way of observing prayer on a regular basis is to attend Mass once a week. When my parents were young Mass was said throughout the week and some people attended Mass at least twice a week as a demonstration of their faith. As a family we attended Mass each Sunday, alternating between St Brendan's at Panmure and St Mary's at Garvoc. The other main form of prayer that was practised in our house, and in other houses in our parish, in the 1970s was The Rosary. I discovered much about how other people said the rosary and what their houses were like when we took part in the communal rosaries that were said as part of The Missions. I was serving on the altar when the Missions priests, often Redemptorists, came to St Brendan's. These were priests who hailed from outside the district and who toured the countryside to give volatile pep talks to congregations about turning away from sin. They shouted and shook incense at the crowd, who mostly listened out of politeness. The reputation of the Missions priests preceded them, and some members of the congregation felt lucky to be receiving such stern epistles. The other component of the Missions was that a roster was set up for communal rosaries. Each week people would visit one family's house and say the rosary together. These occasions were eye-openers for myself, partially because I was able to see how other families prayed, but I could also see how wealthy or poor some of my neighbours were. There were kitchens with torn lino, hard wooden chairs, and a gravity on the faces of some farmers that suggested their lives were always like this. Going into my neighbours' houses to pray was both a humbling and sombre experience. Having a joke wasn't allowed when we were saying the rosary.

We said the rosary each night and everybody needed to be present in the kitchen. After tea had finished, Dad gave the call, 'let's kneel down and say a decade of the rosary.' We would say five, according to the season. They might be Glorious, Sorrowful, Joyful, or Luminous Mysteries. Dad would lead us through the decades, his monotone voice occasionally rising and dropping in tune to his energies at the end of the day. As a child I loved saying the rosary while watching the flames of the open fire in our kitchen. There was something about the combination of heat from the fire, the fire-related imagery of the rosary and the repetition of Hail Mary's and Holy Mary's that appealed to me on a primal level. It didn't matter that I was kneeling on hard lino. I knew the words. I could say the prayers without thinking. It was like breathing. Later, as a teenager, I began to resent this nightly intrusion into my life and eventually Mum and Dad stopped saying the rosary as my brothers and sisters also rebelled or left home. And yet now, whenever I think of The Rosary I am taken back to those hard kitchen squares, Dad's voice and I am reminded that meaning can be found in small country houses across the world.

Catholic daydreams

Lost in language
my brothers and sisters
flick food scraps at each other

as the circular rhythms
of lead and response
echo across paddocks,

the kitchens of large families
humming with Hail Marys
the wind, like a semaphore

tunnels down chimneys.
my father's dairy farming fingers
slip down the beads

as if each bead was a grip
on the Joyful Mystery
of ten children charging through

the Hail Holy Queen,
the tempo picking up
according to what was on TV.

Yet after we had finished
we would often remain kneeling
heads down, studying the lino

and those Catholic daydreams.

As well as being a room to keep warm in, the kitchen was where we gathered. It was where visitors sat to talk of the Crossley dances, cousins and people around the district. It was a space local farmers nervously stepped into, dropping their hat in a corner and replying politely to Mum's questions of a cup of tea. It was where Dad was pulled up by an older sister who spotted the gaps in the lino tiles that he had laid down the week before. It was where my sisters talked quietly to boyfriends after we had all gone to bed. Sometimes the search for a glass of water propelled me into the kitchen causing one of my sisters and her boyfriend to sit up promptly. Sometimes one of the boyfriends tried to be mates with myself or one of my other brothers, only to their eventual embarrassment. One night, a sister invited a new boyfriend to the house. The following night she arranged for her regular boyfriend to come over where she would have a quiet talk with him in front of the fire. However, that night, my younger brother Phil rushed to the knock at the back door, greeted the regular boyfriend with the news that his sister had seen another man in the house the night before. The regular boyfriend was left speechless and smiling. He pushed back the sliding door and stepped into the heat of the kitchen where everyone was told to leave so that my sister could give him the news.

Mostly, the kitchen was Mum's room. It was where our lives were given direction and where she spent the majority of her time inside the house. One night shortly after the Panmure Football club had won a grand final, a group of players and officials turned up unannounced at our house. Dad was vice-president of the club at the time and so he had a lot to do with the winning team. The men turned up with beers and sang and talked into the night. At some stage Mum sent all of us kids to bed while Dad joined in with the singing and drinking. I could hear the laughter and voices from the front bedroom that I shared with Mick and Jack. Part of me wanted to be down there with them as I knew these men, some of whom I looked up to as players in the footy team, and yet I knew that sitting around drinking and talking all night was unusual in our house. At some stage they would have to leave. At six in the morning, Mum had had enough. She got out of bed, pulled on her dressing gown, stormed into the kitchen and told the lot off.

'What time do you think it is! We've been kept awake all night by you men shouting and singing and we haven't been able to sleep at all. Think of the children here trying to sleep!'

She glared at Dad. One of the men hid under the laminex table as Mum spoke.

'Go on, get out the lot of you! Go home!'

And leave they did, sheepishly and quiet. Dad walked over to the dairy to start the engine up. For weeks after the night, people were avoiding Mum's eyes at Mass and at the Panmure general store. She had told the men where to go. The kitchen was back to being hers.

A bedroom

The bedrooms that siblings share are often essential to the growth of brothers. All that time with a closed door. Arguments, education, music, dancing and secrets all occur because the brothers have at least one thing in common – how to work out their place in the world. I shared two bedrooms with my older brother Mick, but one was more influential for both of us. It was the bedroom we shared where we both developed our interests in music and reading and where our individuality from our parents became more pronounced. The bedroom was like a classroom where Mick introduced me to heavy metal music, punk and New Wave of the late 1970s. He had a record player with a brown see-through plastic cover perched on a chest of drawers, posters on the walls and old copies of *Ram* and *Juke* stuffed under his bed. All the tools needed for a farm boy to get by.

The bedroom was not big, although my memory has enlarged it over the years. It could accommodate two wardrobes, a chest of drawers, two single beds and a scattering of clothes on the floor. Clothes spilled out of the wardrobes, milking clothes stained with cow shit were left where we took them off. The peeling lino revealed scarred floorboards and a jagged lino seal divided the room – his stuff and mine. There were also possum stains descending the walls in long dribbly lines, a hole in the floor beside my bed that let the cold air rise. I had a lumpy bed with broken springs and so I slept in an undulating position as if I was lying across a hill. The view out the window was of paddocks and further off a line of bush. In retrospect it seemed to be a typical anonymous country bedroom that lacked some comforts yet it was a bedroom from which each of us grew.

Every weekend it was one of our turns to help Dad milk the cows. Mornings began early with Dad thumping down the hall at 5:30. Both of us knew we had half an hour to chase more sleep while our father rounded up the cows on the motorbike. Invariably we slept in, especially on cold and wet autumn and winter mornings. Frustrated and impatient, he returns to the house in his rubber boots, yanks at the back screen door and shouts at us to 'get out of bed!' His voice thunders around the rooms of the house waking everyone. I can hear the rattle of the dairy engine, sometimes a bull bellowing. There is shame attached to sleeping in. We cannot be trusted or depended upon. If neither of us gets up after Dad leaves by slamming the screen door, Mum struggles into the room in a quieter apologetic voice – 'C'mon, Get up. Your father's angry. Both of you have slept in again.' When either of us stumbles down the back path, past the clothes lines and roundabout and makes it past the thrum of the dairy's engine, we are given another talking to. Sometimes he gives us the silent treatment where we milk side by side for an hour. He looks away from us watching what cows are doing in the back paddock or how a heifer walks out of the yard. He has other things on his mind, and it is not his sons who can't get out of bed.

Typically, we are altar boys at St Brendan's Catholic church in Panmure. It is a cream weatherboard church with a neat lawn mown by a roster of local farmers and a row of craggy cypress trees on the western side of the church. I feel a special sense of pride about serving on the altar at a church with the same name as myself. Mick and I are made to wear our best clothes: colourful body shirts and flares. My parents always believed in community service; Mum with the CWA and Red Cross, Dad with the local football club and fire brigade. Serving on the altar is seen by them as our service to the catholic community and both of us serve on the altar out of a sense of duty for four years. We carry the cruets of water and wine to the priest before the transfiguration and ring the bell during the blessing of the gifts before communion. Sitting up near the altar takes me closer to the crucifix and the presence of the priest, but not closer to God. While I enjoy having a view of the congregation in the pews and of holding the brass plate under the mouths of people when they receive communion, I also become tired of it. I look to the girls I am attracted to and blush easily if they look my way. After Mass, Mick and I clear the altar and wait for the priest to dismiss us from the sacristy. Thankfully, the priests we serve with are reasonable, if not a bit strange. They know many things about God but nothing of our lives and the nights we spend in our bedroom listening to 'Stairway to Heaven' and 'Paranoid'.

Mick's interest in school wanes and by the end of Year nine he has persuaded Mum and Dad to let him leave school and begin an apprenticeship on the farm. He leaves the regimen of the Christian Brothers in Warrnambool for a more carefree life of milking cows, carting in hay, cutting thistles and picking up stones. He rises at 6am and often doesn't finish the day until 6pm. Dairy farming is not an easy job and I often think he must have really hated the strict routine of secondary school so he could move into a job where he was working outside in the rain and wind. In winter and spring, he is allowed money from the sale of calves. During calving season, four or five calves might be born each day. Mick is allowed thirty dollars from two or three calves per week on top of his wages. The calves that are sold are mostly bull calves, but also weak 'bobby' calves, lame calves and sometimes calves abandoned by their mothers. They all end up at the knackery where they are turned into pet food. With the calf money Mick receives, he spends up on clothes, records and music magazines and his self-funded education accelerates.

Two music magazines became influential to Mick's, and in turn, my musical education. *RAM* and *Juke* were two broadsheet musical newspapers that published interviews with musicians; articles about bands, alternative top 40 lists and photographs of our favourite guitar heroes. Before the internet and alternative radio stations, there were alternative newspapers and in the cities, zines. These were the hunting grounds of Mick's quest for the latest news about Radio Birdman, The Tactics, Richie Blackmore's Rainbow and a host of heavy metal groups including Led Zeppelin and Foghat. We lay on our beds listening to the extended guitar solos, danced to the thumping riffs or sang along to 'Hey Joe' by Hendrix. Outside our bedroom door, Mum would be preparing tea or Dad would be on the phone and a thump on the door would resound, followed by the shout of 'turn that music down!' As well as the influence of the music magazines, our appetite for music was whetted further by the rhythmic drum roll of Countdown's introduction and Gavin Wood's voice over announcing who was on the show that night. Our lives were nurtured by the routine of milking cows and 6pm of a Sunday night. At last we could see the bands we had been reading about, live or recorded. From David Bowie and Roxy Music to Cheetah and Marcia Hines, Countdown introduced us to fashion and an aesthetic of how a person looks when they walk down the street. As the punk movement became larger and more frenetic in the late 1970s, Mick's clothes reflected the trend. He was still a farmer yet his white shirts were often ripped. He wore long black coats, lace singlets. When the Sex Pistols sang 'Anarchy in the UK' on Countdown both of us were entranced.

Mick had already bought 'Never Mind the Bollocks' and both of us had pogoed to it in our bedroom. Yet until I saw them perform, they had remained a distant novelty act. Watching Johnny Rotten snarl in black and white, Sid Vicious playing the bass with a cigarette drooping from his lips, and my foot on the edge of the scraps bucket in the kitchen, I knew some aspect of my life was changing.

It was also during this period that my teenage reading possessed its own urgency. I was gripped by a need to discover a world beyond the farm; an elsewhere I was yearning to walk toward. Many of the teenagers around me seemed happy and content to live in a world bordered by football and farming, and while I shared those interests, I also knew, through music that there were places beyond our football league. From an early age, I knew what it was like to be marked by nervousness before waves or a reluctance to act like a dickhead in front of friends. My male role models were hard-working, crease-necked men who drank and waited for dinner to be served to them. On the surface, they were polite and laconic, often pillars of the local community. The codes of behaviour in the country may be unwritten for men yet they are often fiercely upheld, especially against any no-hoper who challenges them. Meanwhile there were marriages breaking up around us, men chasing their sons with stockwhips, men drinking alone in isolated bush shacks. Any woman who lived alone in a country farmhouse was often on the watch. It was within this environment that I began to read about skinheads.

A series of books by Richard Allen, the pen name for James Moffatt, alters my reading dramatically. In the 1970s, Allen became popular with his novels about sharpies, skinheads and punks living in housing estates in London and the north of England. With titles such as Skinhead, Sharpie, Sorts, Boot Boys, Skinhead Girls and Suedehead, Allen tapped into the disaffected youth of Thatcher's England. In the novels there were fights between rival gangs, fights over girls and the despair of unemployment within families. The novels not only fed into my awakening sexuality, they also introduced me to concepts of social justice, generational unemployment and some truths of what the 'mother country' was really like. This was despite the fact that Mick and I were petrified of the few skinheads we saw around Warrnambool; so much better to read about skinheads than to run away from them. Despite the limited writing style of the novels – both genders were stereotyped and violence seemed to be glorified – I read all of the books. They held an elsewhere that I could understand; a place I knew about that set me apart from my friends at the footy club.

Punk books and punk music. Mick's exploration of the culture eventually becomes the catalyst for him to leave the farm. His side of the bedroom was littered with punk fanzines, cassette tapes, and stacks of records by The Stooges, The Slits, The Vibrators and The Boys Next Door. An oversized poster of Johnny Rotten stared from the wall. Quietly spoken, Mick's embrace of punk was both inner and outer. He wore the clothes but he was mild-mannered, responsible yet with a daring streak. His first car was a HQ Holden which he crashed on the first New Year's Ball he went to after driving drunk into a drain. Once the car was repaired, he used to drive me around the back roads of Panmure and Laang. We listened to Patti Smith on his car tape, pulled out white posts and turned stop signs around to face the wrong way. We were bored by the lack of things to do and the summers which dragged on. Weekends he wore his black clothes and boots to 'the Cri', the alternative pub in Warrnambool where uni students hung out. But anyone who stands out from the crowd in a country town will always cop some flak. People would shout at him wearing torn jeans and leathers from passing cars hanging laps of the main street. One morning I woke opposite him to see his face swollen and bruised. He had a black eye and his upper lip was three times its normal size. He had been taken to in the toilets of a popular disco, one of a number of bashings at the time. There were no charges and no complaints were made. He continued to milk cows and play in the ruck for Panmure with a quiff and a Shazam symbol cut into the sides of his number two hair cut.

Many of my brothers and sisters have completed a formal education but Mick didn't. His own education, and to a lesser extent mine, occurred in a small bedroom in the country where he listened to records nobody else in Panmure had heard of. Every teenager needs a bedroom with a door that will close. Once our door closed, we retreated into the world that we craved, aspired to. Never mind the mess on the floor; it was the music we listened to, the gossip about locals that we shared, and the books we hid under the pillow that really mattered. At night, Mick and I lay back on our beds and looked up at the posters of The Rolling Stones, Johnny Rotten, Black Sabbath. They were the images that we stared at, and in doing so dreamed of, like the novels of Richard Allen, we dreamed of another life, of possibilities beyond the farm and the cows outside. The posters were like prayers that we returned to each night, and which gave us more meaning than the rosary could ever give. The bedroom that we shared was that kind of place – it reflected who we were.

The places we went

The places we went as a family were never too far from Vickers Road. The farm was in our lives physically and mentally. I don't think the farm ever left Dad's head. There was always a paddock in his head to keep him occupied. Each Wednesday, Mum and Dad drove the half hour into Warrnambool for grocery shopping and for Dad to hang around the sale yards. He rarely bought cows but he liked to look at the cows in the ring, stand around and talk with other farmers. As a teenager, he used to drove cattle to the sale yards. At first to the sales in Koroit and then later, he worked for other cattle carriers dropping off cows in Warrnambool. As a result, he knew an inordinate amount of people at the yards and on the few occasions that I went with him, he was forever being stopped by other men for a chat. I was introduced as 'the lad'. It was a male environment, I don't recall seeing many women at the saleyards. Sometimes Dad called in to the bar that was at the sale yards and had one or two glasses, but like some other farmers, he didn't linger. There was always another job or a person to talk to.

    I watched the men with their red cheeks and dryzabone coats leaning on the metal railings, who in turn, scrutinized the heifers and steers that came trotting into the sale ring. Occasionally, a farmer would raise a finger for a bid, but often they would be muttering to whoever was near, or looking distractedly at the concrete. The cattle caller who sat in a booth over-looking the sale ring was like a ringmaster at a circus. He had the tone and rhythms of a race caller, rattling through a description of the heifer ambling around the ring and the seller who would be identified with initials such as F.C & M.D Ryan of Panmure. Place was an important signifier when selling cattle and a mental map was formed in my head as the caller mentioned Mepunga, Cudgee, Toolong and Illowa. It was similar to the names I saw on the doors of cattle trucks at the saleyards.

Farmers were known by the town or area they came from on the side of the truck door. It was always the man's initials first.

The known world of Warrnambool was both a comfort and a living example of the local knowledge that Mum and Dad depended on when they were shopping. It was not only easier to visit the same shops each Wednesday, it was also a way of keeping in contact with shop owners, some of whom Mum knew from her childhood in Warrnambool. Mum shopped at Swinton's for groceries, bought new shoes at Bill Fish shoes, took our shoes for repair to Mr Boyle, stocked up at Mr Forbes' for fruit and vegetables and at the end of the day waited for Dad to return from the sale yards and pick her up under the T & G clock tower on the corner of Liebig and Lava Streets in Warrnambool. It was a mental map that Mum followed around the streets of Liebig, Kepler and Lava streets; a rhythm that she returned to each Wednesday; a routine that located her day. There were other known places that Mum shopped at such as Mac's Snacks, The Savoy, and Younger's department store. Each Wednesday was a day the whole family looked forward to; relief for Mum from her days of washing, and for my brothers and sisters and I, a day to return to the civilized world.

When Target first opened in Warrnambool in the 1970s, it became a draw card for us as we hadn't seen a department store as big and light-filled as the new Target. My brothers and sisters and I could easily spend an hour or two browsing the clothes and toy racks or flipping through the racks of albums. Sometimes we remained in the store until it was time to go home and the signal came from Dad. He arrived from the sale yards, thinking about milking time and whistled loudly as only he could to get our attention. Nearly everyone in the store turned to see who had whistled. With our heads down and faces burning, my brothers and sisters and I trudged from the racks and walked down the central row to where Dad was standing and grinning. Other shoppers looked around at us, smiled and laughed, at the yarding of the family. No doubt, it saved Mum and Dad time walking around the rows looking for Annie, Theresa, Michael, Brendan, Kathryn, Jack and David. There was no other whistle as shrill as Dad's and whenever we heard it, regardless of how embarrassing it was, we knew it was time to go.

In summer, the Hot Rods started up at Allansford's Premier Speedway. Sprint cars, saloon cars and occasionally motorbikes roared around the oval track flicking up stones and infecting the night with the rich smells of racing fuel. Although the nights might start out warm, they were often cold by the end and teenagers used to stand around wrapped in blankets to conceal cans of beer and wandering hands. Dad took us to the Hot Rods occasionally but we often went with friends for a Saturday night out. Apart from watching the cars speed around, the other main attraction was to find some beer and to check out some girls. Allansford's lone pub did a roaring trade on Hot Rod nights with many under-age drinkers finding alcohol through older friends or brothers. After a slab or a dozen cans were bought from the pub, groups of teenagers made their way back through Allansford's streets to the Speedway. The most direct route to the speedway was by the rail line and as the two train times were memorized by most local teenagers, it was easy enough to walk back along the rail line and drink in the car park before returning to watch the races. The Hopkins River separated the town from the speedway and a high rail bridge forded the river. Below the bridge the water cascaded over rocks and around snagged trees before slowing into deeper river holes. The challenge was to walk across the rail bridge with a slab on your shoulder before a train came along. If you were on the rail bridge when a train came along, there was no option but to give up the slab and jump ten metres into the waters below. One night after a friend and I made it over the rail bridge with our cans and were proceeding to drink them crouched down beside a car, two policemen sprung us. They picked us up and gave us a good going over with their fists and my friend was beaten over the head with a baton. No doubt they were on the lookout for underage drinkers at the Hot Rods, as with the dark spaces and many teenagers wandering around the backs of grandstands, fights flared up or cans were consumed. Anything was possible at the Hot Rods and it was a rite of passage for many people to get drunk, have sex or act tough. I wasn't crazy about watching the hot rods race yet I sensed the whiff of danger in the mix of dust, diesel and the growl of V8 engines. They attracted a certain type of male and female; men and women with an edge to their faces, mullets, tatts and in the 1970s, skinheads. I was out of my depth standing around looking at a carefully polished chrome engine, yet, as a teenager, I was attracted to anything that would take me away from the cows.

In contrast to the rebellious attractions of the Hot Rods, a more mundane ritual demanded our presence a short distance from the farm. Attending Mass on a weekly basis was one of the expectations for being a Catholic. While my brothers and sisters and I were running around trying to find shoes and good clothes and Mum was putting her make-up on, Dad would walk out to the car and begin blowing the horn. Eventually ten of us piled into the station wagon with two children sitting in the rear section, without seat belts. If Mass was at Panmure, Mick and I were dropped off at the sacristy where we would get dressed as altar boys to help the priest. Dad drove around to the right side of the weatherboard church and parked in roughly the same space as he had the fortnight before. People parked around the church out of habit, or out of a need to make a quick getaway. If a family parked in a different space, it was noticed. Dan Kelly always parked his old blue Mercedes under a pine tree. Ten children spilled out of the doors and hurried across the grass as the priest was kissing the altar. The pious and religious families always sat in the front rows while the single men and teenagers stooped in the back rows and sometimes nicked out for cigarettes while communion was being given out. Other families sat in the same sections out of habit and expectation. Mothers carried crying babies to the rear of the church. Local pillars of the community collected money for the plate and carried the stainless steel plate of envelopes and cash to the altar with the solemnity of a funeral. The priests intoned and the hour dragged. A large statue of Jesus on the cross was nailed to the wall at the rear of the altar at Panmure. I looked at the blood on Jesus' feet and tried to imagine the reality of having a nail hammered through his ankles. The idea of suffering and endurance was ever-present in the Catholic Church and it seemed to suit the stoic nature of the congregation whose lives were ingrained with the rituals of hard physical work.

After the Mass was over, people stood on the concrete outside the church and analysed local football scores from the day before. Men stood in groups laughing or quipping to each other, while women stood in what circles they could manage between the men. Some men bent a knee to support themselves against the weatherboards and smoked rollies listening to others deliberate about cows or machinery. Often the priest wandered into the crowd and struck up an awkward conversation with some of the older men. Other families raced to their cars to leave for lunch and *World of Sport* on TV. Dad had a habit of talking about cows to anybody who would listen, but mostly to one or two farmers who also liked to test out their political arguments on him. Consequently, our family was often the last to leave the church grounds. We would all be sitting in the car waiting for Dad, trying to get his attention through the car window while my brothers and sisters and I punched, yelled and squashed against each other. Mum raised her voice to get us to be quiet and whatever sense of calm she had attained during Mass, slowly withered.

I was about fourteen when I decided that I couldn't believe in the idea of a God that the Catholic Church promoted. It was about the same age that I decided that as much as I liked being on the farm, I couldn't be a farmer. I didn't want to be tied to the farm seven days a week and have to milk the cows twice a day. I wanted to be able to travel and not have to return to a farm at 3:30 to get the cows in. Even though I went to a Christian Brothers college, enjoyed the history of religion classes, said prayers in class, said the rosary at home, I couldn't bring myself to accept the contradictions between religion and the people around me. The religious life of accepting the teachings from the Gospels, of going to confessions regularly and to be seen in the local community as a dutiful Catholic jarred against my interests in heavy metal music, football and girls. As an altar boy, I often fantasized about the girls and women in the congregation. After Mass, I saw how certain people shunned others and how older men might look at teenage girls who were developing physically. As a boy I had enjoyed singing in Mass and sitting beside Mum and like any child, I wanted to please my parents. But those ideas of loyalty, servitude and obedience gradually paled as I grew older. After serving on the altar, I continued attending Mass, but I sat down the back with the other teenagers and older men. Sometimes my friends and I whispered to each other about Saturday's footy game or when we were older, how hungover we were. In comparison, the priest on the altar became a strange man raving about St Paul and the apostles – a man who was totally disconnected from the minutiae of our local lives. By the time I had my licence, I was attending Mass only out of obligation to my parents, and to catch up with friends afterwards. I knew what I had to do to appear to be Catholic, but like many, my inner thoughts and convictions were elsewhere.

While Dad's thoughts about the farm may have been in his head, his need to be always near the cows was practical and emotional. In summer, his main concern was whether the cows would have enough water in the afternoon. Our bore water supply on the farm was unreliable in the early years and there were breakdowns with the windmill near the back paddock. Dad took it upon himself to fix most problems on the farm and several times, Dad, Mick and I had to drag rust-coloured pipes up from underground, replace the damaged water pipes and reconnect new pipes with the underground bore water supply. It was as though we were reaching down into the core of the farm, reaching down into our history, our livelihood. On hot days, a herd of milkers could easily drink a trough dry if a windmill had broken down or there was a burst pipe. The cows stood in a circle around the corrugated iron and cement trough, swishing their tails and flicking their ears at flies while they looked at you for answers. Their milk would be down that night and they would be unsettled in the cowyard. But Dad also didn't like being away from the cows and the farm out of love for the animals and what the farm meant to him. He didn't always talk about this love, but in later years he would joke around smiling and half-singing, 'ah me darlings, me Jerseys.' Consequently, any Sunday drives with the family were always cut short by having to return home to milk. Sometimes we piled into either the blue HR Holden or in later years the lime yellow Valiant and Dad drove us to the local beaches – Peterborough, Port Campbell, Warrnambool and Port Fairy. Driving to Peterborough we passed through the small towns of Naringal, Nullawarre and Nirranda; towns with a hall, a tennis court, a collection of houses and a sense of the beach being close by. Mostly flat dairy farming country, but with the occasional beef farm and towering pine trees lining the roads. I was impatient to pass through these towns for the salt air and the first glimpse of breakers on the beach. When we were returning home in a hot car with no air-conditioning and squashed into a seat with four brothers and sisters, each small town we passed through was mentally ticked off in the rush to get out of the car. Quite a few local dairy farmers had holiday houses at the beach and these houses were pointed out to us by Mum and Dad and so signified a local connection to Peterborough. But each subsequent visit to Peterborough only seemed to remind me of the farmers who inherited their farms, and the farmers who had to scratch a living to pay a lease, or a mortgage and a herd of cows.

Sometimes it was the accumulation of images I saw when I looked out the car window that has remained with me. After all, this is one way that memory imprints a landscape within us – by what we see and how we think about it, different to how we experience it. Often those images were of barbed wire fences, orange brick farm houses, cows' noses down in paddocks, windmills and haysheds. Other times they were more significant and mysterious such as a white cross by the side of the road just past Port Fairy. This wasn't a roadside shrine to someone being killed in a car accident, but the grave marker for George Watmore 'speared by Blacks, 1842.' I had glimpsed this cross many times on our family drives out to Port Fairy and Portland and no doubt I would have asked Mum and Dad about the story behind it. Their answer may have been that he was a farmer who was attacked by Aborigines or a farmer who died doing his job. They didn't talk about the massacres of Aboriginal peoples, of which this white cross was linked to. My parents also wouldn't have known about the violence associated with European settlement as indigenous history wasn't taught in school for them, or even much later in the 1970s for myself. For many people, the white cross became just one more thing with an unknown story to be seen out the car window- a wind-battered hay shed, an old dairy, a clump of trees where a house was. When I first saw this white cross out the car window, I immediately felt sorry for George Watmore. Apparently Watmore was a shepherd who refused to hand over promised food rations to a local Aboriginal clan. Watmore's death, seemed to me in the 1970s, to represent an ultimate danger in farming – that Aborigines might kill you. It was a fear I was later to realize was brought about by by my own ignorance of history and naivety. It was also a fear maintained by silence. My parents and cousins never talked about George Watmore's cross. They couldn't explain the landscape behind it.

Providing entertainment for a large family was always an ongoing issue for Mum and Dad, especially when there wasn't a lot of money around. Social occasions were mainly confined to the Panmure Football Club and as we got older, discos and cabaret balls at the Panmure Hall. Dad did take some of us to the drive-ins at Warrnambool and Terang. Often these movies were not to his taste and after finding a park, and hanging the speakers on the car window, he would curl up in the back seat and have a sleep while Mick and I or Annie and Theresa were glued to the larger than life images on the big white screen. One night he drove Mick and I to see Led Zeppelin's *The Song Remains the Same* on a double-bill with *The Jimi Hendrix Story*. Mick and I were rapt to be seeing our heroes on the screen and although *The Song Remains the Same* included some epic songs with fantastical imagery that I didn't quite comprehend at the time, it remains with me as a pivotal film of my early teenage years. The music in both films was loud and confronting with soaring guitar solos that Mick and I could hardly believe we were watching. Dad lay on the back seat of our blue HR Holden snoring while Jimmy Page and Robert Plant played to rows of cars in the darkness, and beyond the cars, the shadowy expanses of paddocks and cows ambling in circles looking for feed. Their larger than life celluloid faces on the screen remained in my head for years to come. These were the musicians I had read about and shook my fist to in our bedroom and now they were looming over the paddocks of Terang. However, sometimes it is as though memory has distorted these images of Led Zeppelin and I am no longer seeing Jimmy Page or Robert Plant's face at the drive-in, but the faces of certain farmers from cabaret balls, the footy or the Panmure pub – grinning faces I can't avoid and who haunt me with a presence as visceral as a Jimmy Page solo.

    Cabaret balls and kitchen teas were commonly held in small Mechanic's Institutes or country halls around the district. A Ball might be held as a fundraiser for a footy club, as a New Year's Eve event or as part of a series of Balls where women could compete for the prized Belle of the Ball Award. Mostly Mum and Dad attended cabaret balls at the Panmure Hall, sometimes Nirranda, Naringal or Purnim Halls. People booked tables, brought in plates of food and eskies of beer were stashed under the tables so that the old-time dancing could happen on the sawdust-covered floors. The music varied from a small string ensemble to country and western bands crammed onto the stage playing old classics that people could dance the Pride of Erin to, or the Foxtrot, or Progressive Barn dance. Sometimes country and western stars such as Johnny Chester played, but often the groups were made up of farming families such as the McKinnon's Orchestra from Ecklin, or wiry farmers transformed by brylcreem, a lairy shirt and a semi-acoustic guitar singing 'Sea of Heartbreak' or 'I've Been Everywhere Man'. Children were welcome at the cabaret balls and the sight of a mother dancing with her ten year old daughter was not uncommon. My brothers and sisters and I would be running around with other local kids, playing outside the halls at night while the adults talked and drank inside. One night at the Purnim Hall I was swinging upside down on the metal railings of a fence when I slipped and gashed my head open on a jagged piece of concrete. I felt something wet and warm on my head and when I looked at my hand it was covered in blood. I ran into the hall crowded with dancers and found Mum sitting talking to her friends. I was crying and there was blood dripping down my clothes and onto the floor. Quickly, I was ushered outside and cleaned up in the toilets. The gash wasn't so bad that I needed stitches, but it was enough for me to have to sit out the night with Mum and her friends until it was time to go home.

The kitchen teas and cabaret balls that we went to have left an indelible impression that has only become clearer over the years. It is a nostalgic impression of communities celebrating occasions, coming together after a football celebration and yet these events revealed something to me about human interaction – how people got on with each other, the furtive glances across a crowded hall, the long, restless nights of waiting for the music to finish, groups of men standing around trestle tables drinking and at ease with themselves. Not only did many locals look different once they were dressed in suits and gowns, it was also their enthusiasm to be transformed on a night into something or someone else that sometimes made these nights memorable. Cross dressing Balls were popular with football clubs and there is a photo of Dad in a dress, red lipstick and a wig and Mum standing beside him in a black suit that illustrates their willingness to do whatever it takes to be part of a community. Local footballers dressed as women was always seen as a good laugh, perhaps because it was considered the most fantastical idea. The kitchen teas were more formal nights out where families were almost paraded before a community who were giving the couple their approval. Wrapped presents were laid out on a trestle-table and the bride-to-be was congratulated and her ring admired. It was customary to ply the groom with drinks so that he made a good speech at the end of the night. However, not all country people and farmers were articulate and so there were many speeches where men stumbled with their words on stage and made short work of the few words that they could muster. Mum and Dad danced at different stages throughout the nights but Dad spent time talking with other men down the back of the hall. There were fights and scuffles which usually happened outside and tensions were evident when certain families walked in and looked around to see who else they knew. Small towns can be places that strengthen community and they can be places where a sense of community can be slowly torn apart like a marriage bruised by familiarity.

Down to the river

Mt Emu Creek stretched and looped around the river flats on the western boundary of our farm. In summer, my brothers and sisters and I swam and dog paddled in the narrow water holes of the river watching black fish, catfish and eels slide past. There were a lot of fallen trees as well as moss and reeds in the river that used to flood in winter but for most of the year the river was not much deeper than waist height. Some of the banks were steep with tussocks growing down to the water's edge. Huge river red gums grew along the banks and their exposed roots gave us plenty of places to muck around in. Sometimes we walked along the banks into the neighbour's farms, crossing the river by walking along trees that had fallen in, wading through waist-high tussocks, always mindful of snakes. Sometimes there was a kerfuffle in the tussocks and a rabbit or fox startled us by sprinting out and onto the open paddocks. Hours would drift toward afternoon tea time as we walked in single file, discovering new swimming holes, more tussocks, more paddocks of cows. Some waterholes were over twenty metres across. Shaded by the extending branches of the red gums, these waterholes were a sanctuary to another time and place. Water hens and ducks kicked away at the sound of our footsteps. There were hoof prints of cows in the mud suggesting that they too appreciated these peaceful places. We swam and mucked around in the cool dark water, seemingly isolated from our jobs on the farm. There was the occasional hush of cars and trucks on the Princes Highway two kilometres away, the caw of a crow, but mostly there was the heavy quiet of the paddocks surrounding us. We had walked beyond our own farm and it felt exciting to be exploring, to be going somewhere we were not allowed to. When Mum or Dad asked us where we went, we were vague and replied 'just down to the river'. As I grew up, I went fishing and eel spearing with Mick and gradually came to know something of the river. Yet like shooting rabbits, fishing was something we tried our hand at, but our hearts weren't in it. We lived for music and football and later on, motorbikes and cars.

When the river flooded during winter, the lower river flat paddocks were often fully submerged. Waters from up north would flow into Mt Emu Creek which had its origins around Ararat. With the heavy rains of June and July, the increased flows from other tributaries and water courses pushed the water out into our sodden paddocks. Sometimes water flowed over a low-lying stretch of Vickers Road and we hoped that it would be so deep that Mum wouldn't be able to drive us to the school bus stop on the highway. However, the water flowing over the road from a drain in the bull paddock was always passable. We played in this stretch of water in our rubber boots, feeling the current as it swished around our ankles. We threw stones into the faster flowing water as it eddied out of a culvert and under the barbed wire fence. Sometimes one of us fell in and we trudged back to the house with soaked trousers and socks. The paddocks smelled of mud, wet grass and brown water. Ibis glided down to the edges of drains, tip-toeing around, and picked for worms with their curved beaks. The contrast of their white feathers against the mud and green paddocks became a welcome sight for me, as their return represented the good things about routine. When I looked to the river from the ridge our weatherboard house was on, all I could see was a sheen of silver where the river-flat paddocks used to be. When the sun shone the water glistened and sparkled. When a cloud passed over, the water reflected a dull metallic shine. It could be days or weeks before the floodwaters began to recede. The river red gums by the river seemed isolated from each other as the floodwater flowed between them. When we drove over the wooden bridge on Vickers Road, I looked down to the flooded river in fright at the water level often one or two feet below the bridge. Dirty water swirled and eddied away downstream, and the river often rose two or three metres with heavy rain. At night,

I dreamt of being chased in and out of the floodwaters, of our car becoming stuck on the bridge, of the river rising towards me. These days, the river rarely floods as the waters from up north have been diverted, and so the river is rarely flushed clean. Long stretches of green algae cover the river so that it resembles a golf course in places. The run-off from dairies is prohibited from being emptied into the river, but the run-off from so much fertliser in the paddocks is also contributing to the algae in the river. Something seems lost now that there are no floodwaters to wade through.

The lost world of the walk-through

The first of our dairies on the farm was a walk-through dairy. Later this dairy would be replaced by a nine-a-side, double machine herringbone-dairy and then finally a thirty-two cow rotary dairy. The walk-through had six bails in a row for the cows to be milked in. They were called walk-throughs because after the cows had finished milking, a door was opened for the cows to walk though into a race with wooden rails that guided them back onto the muddy lane and then into their night or day paddock. We opened the door of the bail with a long wooden rail that would push the door latch open and then be pulled back to close the door latch. Heifers and impatient Friesians used to bang their bony heads against the door either while they were being milked or when they thought that they had given enough. On rare occasions, a cow managed to force the door open and leap out into the daylight with the milking machines slipping off their teats as the cow ran down the race. Such incidents upset other cows as well as annoying Dad who would shout and swear, 'Come back here, you bugger!' and sometimes give chase if the cow had not given enough milk.

Each cow was kept in the bail by a leg rope which was tied to the outside lower leg of the cow. The leg rope ensured that the milking machines could be put on the cow without the person milking being kicked. The leg rope was anchored to a metal ring on the wall and once the rope was hooked around the cow's leg, and a slip-knot tied, most cows weren't able to kick it off. Some heifers kicked in an arc and we had to be careful not to be kicked as we pulled the machines off such cows. As well as a leg rope, there was also a chain with a circular hook at its end that was used in some bails. Quieter cows could be milked without a leg rope but these cows usually didn't mind having their leg pulled back so the machines could be attached. Milking in a herringbone and rotary dairy solved all these problems with access to the cows' udder from behind the cow rather than from the side. The galvanized steel rails in a herringbone or rotary also stopped the cows from raising their legs to kick, although some cows will always find a way to kick. Mostly, the cows stood in the bail watching the door, chewing their cud and swishing their tails at flies while they were being milked before ambling slowly out into the light of the day or early evening.

The cows were fed crushed oats from metal chutes above their heads. The chutes were opened by a pulley and cord system which was operated by giving the feed cord a swift pull once the cow had walked into the bail. Hungry heifers and large-boned Friesians would bang their heads against the chutes to try and shake more oats into the wooden boxes that they ate out of. Before each milking, the chutes would have to be filled with oats. This would be Mick's job or mine on weekends. The oats came in hessian bags weighing 80 kilograms. It was hard enough standing on a stool and lifting a full bag of oats up into the chute, but the worst part was the feel of the oat dust on my skin. My face and arms were covered in a powdery dust and itched like hell afterwards.

Milking in a walk-through was where we became intimate with cows. They stood on our rubber boots as they were jostled into the bail. We sat on small wooden stools beside their stomachs, washed the cows' muddy teats with warm water and squeezed them to bring down their milk, resting our heads against their flanks while grappling with the machines as they shifted the weight on their feet, or lifted their legs to force the machines off. Sometimes if a cow had a hard back-quarter, one of the cow's teats would have to be hand-milked to ease the inflammation inside. Dad and his siblings grew up hand-milking and he always said that women made better hand-milkers than men, partially because of their flexibility in squatting and bending down, and partially because of their gentler temperaments. With sixty-eighty cows crammed into the small holding yard, the heat of their grassy breaths was up close and in our faces.

While we waited for an old Jersey to finish in the walk-through, Dad would walk out into the herd, pat the cows' backs, and talk to them while pushing a reluctant heifer closer to the bail. But cows could be stubborn. Sometimes Dad and I or Mick had to get behind a cow and push with our shoulders to coax the cow into the bail; much like pushing a racehorse into a barrier. In the early days, we knew each cow by its name, Catholic names, such as Mary, Josephine and Theresa. Each cow was known by its mood as well as colour, how much milk it gave and whether it liked to be milked early or late. This close connection with the cows made the job of milking less of a task and more of a way of reacquainting myself with these animals that became pets to us all.

The wooden rails separating each bail were softened and greased by the cows' flanks. The soft wooden posts holding up the dairy were rubbed smooth from our shoulders as we leant against them and waited for the cows to finish. Dad often rubbed his back against the posts, much like a cow or bull does against a fence post. His pale Irish skin always seemed to be itchy and flaked easily in summer. The holding yard where the cows stood waiting to be milked was without a roof. The walls of the yard were made from sheets of corrugated iron nailed to rough cut beams. The corrugated iron sheets shuddered and sang as the wind from the west pummeled the herd shivering in the cold. In our early days on the farm, the cows were mostly Jerseys, on account of their high butterfat yield. The few larger-boned cows that we had – Ayreshires, Guernseys and Friesians always hung back to the rear, trying to postpone the time they would have to be coaxed into the bail. We were always directed by Dad to mix them up in the bail, put a larger, older cow beside a young heifer. Try not to have three heifers all in a row, otherwise the machines would be kicked off in succession.

Water was continually being used around the cows; to wash their teats, wash the machines, hose down the shit from around our feet. The holding yard had to be hosed and squee-jeed; all the watery cowshit pushed down into a one foot opening at the rear of the yard that ran into an open drain in the bull paddock. I looked after a vegie garden that flourished on either side of the drain. Pumpkins spread like rumours over the boggy grass and cape weed. Tomatoes, lettuce and sweet corn were planted in rows. The garden sloped down towards the drain that meandered in a westerly direction towards Mt Emu Creek. I fenced off the garden from the bulls with a single strand of wire and electric fence droppers. Our bulls were mainly Jersey, who demanded our respect, yet they were rarely interested in lettuce, tomatoes or pumpkins.

Mick and I used to fight over whose job it was to clean the yard, as it was much easier than washing the machines in a bucket of warm water after milking at night or in a trough following each morning's milking. Washing the machines at night involved dragging a white bucket of hot water to each of the six machines and scrubbing the muck from the galvanized teat cups and black rubber hoses. It was a messy job with water spilling onto our jeans and shirts and it had to be done bending over the bucket. After each morning's milking, we pulled the machines from the rubber hoses and washed them in a stone water trough, a job that still involved a lot of warm water being spilt on shirts and jeans. By comparison, hosing down the yard and squee-jeeing the larger clumps of cowshit into the small hole that lead onto the bull paddock was meditative work. The radio was always on, with Casey Casem's upbeat 'American Top 40' on Saturday mornings. Other times it was the hits from the 60s and 70s on 3YB. Listening to the radio, imagining what I might be doing in the future, I could lose myself to the repetition of pushing cowshit in lines toward the rear of the holding yard. Dad joked that we would all end up sweeping gutters, and he did prepare us for it well. Much later, when I did work for a Council Parks and Gardens Department and had to sweep a gutter as part of the job, I remembered his warning.

Whenever there was an opportunity, Mick and I competed against each other. It wasn't an ambitious competitiveness where one brother takes joy in defeating the other. It was more of a case of pitting our strength or cunning against each other. When we were younger, it was more of a game to see who could kick a football the longest or who could swim out further into a swimming hole in Mt Emu Creek. Other times it was simply because we spent a lot of time together walking down the paddocks to cut thistles, to pick up stones and serving on the altar as altar boys. After a night's milking, we turned into the approaching darkness and raced each other over to the house for tea. The light of the kitchen was visible through the branches of the cypress trees that shadowed the house. Inside the kitchen was warmth from the open fire, the stove and Mum dishing up. Outside the cold night was closing in around us. Running in our rubber boots made this race more difficult, but we'd do anything to be inside out of the cold and the smell of the cows on our clothes. We slugged along the gravel track, pushing against each other, trying to send the other off-balance past the roundabout, the towering cypress trees, past the chook shed, the 44 gallon drums for the cattle dogs, past wet smells of the woodheap until we reached the grey cow yard bricks of the garage where the finish line materialized like magic in our minds.

Four women

Fresh out of school and with the excitement of her first paying job, a teenage girl pushes a crippled boy in a wheelbarrow around the wide streets of a country town in the early part of the twentieth century. The boy is afflicted by polio and he has spent months in a Warrnambool hospital ward receiving treatment to straighten and enliven his crooked legs. The teenage girl works in the boy's family home as a maid, helping to cook meals, scrubbing floors and attending to the needs of the boy. She boards with the family in a room of her own, yet this is a town that the teenage girl has breathed, has known. Some years earlier, her own family farmed near the Mount and milked cows on the heavy volcanic soil. She helped her father drag and lift metal milk churns to a wooden platform on the corner of her road. The milk churns were stamped with a number, C23, a number that let the truck drivers know who the churns belonged to, as well as being a number that the girl would memorize for years to come. Just like the job she had each day of pushing the boy around the gravel streets; his laughter and jokes of leaning out of the wheelbarrow when she took the corners tight. This first job that she had after leaving school was a homecoming of sorts to her. She knew this town with its red brick two-storey hotel and its weatherboard Post Office and she knew this boy and what he was trying to do with legs that wouldn't work. The boy's name was Alan Marshall, the town was Noorat and the teenage girl was Letitia Willis, my grandmother.

Letitia, or Nanna as she became known to our family was born in 1891, one of twelve children borne to John Willis and Letitia Carmody. After Nanna finished working for the Marshalls at Noorat, she returned to live with her family on the small dairy farm they rented at Tower Hill. John 'Rudd' Willis was a small time 'gentleman' dairy farmer who had an appointment each Thursday at a hotel in Port Fairy. Much of the work on the farm fell to Letitia's brother Alan, who milked the cows and planted onions and potatoes on the volcanic plains around the collapsed caldera of Tower Hill. Nanna's grandmother, Margaret Harris, a daughter of a convict, was running the Queen's Ferry Hotel near the Merri River at Dennington, just outside of Warrnambool. The hotel, which was built in 1856, was on the main road to Port Fairy (formerly Belfast). Nanna lived in the hotel for some time working as a maid and as a cleaner; jobs which would not have been easy for a single woman. By the time I was born in 1963, Nanna's husband, Louis had died and she was living in a weatherboard cottage in Warrnambool. Parts of her life remain a mystery to me, as does the character of the slender girl with glasses who pushed Alan Marshall around the streets of Noorat.

After Nanna and Louis were married, they moved to the weatherboard cottage in Warrnambool. They had five children together: Dorrie, Alan, Grace, Kevin and Mum was the youngest. Nanna was forty-five years old when she had Mum, who no doubt was referred to as the 'surprise'. During this time, Louis was a blacksmith who worked at a business on Fairy Street a short walk away from their house. According to the stories that I have been told, Louis had a great love of his own family, so much so, that he spent most nights eating dinner with his parents instead of his wife and children. He was known to have a temper and Dorrie told me stories of him threatening Nanna with an axe, and of the children having to be sent to the neighbours while Louis smashed up the crockery in the kitchen. When I asked Mum about these stories she said that she never witnessed any violence, but that she did remember being sent to the neighbour's house. When I asked her if Louis drank, she replied, no he didn't drink, but he might have been in a better mood if he had.

Mum's elder sister, Grace, turned nineteen the year Mum was born in 1933. An abiding story that has often been told was once when Grace picked Mum up as a baby, Mum promptly weed all over her. After Grace left school, her first job was working as a factory hand in the Warrnambool Woollen Mill. Apparently, Grace was an outgoing woman who loved going to the weekly dances in Warrnambool. However, she contracted tuberculosis at nineteen, which some people said was caused by the dust and fibres from blankets at the Mill. However, cases of TB were not unknown in Australia at the time and it would mostly likely have been caused by other means. Her treatment for TB meant trips to Melbourne at St Vincent's hospital, including some lengthy stays. They were trips that Louis and Nanna could not afford and so it was left to Nanna to hitch rides on trucks to Melbourne. Louis rarely visited his sick daughter in hospital. St Vincent's hospital backed onto the streets of Fitzroy, at the time a rough suburb of poverty and homelessness. One night, a truck driver on Gertrude Street dropped off Nanna. There were men fighting and drinking in the street. Nanna was a careful woman from a country town and she had to walk past their jeers and shouting to reach the boarding house where she was staying. These were scenes that Nanna had to face repeatedly until Grace succumbed to TB during a stay at a sanitorium for the treatment of the illness in Broadmeadows. The tragedy of Grace's death was enough, but as money was scarce in 1934, Nanna had to catch a ride back to Warrnambool in the front seat of the hearse with Grace's body in the rear. I can barely imagine the pain and heartache Nanna had to endure on that long drive along the Princes Highway through Geelong, Colac, Camperdown, Terang, Allansford and onto Warrnambool. Having to sit up front in the hearse with her daughter, Grace, lying in a coffin behind her would have been a car ride Nanna could never forget. Every parent wants to bring his or her children home from any stay in hospital and that return journey for Nanna must have been heartbreaking.

Although I had seen a tinted black and white photograph of Grace in a pile of family photographs as a child, the nature of Grace's death was kept from our family for a number of years. If I asked questions about how she died, Mum often said that she was only nineteen when she died of TB. But sometimes the facts are not enough. In fact, it is only as an adult and as a son who likes to ask questions that I have been able to discover the story of this tragic return home to Warrnambool for Nanna. It has never been a customary thing in our family to dwell on the past or on tragedies. My parents have always lived for the present and the possibility of what the future might bring. Stories of my parents' families have only come to light through their ageing and the relaxing of barriers that ageing often brings. Emerging from a Depression-era experience seemed to steel the resolve of my grandparents and so misfortune and bad luck were either accepted and not spoken about, or incidents were stoically denied the air that was required for families to breathe down through the generations.

As if Grace's death in 1934 was not enough tragedy for Nanna, she had to cope with further setbacks. After enduring the black-outs and food rations in Warrnambool during World War Two, the worry about her son, Alan, fighting against the Japanese in New Guinea, Nanna's younger son, Kevin, was killed in a car accident in Warrnambool, just after war was declared over. He was twenty-three. Nanna and Louis were too upset to collect Mum from St Anne's school so they sent a neighbour to tell Mum. Mum recalls it being strange that their neighbour, Mrs. Spong, had been sent to collect her from school and on the way Mrs. Spong could only say that Kevin was sick and that was why Mum was needed at home. When Mum opened the door to see Nanna crying and strange women in the house she realized that Kevin had died. Louis was away telling his own family about Kevin's death. Kevin had been a singer with a future ahead of him. He sang Irish ballads and had even made a 78 record. He had also enlisted to fight in World War Two but he never saw any action. It was a custom of the time that hats would not be worn on the day that a family member died. Nanna refused to wear her hat the day Kevin died. I was given the name, Kevin, as my middle name.

My earliest memories of Nanna, of accompanying Mum to visit her in a nursing home named Corio on a hill overlooking Liebig Street in Warrnambool, were tinged with sadness and mystery. A high sandstone wall ran around the perimeter of Corio, which had once been a grand Victorian style home. It is a short distance from where my parents currently live. Each time I drive past the sandstone wall Nanna's last days come back to me. She didn't drive and so throughout the 1960s she was separated from our life on the farm. Visits to her house in Warrnambool had been sporadic and so when she was moved into Corio, she seemed like a stranger to me. She often seemed to be resting in bed with what I thought was a pained expression on her face while she listened to Mum talk about our lives on the farm. She was a tall woman with an elegant neck. She wore thick-rimmed glasses and spoke with the caution of a woman who had been educated. What education Nanna had been fortunate to have, I didn't know, other than that family tragedy had been an experience and an education that had coloured her life. I imagine it was a life common to many women of the post-Depression era whose futures were often determined by hardship and what they couldn't do. Much of her life remains unknown and all I have to go on are my mother and her sister, Dorrie's memories of her living with Louis. It doesn't seem enough. Her death at Corio was a world away from the plucky teenager pushing Alan Marshall around the streets of Noorat.

■

Three of my grandparents died before I was born and so the knowledge I have of them has been passed down to me by my parents. Knowledge that is unreliable, subjective and which alters like sunlight passing across a wall. Sometimes it depends on whom I am hearing the stories from. Sometimes I don't know what to believe as in later years, Dad's stories of his father present themselves as anecdotes sprouting like weeds in the spur of the moment. Dad's mother, Granny, died in 1984 and so I came to know her well, well enough for her to feature in my dreams after she had died. On both sides of the family, my grandparents' lives involved daily struggle, more so for the women of the family. For it was the women who cooked, put to bed drunk husbands, cared for the children, milked the cows or saved the deposit for a house. The 1920s are often romanticized in film and television, yet I sensed there were few things romantic about milking cows in Morwell in 1925, or cleaning houses in Warrnambool as Nanna did so that one shilling per week could be put away for a dreamed-of house.

Granny grew up on her auntie's farm off the Three Chain Road at Crossley, ten kilometres from Koroit in the western district of Victoria. Her mother died when Granny was three and her father moved to Penshurst taking his four sons with him while leaving his daughter Joan at the Noonan's dairy farm. Her father remarried and his second wife gave birth to another seven children at Penshurst. All her life, Granny lived apart from her family. However, she wouldn't have to go far to begin her own family. The Noonans were neighbours to the Ryans, where Pop, my paternal grandfather grew up. He only had to lift the barbed wire fence to begin courting the girl he had been watching grow up. When they married, Pop was twenty-four and Granny was seventeen. In time, Granny gave birth to eleven children, two of whom died at a young age: Joan from Pink's disease aged eleven, and Adrian died from cancer on Christmas Day 1956. Pop and Granny rented a number of dairy farms before they settled at Yarpturk, near Koroit. A large part of their family life was spent at Badham's Lane in Moyne, where Dad was born. The house was without electricity and set back in the paddocks near the Korongarah flats between Moyne and Killarney. Hawkers frequented the farm selling bread, Indian curries and trinkets. Each year apiarists travelled south from Ararat to farm their bees on the rich strawberry clover Korongarah flats. They paid Pop in gallons of honey for the use of his land.

No doubt Granny put up with a lot rearing a large family with Pop frequently absent with his drinking, and when he did arrive home, Granny had to untie his boot laces as he lay snoring on their bed. Granny was a regular milker in the dairy, as were Dad's sisters, Rose, Nellie, Mary and Kate. A large woman with wavy, grey hair and a ready smile, Granny could be forthright in her opinions of local people. She spoke with an authority Dad rarely challenged in front of us. Later in life, perhaps due to the work and rough conditions of the houses she was living in, Granny developed asthma and had to be hospitalized several times, including on the day of Mum and Dad's wedding and Mum's first birth, with my sister Annie. On that night in November, both Granny and Mum were in the same hospital, giving Dad two reasons to be there.

Granny's kindness and stoic nature endeared her to many people. Well after Pop had died in 1961, Granny was famed for driving a cream and maroon Humber slowly around the streets of Koroit. Sometimes one of us kids would be farmed out to stay at Granny's house during the school holidays. Away from the noise and competitive arguing with my brothers and sisters, I could have whole days to myself wandering around her back yard, talking to her budgerigar, sometimes walking up the quiet streets of Koroit to look in the shops. They were precious days when I seemed to have the world to myself. There were no cows to be milked, no pigs to feed, no brothers to fight with. At meal times, I let myself be mesmerized by the gold flecks on her white laminex kitchen table. There was the local radio station on, Granny's questions to me about school and the prospect of cream cakes and ice creams that Granny indulged us with whenever she could. It was at Granny's that I saw my first episodes of 'Number 96', blushing at the sight of Abigail's breasts while Granny talked to a friend who had called over for a cup of tea. She let us stay up late and gave each of my brothers and sisters who stayed with her the space we craved growing up in a family of twelve.

Every school holidays she drove out to visit our family on the farm in her Humber. Koroit is approximately forty kilometres from Panmure and Granny's top speed was forty kilometres an hour. After Dad had been told that Granny was coming, my brothers and sisters and I looked to the cars on the Princes Highway, two kilometres away, for signs of her Humber. From our farmhouse we had a wide view of the highway and any slow moving car caught our attention. Is that her car? No, it's going past the turn off to Vickers Road, here she is. We watched her drive slowly down Vickers Road, followed the dust from her car as if it was a smoke signal. Kids ran through the house shouting, Granny's coming! Granny's coming. However, the main reason that my brothers and sisters jumped up and down at the news of Granny's visits was the ten ice creams she would bring with her. It was Granny's tradition to stop off at the milk bar in Panmure, buy the ice creams from Peter Bourke, who also looked forward to her visits, and bring them to us, parcelled into a box. We would mob her as soon as she was stepping out of the car. Mum would come out to wave us away and let Granny come in by the back screen door. Once she was sitting at the red laminex kitchen table, the ice creams would be carefully passed around to each of us. They were mostly icy poles, raspberries or banana splits. Apart from the ice creams, her visits also had an effect on Dad – for once he had to stop working and come into the house from the paddocks to talk with her at afternoon tea. Granny seemed to exert a calming presence on Dad as he put his arms behind his head and leant back to hear the news of the people from his district. By moving out to the farm at Panmure, Dad had consciously moved away from the people and farms he had grown up with. His people were on the far side of Koroit. Granny's drives out to Panmure were the equivalent of crossing a state border: the country was different; there were less connections between her and the family names. Like people everywhere resuming family connections, Granny talked to Dad about who had married, who had had a baby and who had died. For the cost of a few icy poles, Granny kept a family invested.

∎

Mystery and absence of information are common factors within families, even more so when it is a generation's preference to not speak to children about personal matters, love, attraction, desire or tragedy. The silences of Nanna and Louis Beattie were offset by the talkativeness of their daughters, Dorrie and Mum. The stories that each of them have told me have become the news of what I have had to go on.

Dorrie was my godmother, and as such, she always seemed to have a soft spot for me. As well as being farmed out to Granny's house in Koroit during the school holidays, sometimes Mick or Kathryn and myself would spend time at Dorrie and Ernie's orange brick house in Koroit. Compared to our own ramshackle garden of bushes and jonquils, Dorrie's garden was resplendent with roses, dahlias, daisies and annuals bordering the driveway each time I visited. Their red Holden Premier parked in front of the wooden garage was also immaculately clean. They had lived on a soldier-settlement farm at Tarrone for many years before moving into Koroit, a move which took Dorrie twelve months to get used to. Bowls, cards and fishing were their regular pursuits. One night Dorrie and Ernie took me fishing with friends at Killarney beach. While they were sitting behind the hummocks to the beach and sharing beers and cigars, Dorrie passed a thin brown cigar to me. It was the first time I had smoked. I was thirteen at the time.

They had married at the outbreak of World War Two and after Ernie's return from serving in New Guinea they moved to a farm at Tyrrendara near Portland. The house was primitive with no hot water. Bread was cooked daily, even soap had to be made. One year Tyrrendara won the footy premiership and there was a big celebration planned at the local hall. Ernie had been drinking in the afternoon so he and Dorrie hitched a ride to the celebrations with some neighbours in the back of a cattle truck. The driver took a back road to the hall, one they had been on repeatedly. Recent rain had softened the road and its sandy edges had turned into slush. Not surprisingly, it didn't take long for the truck to become bogged. They were all stuck in a cattle truck under a black sky miles from the hall. Dorrie was wearing an evening dress, Ernie a suit. Ernie and one of the men began walking toward the light of a distant farmhouse. The wind kicked up and Dorrie sat in the cabin of the truck in her evening dress, shivering, and told her life story to a man she barely knew. They talked on through the hours until Ernie returned with a tractor and they were able to tow the truck free of the ruts. The sky was beginning to lighten. They drove to the hall hoping there might still be music to dance to, but when they arrived the hall was deserted. The celebrations were over. Streamers and empty beer bottles were scattered across the wooden floor. With nothing else to do, they turned the truck around and drove towards home past the spot where Dorrie had spent the night talking and waiting. When they were dropped off, Ernie thanked the driver, Dorrie climbed down from the cabin in her evening dress and together they walked over to the dairy after their night out to prepare for another morning's milking.

Dorrie was twenty years older than Mum and while Mum has certainly shared stories of her childhood with me, it was Dorrie whom I asked about family history. It was Dorrie who told me stories about Louis walking several blocks to eat with his parents instead of his wife and children each night. My parents belong to the generation where it is not acceptable to say a bad word about other people, that the past is over, it is not important. Dorrie was an exception to this belief, although she often deferred to it by saying, you don't want to know about this, before renewing the past with a story. She always enjoyed a laugh, gossip and people who were characters. Often when she came out to the farm for family gatherings she enjoyed a beer. Unlike Mum, Dorrie would sit on kitchen chairs under wonky umbrellas out of the sun with the men, stirring them up, taking as much as she could give. She had a strong moral sense and occasionally she would fix you with a stare behind her glasses before she relaxed into a grin and a sip of her beer. Later in her life, I drove out to Koroit for visits and the cricket commentary would be turned up so loud I could hear what Richie Benaud was saying in her garden. Dorrie had taken her hearing aids out. I knew that by listening to her stories with cups of tea and dry biscuits with tomato and salt and pepper the past was alive for me. It was a place possessed by stories, half-truths and images repeated like the look on Nanna's face the night she had to lock Dorrie and Grace in the lounge room away from Louis who was in a rage.

One of her favourite sights was the view of Killarney beach from the eastern bank of Tower Hill. Looking south from the bitumen road that skirts Tower Hill is a panoramic sweep of dairy farms, the dark, volcanic soil of fallow potato paddocks, farmhouses and the vivid blue of the ocean. This is where the Irish first settled when they emigrated to Australia after the Irish famine of the 1850s, either as free settlers, or pardoned convicts. It was a view Dorrie never tired of recalling or repeating as if the view of breakers at Killarney beach could be a prayer she returned to for balance and common sense.

■

Mum was studying shorthand and typing while completing her Proficiency and Intermediate years of schooling at St Anne's when she was approached by a local business to leave school and begin working for them. Ray Barnes from Ray Barnes' bakery had contacted the school as he was in need of an office girl. His regular office girl was leaving the business to get married. This was the custom in the 1950s. Once a woman was married it was expected that she would leave work so that she could begin a family. The nuns at St Anne's College recommended Mum because they knew that the cost of her education was a worry to Nanna and Louis. This was despite the fact that Mum really liked school and would have kept on going, if she had been given the chance. When I asked Mum if she knew of any woman who returned to work after they were married, she replied no, it was just something you did. She worked in the office at the bakery for ten years, finishing up in 1960, the year of her marriage, and the birth year of her eldest daughter, Annie.

Prior to their marriage, Mum and Dad had bought a weatherboard house in a paddock at Crossley, a short distance from Koroit. With Mum's savings, Dad's work at the Nestles factory in Dennington they were able to buy it outright for eleven hundred pounds. While there was some furniture left behind by the previous owners, the Ritchies, the house was without a telephone and hot water. There was an outside toilet and an old copper in an outside laundry for washing clothes. A white picket fence ran out front of the house which faced onto the Koroit Penshurst Road. Mum planted roses and daisies while Dad grew onions and potatoes in the small paddocks beside the house and in their second year at Crossley Dad sold the potatoes for eight pounds a bag.

The image of a woman living in the country on her own while her husband is away is a well-known literary trope and has a long history in Australian literature. While Mum and Dad were hardly pioneers battling snakes and the monotony of the bush, Mum did experience the isolation and loneliness that many country women have coped with at different stages of their lives. There were families nearby such as the Conroys, the Gavins and O'Gormans plus a host of single men and women living alone or with siblings. Mum didn't have a licence and these neighbours were not Mum's people, and despite Crossley being familiar to Mum through the dances at St Brigid's Hall, Crossley was not her district. Mum was a townie and these people were Dad's people, such as Mrs. Carey who raised ten children before she died at forty- five. Dad was at home with these people as he was with the stories about them. Even now, when I take Dad for a drive around the district he can still remember the search for a man who went missing and who was later found hanging in a tank after he committed suicide.

Mum's struggle with living in a house without hot water and often alone with a young baby came to a head with her second pregnancy in 1961. One week before she was due to give birth, Mum's doctor asked if there was a history of twins in the family. With no history of twins, Mum had to suddenly get used to the idea. She was totally unprepared for it regarding clothes, bassinettes and feeding two babies instead of one. The doctor cautioned Mum to remain close to Warrnambool but she had to return to collect her belongings. She was three weeks before the due date and a neighbour consoled Mum by saying it's better to be having two little ones than one big one. The next morning she told Dad that she didn't feel well and he replied on his way to work, it's probably nerves. Her waters broke after lunch while Annie was sleeping. Mum knew that she had to act quickly so she left Annie and walked up the road where some old fellas were talking but she didn't like to say anything to them. She kept walking towards the Conways but they were not home, so she scrambled further up the road to a dairy where a farmer was milking. In shock at the news that Mum gave him, Reg Cox stopped milking and drove Mum back home in his ute to collect Annie, placed her in the back of the ute in her bassinette and drove up towards Pink-Eye Moloney's wife. Pink-Eye was given his name because he grew mustard during World War Two which was exported to Europe for the manufacturing of mustard gas. Mrs. Moloney drove Mum onto St John Of God's hospital in Warrnambool where she gave birth to Michael and Theresa an hour later. Michael was underweight and he was said to fit inside a shoebox.

With three children under one, the house at Crossley wasn't going to measure up. Mum and Dad managed to sell the Crossley house for fifteen hundred pounds which was enough to pay off their mortgage and put a deposit down on a new house in Warrnambool. In more recent times, the house at Crossley has been cleared and all that remains of it is a small ditch in a paddock. It is a space that Dad reminds us of each time we drive past. I am always moved by the spaces within paddocks that suggest a previous house by a clump or circle of collapsing cypress trees. Many people would not know or perhaps care about the space where the Crossley house once stood; or how alive spaces within paddocks can be to the memories of people who have lived within them.

Children defined my parents' lives so much that they became the currency and mobility that Mum attained throughout her life. It was through having children that my parents were able to move forward. Having to give up her formal education in order to work and then having to give up her work in order to marry and have children, I often think of what would have happened for Mum if she had been allowed to remain at school. Would she have gone to university? Most likely not due to her family's lack of money and the expectations of women in the 1950s. Not one of my sisters has had to give up work in order to marry. Mum, Dorrie, Granny and Nanna all lived their lives before the advance of feminism and equal rights for women in the work place. In this way, they were hampered by their lack of choice and their ability to learn from other women. And yet, each of them lived lives of hardship, sometimes in spite of their husbands, and have left me with a sense of the dignity of country women.

Mother and daughter

A photo of her from the brown suitcase –
a fourteen year old in pigtails, pleated tunic,
Saturday morning optimism.
Her primly-dressed mother beside her
setting the pace. Their lives held
by the mother's formal gaze, a wariness
owing to the black and white era.
One of the few creased photos of my mother
before her office job, before marriage.
She has the innocent air of being in-life;
an ordinary moment developing, unaware
that much later she would stagger
from a farmhouse to a neighbour's dairy
about to give birth and wanting a lift.
Perhaps the photo lacks the truth
of men throwing chooks through the windows
of the Kirkstall Hall dances, or the lifts
my father gave her to the Pictures
her mother, up front, sitting in between them.
What can be trusted – the intent of her eyes
the future I throw back at her.
A mother and daughter stepping out
of a busy country street,
going somewhere without being able to arrive.

Shadow figures

After seven years of wearing white overalls, a hairnet and walking the washed concrete floors at the Nestles factory in Dennington, Dad walked out the door to become his own boss leasing a farm nobody else wanted. On that day in 1966, one of his work colleagues, Jack Moloney came up to Dad and said, 'Frank, I would love to do what you have done, but I don't have the guts to do it.' Perhaps it did take courage for Dad to leave Nestles, its certainty and safety, for the unknown territory of leasing a rundown farm at Panmure. Dad didn't forget Jack Moloney's comments; they were the words of a factory worker Dad kept replying to throughout his life. When I was working at the Kraft cheese factory in the 1980s, there were men who had been working there since the 1950s. Men of Dad's era who had not been able to let go of what a factory offered.

The owners of the farm, Ron and Nancy Vickers, had milked cows at Panmure since the early part of the twentieth century. Bob Vickers, the father of Ron and Tom, had cleared much of the bush from the paddocks, chopping down eucalypts and carting out the logs with a bullock and dray. Bob and his wife had built an old weatherboard with wide verandahs in the middle of a paddock on our neighbour's farm, which was also referred to by them as the 'home place'. When I was younger, I used to sneak into Bob Vickers' paddocks with my brothers and sisters and walk along the gravel lane that wound up to the rise the old house was positioned on. I remember its high ceilings, empty rooms thick with dust, the bird shit splattered tables and chairs. We loved to explore the rooms and furniture looking for souvenirs, imagining the people who might live in an old weatherboard in the middle of a paddock. To the west, there was a picturesque view of Mount Emu Creek, and further to the north-west, the low treeless hump of Mount Warrnambool. Two landmarks in my upbringing I would later write about, trying to understand a river and a mountain I would watch each day.

In November 1965, Ron Vickers died in mysterious circumstances. Throughout my life I had been told that he had died of a bull ant bite; a death that only seemed to go with my visions of a wild and untamed country that I imagined before we moved onto the farm at Vickers Road. Despite the nature of Ron Vickers' sudden death, Ron's health had been in decline for some time. For years after we took over the farm, empty whiskey bottles could be found lying around the paddocks, in clumps of thistles, and would be brought to the surface in floods, or when Dad began ploughing the paddocks. The empty bottles around the farm challenged my ideas about hard-working farmers; men who might drink a bit, but who were expected to handle their liquor. Ron Vickers' death from a bull ant or beetle bite, the empty bottles rising to the surface throughout the paddocks and the rough state of the farm in 1966 only seemed to emphasize the tragic-comedy elements of farming that Henry Lawson wrote about in the 19th century.

When tenders for lease were called for Ron Vickers' farm in 1966 Dad asked his friend at Nestles, Dan Scullion what he thought of the farm and its lease price. Scullion was an ex-farmer who had lost his dairy farm at Garvoc, five kilometres from Panmure, due to debts and drinking.

'What's the country like out there?'

'God it would be rough.' Scullion replied. 'But I think it would be worth having a go. You'd make a go of it.'

Dad chuckled and tore the notice out of the newspaper. He had already been knocked back on offers to lease a soldier settlement farm at Heystesbury. He had little in the way of savings, but he had a great desire to farm.

After Mrs Vickers agreed to sign the lease for Mum and Dad to take on the farm, Dad visited the manager of the Commercial Bank in Warrnambool to ask for a loan. Listening to Dad's details of the request, the manager replied, 'No, no, no. You'll go broke. There's no hope for you in leasing that farm.' Dad walked out disappointed but came back the next day and the day after, yet he was met with the same response. He spoke to a friend, Vin Mugavin, who was a farmer at Woodford, and who suggested he visit the manager of his bank, the Commonwealth Bank, in Warrnambool. Dad made an appointment with the bank manager and explained the particulars of his request, which included buying a herd of cows as well as being able to pay the quarterly payments to Mrs Vickers. The manager replied, 'Mr Ryan, you don't want to see a bank manager, you don't want to see me. You want to see a fairy godmother.' Frustrated by the manager's use of sarcasm and refusal to grant a loan, Dad jumped out of the chair, smashed his fist on the manager's desk, swore at the manager and shouted, 'I don't want to see a fairy godmother! I want to see a bank manager!' He smashed his fist on the desk again, rose to his full height and stormed out of the office, slamming the door behind him so hard that by the time Dad was out on the footpath, he could still hear the door shuddering.

Two days later, Dad was speaking to Vin Mugavin who relayed the bank manager's comments about Dad to him. The manager described Dad storming out of the office and said, 'I've never seen anyone like him. That's the wildest bugger I've ever talked to.' Many people would have been humiliated or disappointed by the treatment Dad received by the managers and given up. While the bank managers would have been right to be cautious about lending money to a person without credit or savings, the fact that Dad had a steady job at Nestles might have ensured he would receive a loan in today's economic climate. Undeterred by the knockbacks, Dad persisted in going back to the manager of the Commercial Bank who eventually relented and said, 'I'll take you on, but you'll go broke. There's no hope for you.'

Days later, Scullion and Dad were driving out from Warrnambool to have a look at the farm. They stood and looked at the paddocks of tussocks, stands of bush, tree stumps, fallen down fences and bracken. Scullion shook his head, smiled at Dad and said, 'It's wild, and rough. Who else but you would want it?' After their visit, Scullion drove Dad along Occupation Lane at Garvoc, where his own farm had been, to see his neighbour, Jim McKinnon. McKinnon was a relative of the Vickers family and he was also the executor of Ron Vickers' will. Scullion put a word in for Dad with McKinnon, who was to become a life-long friend of our family, to make a choice between leasing the land to a farmer who wanted to run beef cattle or give it to 'the man from Warrnambool with five kids.'

Scullion was a man I didn't meet but who was often referred to over the years by Dad. He lived in a clinker-brick house on the Princes Highway in Dennington, within walking distance to Nestles. Each time Dad took us out to visit Granny or his younger brother, Trevor, in Koroit on a weekend, he would shout out in the car as we were passing, 'Hello Scullion, good to see you.' But Dad never stopped to go in. I am not sure why, other than we were often on our way to elsewhere. However, Scullion became one of the many men that Dad referred to over the years, and who we never met or only met on the rarest of occasions if we bumped into them on the street in Warrnambool or at the Warrnambool saleyards, where everybody seemed to know my father. It was as if once Dad was married and working on a farm, and helping to bring up a family, many connections to his former life were lost. As a result, Scullion by his very name loomed larger than life in Dad's stories. We had to imagine this man, his life and early influence on Dad. He became a shadow figure in the outline of Dad's early life; a person referred to only by name, yet given respect. For myself, trying to know and understand the influence of such men as Scullion in Dad's life has been like trying to read a paddock in drought.

Dad is from the generation that doesn't talk about their troubles or the family members who might have brought some embarrassment to their family. It was often the men in Dad's family who were the mystery figures; uncles I rarely got to know or understand. As always in the country, there was a decision to be made of remaining on the farm or in the district and of leaving the district to live and work elsewhere. Dad's brother

Adrian moved to Horsham to work on the railways with their sister Nellie and he was a brother who kept his distance from the remainder of the family throughout his life. He was always the brother who lived in Murtoa who we never visited, and who never visited us. According to Dad, there was no real reason for this estrangement from the family, 'he was just cranky'. At Dad's mother's funeral, Adrian remained sitting in his car at Tower Hill cemetery rather than stand around the grave and talk to his brothers and sisters. He may have suffered from depression. He lived alone in a unit in Murtoa and drank. The facts don't add up for the mystery of an uncle I never met. But do we ever know our uncles and aunties foisted on us by birth? People who we share physical resemblances with, but who can be as remote as the dreams they have followed through their lives.

Dad's father, Michael 'Pop' Ryan was only in his 60s when he died of cancer in 1961. From the photographs that I have seen of him, he was a large man with a ruddy Irish face and fair hair. In the pubs around Koroit and Port Fairy he was known as Shine Ryan, but Dad always referred to him as Pop. A colourful character perhaps, but within his own family, his authoritarian presence was more sobering, even negative towards providing opportunities for his children. According to Dad, Pop always said that in an argument if you were still talking, you stood a chance of winning. Like many farmers, he was a man also driven by routine, both personally and through the expectations of a community. Each Thursday, after shopping, Pop would meet other farmers at Mickey Bourke's hotel in Koroit. The sessions at Mickey Bourke's, a pub famed for its antique furniture and loyalty to the Catholic community, would last until stumps at 6pm, after which, the men would adjourn to a local's house to continue drinking and playing cards into the early hours of the next morning. All around Koroit, farmer's wives, like Granny, had to milk the cows on a Thursday evening. Often the farmers' sessions continued on into Friday until their wives could come and pick the men up from whichever house or pub they had finished up at. Two-day blinders were accepted in those days for farmers accustomed to hard work in semi-remote dairy farms. They still wore their suits to Mass each Sunday and perhaps it was easier to eke out a living on dairy farms with smaller herds. Yet it is no surprise that although Dad has enjoyed a drink over the years, he has never been a big drinker like his father. In many ways, he has lived his life in reaction to his 'doom and gloom' father.

Yet Pop also had a moral view of life. One of his sayings that Dad quotes is - 'I'd trust a thief before a liar.' The implication being that a thief might change their life after being in a low spot whereas once a person made a conscious decision to tell a lie, they would never change. Undoubtedly this viewpoint has a Christian background, and is a moral that Pop would have heard regularly at Mass, Thou shalt not steal. Pop's interpretation of the eighth commandment actually challenges the accepted view. However, there is clearly a difference between white, everyday lies and deliberate lies that affect other people. When Pop was dying of cancer in the Warrnambool hospital in 1961, his son Trevor was involved in some trouble in Koroit. Pop was close to dying and Dad went in to see him in hospital. Pop had heard about the trouble and he asked Dad, 'Was the Lad involved in that trouble?' Dad couldn't bring himself to tell his father that Trevor was involved so he said, 'Oh there's been a few caught up in it. They don't know who's to blame at the moment.' Dad's lie, which spared his dying father of more grief and sadness, was a lie of character, a lie which revealed much about my father.

At the time, Dad had been working on the farm at Yarpturk and almost every day for twelve months he had listened to Pop complaining of pains in his stomach. But Pop wouldn't see a doctor. People of his generation stayed away from doctors and hospitals. Eventually, he saw a doctor in Warrnambool on a Wednesday. On Thursday he was 'opened up', by Sunday he was dead. He was sixty-seven. Pop, Adrian, Scullion and Dan Madden; names I heard a lot about and people I didn't get the chance to meet. Men who figured large in my father's life yet who remain allusive and mysterious as many country men.

Skull stumps

Dan Scullion's description of the 209 acres on Vickers Road Panmure captured the essence of the country. It was wild, and as Dad would later say, hungry country. Thistles and blackberry were rampant. There were four big paddocks, 'no grass, just rubbish and tussocks.' While the paddocks were cleared of trees, there were still a lot of tree stumps, or as Dad called them skull stumps, left in the paddocks. They hadn't been dragged out of the paddocks and this was another job facing Dad when he first surveyed the farm. The weatherboard house on the farm was also in a state of ruin. Paint was peeling from the weatherboards, the tin roof was rusting and there was no hot water in the house. Once again, Mum and Dad were starting from the bottom of the farming ladder.

Clearing the land of tussocks and stones, fertilizing the paddocks with superphosphate to encourage new grasses to sprout were the goals for much of the early years on the farm. The skull stumps of trees were scattered around the four main paddocks, which always made me wonder how heavily forested the farm had been before it was cleared. Snakes loved to curl up in the nooks of the skull stumps or to lay on the warm wood in the sun. One day Dad was walking in a paddock toward the strip of bush that forms a boundary on the southern side of the farm and he counted seven snakes on tree stumps sunning themselves and looking at him as he passed. Many years later, I was with Dad when he was giving a family friend a tour of the farm. We came upon a black snake sunning itself in the crook of a tree skull. Instinctively, Dad bent down, grabbed the snake by its tail, swung it over his head and broke its back on the cattle track. He swung it down a further two times to make sure the snake's back was broken. I couldn't believe what he had just done, and the friend who was also a farmer, of not many words, simply added, 'good work Frank,' and they walked on. I turned around to watch blood dripping from the snake's nose, its black body glistening as it hung over a barbed wire fence. It was the first time I had seen my father kill a snake.

Although he had prepared Mum by telling her that it was an old house, a house she was moving into at the expense of a new conite house in Warrnambool where we had been living, she was in shock when she arrived. Not only was paint peeling from the weatherboards, many of the weatherboards were loose and falling from the walls. Cypress trees planted around the house accentuated the gloomy air of neglect. Dad had to lift the rusted side gate off its hinges so that Mum could enter by the back door. She stepped into a skillion lean-to which comprised the kitchen and small bathroom. Each of the rooms was covered with lino, sometimes patchy and peeling. There was an open-fire place at one end of the kitchen. A further step-up into the house proper took her into the lounge with its thin plywood walls, a bedroom off to the left and at the front of the house two bedrooms including the master. A wooden verandah with a view west over a small paddock to Vickers Road ran across the front of the house. Some of the verandah boards were rotten, especially on each end of the verandah where rain water had leaked from holes in the spouting and softened the faded wood. The laundry was outside at the rear of the house in a weatherboard lean-to. Next to the laundry was the wooden thunder-box toilet which was crowded with cobwebs and the suspicion of spiders. While the bathroom next to the kitchen had a bath and wash-basin, hot water had to be boiled in a copper and brought in from the laundry outside for bathing, washing dishes and clothes. One of the first improvements Dad made to the farm was to have a local electrician, Jimmy Leahy, install an electric hot water system in the outside laundry. Prior to this, hot water was carried into the house by bucket from the copper in the laundry. It was a miracle that nobody was scalded as hot water was tipped into the bath, the kitchen sink or carried in a bucket to mop the worn linoleum floor. For much of our early lives on the farm, our sole source of water was from the tank beside the house, and so we were always reminded to go easy on the water. Bath night became Saturday night, after football, and if you were unlucky to be the last person in the bath, the water was most likely to be as dark as the night.

Dad has often described the type of country we were farming on as 'hungry' country. It is a term that I have seen to describe many other areas of land in Victoria and other parts of Australia and perhaps the term 'hungry country' symbolizes an unforgiving country, a country that doesn't produce the types of grass necessary for dairy milk production. How indigenous people used and farmed the land around Panmure prior to white occupation would be instructive to many of us. Dad has also called the grass rubbishy, bent grass; grass that dries off too quickly, grass that won't sustain a cow. In 1966, there were four days where the temperature reached over one hundred degrees. Dad had cut grass for hay in one of the back paddocks. A neighbour came with a hay press to bale up the hay for Dad, but much of the hay was so dry that it simply blew away as dust in the wind. With the hay bale count down, there would be less summer feed for the cows, less milk production, less money for food.

Shortly after taking over the lease, Dad looked down at his shoes and realized they were 'buggered'. He looked around in the laundry, as he had seen an old pair in a corner, and tried them on. They fitted with a squeeze, but he could wear them. He wore the shoes for twelve months, shopping in Warrnambool, to Mass on a Sunday, to the football on a weekend. One day he was visiting Jim McKinnon at his Garvoc farm and Jim's eldest daughter, Valerie, a woman in her early twenties, kept looking down at Dad's shoes. Dad sensed that she had discovered that he was wearing Ron Vickers' shoes while he spoke to her father. Valerie looked at Dad, but didn't say a word. Dad didn't say anything, and he walked away smiling to himself, filling Ron Vickers' shoes admirably.

Hunger wasn't only confined to the country or cows in 1966. Mum and Dad struggled financially to pay the rent and after being given three months grace on repayments for the herd, the cost of each cow had to be accounted for. Their income for the financial year of 1966-67 was $14,000 of which Mrs Vickers was paid $5,000 rent. The following year their income from the farm was $10,000. While the first year on the farm had provided Mum and Dad with enough to think that running a farm might be viable, the drought of 1967-68 challenged their hopes and dreams of staying on the land. Not only were the paddocks dry and dust storms more frequent, the cows were struggling to provide enough milk to maintain an income. Dad had noticed road work beginning on the Princes Highway between Panmure and Garvoc and he enquired about finding some work to supplement the farm income. Luckily, he was given the chance to drive a roller on the road works. A road roller has the grace and agility of a giraffe and there is the sense that it could topple over at anytime. There was a story going around our family that this is how Dad ended his time at the CRB, by running the roller off the road and into a ditch. However, this like many other family stories is built on myth and memory. Dad drove the roller back and forwards over the gravel and scoria with the CRB for three months during the summer of 1967-68. He would milk most of the cows in the morning and then have Mum finish the milking so that he could drive up the road to work. In the afternoon, Mum who was pregnant with Jack, and sometimes with the help of Mick who was seven years old, would complete most of the afternoon's milking before Dad returned home from work.

Our kitchen cupboards were often empty, especially before shopping day on a Wednesday. It was a constant battle for Mum to fill the cupboards with a growing family and dwindling finances. One Saturday morning Mum told Dad that all she had was three dollars in her purse and that the cupboards were empty. She said that maybe they could drive down to the Panmure store, buy some flour and she could make some scones.

Before they went into the store, Dad checked the Panmure post office for mail and his heart leapt when he discovered that his tax refund had come through from his last year at Nestles. Now we could eat something more than scones for tea. Mum and Dad celebrated by driving into Warrnambool, buying up on groceries and then in the afternoon, dropping us kids off at Nannas' house so that the two of them could go to the football to watch South Warrnambool play. Mum had grown up in South Warrnambool and her brother Alan had played for them in the 1950s. This was my parents' special treat. Mum said that their philosophy was that if they couldn't afford to go to the football, then they would have to stay home. Although the early years on the farm were a financial struggle, Mum and Dad did make something out of the 'wild and rough country' they walked into. For myself, growing up on the farm at Vickers Road, home became more than a house; it became the paddocks, the creek, the mountain, the jokes and squabbles my brothers and sisters shared with each other and the space my parents gave to us all. When I was young, we didn't go anywhere. We couldn't afford to, and we didn't need to. We were always staying home.

Cows and bulls on the loose

Mostly, our bulls were Jerseys; stud bulls bought to improve the quality of the herd or bulls that we reared from A.I. semen. There was one dark Jersey stud bull called Idler that Dad paid a lot of money for. Idler serviced the cows on the farm for a number of years. Dad dreamed of Idler being the difference between having an average dairy herd and quality Jerseys who produce milk rich in butterfat and that would fill our vat. He talked of naming the farm after Idler. Much like he talked of building a tennis court for us kids in the front garden paddock. Instead, after Idler had died, he was loaded onto the carryall, his head and hooves hanging over the edge, and driven by tractor up to the bush where he was dumped onto a bed of ferns. We buried a number of bulls up in the bush, the smell rising from the ferns whenever I walked near, until Dad discovered that he was not meant to be burying them up there. I used to think of the foxes and our dogs having a feast on Idler, and how he worked so hard for us, or spent days just standing around and then at the end, after we had finished with him, we just dropped him off the carryall into the ferns.

Good money could be earned with large bull calves and for a while we joined Hereford bulls with the Jerseys to try and bolster the size of our calves. Watching a large Hereford bull with his curved horns virtually squash a Jersey cow as he climbed on top of her was not a pretty sight. The more popular and successful breeding method that we eventually adopted was the use of Artificial Insemination. A.I. was used to produce not only larger, more profitable bull calves but also a better quality of cow. The majority of our cows were impregnated with the A.I. man turning up to shove his arm into a cow's vagina and insert the semen into the cow through a long steel rod. The cows were generally joined to A.I. in batches so that they would calve at staggered intervals throughout the year. Watching the A.I. man get behind each cow in the bail of the dairy, shove his arm wrapped in plastic into the cow and then pull it out made me realize there were some jobs I couldn't do. Although I had put my arm inside a cow's vagina to feel the slimy hooves of a calf in a difficult birth, I couldn't do what the A.I. man did for a living. And yet, I was surprised by how cheerful and young some of the A.I. men were who drove around the district impregnating our neighbours' herds. Our own bulls were joined with the cows mainly to mop-up the cows that didn't join successfully with the A.I. semen. While joining cows through A.I. is easier on the cows than having a bull jump on them, I used to look at the bulls moaning at the bottom wire of a fence while the cows were in the dairy. The bulls didn't see much action, and yet for us, they still needed to be treated with respect.

It often depended on the character of the bull as to how much caution needed to be adopted when one had to be rounded up. Dad's call of 'C'mon, C'mon' from the dairy got the bulls' attention if they were not already nosing the fence wires next to the cowyard. If a bull needed to be called up to join a cow, Dad would walk out into the paddock, armed with a pitch fork and shoo the bull toward the gate that led into a small holding yard next to the dairy. A bullin cow on heat would be standing nervously in the holding yard, its skin shining from the sweat and the heat its body was generating. My brothers and sisters and I stood in a line in the paddock to corral the bull towards the holding yard. My heart was always racing as the Hereford or Jersey bull with its huge shoulders and loose neck folds trotted towards us. Once the bull saw the bullin cow in the holding yard, it picked up speed and raced single-mindedly towards the cow. It reminded me of the footage I had seen of monitor lizards racing toward tethered goats, petrified by the smell of the monster racing towards them. Once inside the holding yard, the bull walked around the cow, sniffing its back before jumping on top. The act was over within seconds with the bull astride on top, jerking forward, the cow being shaken, and stumbling for a foothold in the mud before the bull slid off, still sniffing the cow's vagina. As a child, it was a fascinating sight watching the bull jump on the cows and it always emphasized for me, the primal nature of bulls and cows, even more so when a bullin cow jumped on other cows' backs. We left the bull with the cow in the holding yard for another twenty minutes or whatever time it took them to lose interest, after which they were let out to go, like strangers, their separate ways.

For many years I have had nightmares and dreams about bulls. In the dreams the bulls are chasing me, or running toward someone that I know. In other dreams they are on the loose, lunging with their terrible shoulders, unable to be caught, unable to be escaped from, a threat that hums with a powerful sense of fear in the background of the dream. Often they are young black bulls, wild and unable to be contained. I have written some of the dreams down but have thought about them, rather than analysed their meaning or symbolism. A bull on the loose on our farm sent a shiver of fear up us all. It was the unpredictability of a bull that unnerved us. They weren't able to be subdued like dairy cows. Their nature was stubborn, often repressed, and shirty if upset. They were capable of anything. The bulls did manage to force their way through the bull paddock fence a number of times and sometimes they ambled around the house munching on unfamiliar grasses. Mum kept the smaller children inside while Dad and 'the boys' went outside to shoo the bull back into its paddock. Sometimes Dad would be away and chasing the bull back was left to me, Mick or whoever else was around. At other times, cows wandered from their day paddocks to eat the grass around the house and dropped moons of cow shit on the front lawn and garden. The division between house and farm was clear and hard fought for. A house and garden needed to be kept clean and ordered. The worst case scenario was to have a cow trotting and shitting down the hallway of our house. This sense of order and control was something that, if provoked, a bull could challenge. Mostly, the bulls muttered to the bottom wires of fences, squatted down to rub their shoulders against a ditch or ambled slowly across the bull paddock, keeping their territorial distance from each other. The only sense of havoc that the bulls created was in my dreams.

The boy in the shadow of the bus

My brothers and sisters and I stand around a tin bus shelter at the intersection of Occupation Lane and the Princes Highway near Garvoc waiting for an old red bus to take us to school. The intersection is on the downward slope of a hill. I look across Bernie Kelly's paddocks to the south, over the red gums hugging the curves of Mt Emu Creek, over the ridges of Monks' farm to the white weatherboards and green roof of our farmhouse. It is not a grand country home or a farmhouse to be admired; it barely has enough rooms to contain ten children and two adults. But it represents everything that I know and feel at that moment. When I see the farmhouse from a distance I begin to relax. If I concentrate hard enough I can see the trail of Jerseys winding up the muddy lane and into one of the day paddocks. Dad is finishing up milking at 8 o'clock and we are catching a bus to school.

The bus heads north into flat stony country. We rarely meet other cars on the narrow bitumen road. We pick up Terry Harney, the Arundels, Healeys and Finnigans. Throughout my primary school years, I have a crush on Lois Arundel but I am too shy to do anything about it. She has blonde hair, the middle child in a large family, and she is one of the smartest kids in our grade. She seems to be unattainable. I watch trails of cows leaving dairies, muddy tracks marking the paddocks like veins. Sometimes I let my eye follow a farmer on a motor bike or a tractor driving across the stony paddocks. I think of what it would be like to be a farmer rounding up cows instead of going to school. After picking up Bradley Porter on a hill, the bus descends into a flat expanse that might have been a lake in another lifetime. There are few trees and the ridge lines of rocky paddocks to the north recede in waves toward the horizon. The Harris brothers are waiting at a treeless intersection that could be anywhere. The bus turns right in the direction of Terang. We pass The Sisters – two lonely humps in the rocky paddocks that I stare at and fail to understand.

Each morning becomes a familiar repetition of the rhythms of the bus ride. Songs and squeals along narrow winding roads, glancing out at the rock-strewn paddocks and those passages when nobody needs to be picked up. The driver puts his foot down and the bus falls quiet as we edge closer to Terang. Sometimes, I am sick with worry for the day ahead, but mostly I am happy to be attending school. I have friends, I can play football, generally, I fit in. In the afternoon, the sun is chasing us home and the bus becomes quieter as each family hops off. I stare out the window at the paddocks, the farmhouses and dairies. The shadow of the bus stretches against cypress plantations. I can see a boy sitting in the shadow of the bus and wonder if this is how other people see me.

In 1969, I start Grade Prep at St Thomas' Primary School in Terang. A Sisters of Mercy school that started in 1907. It caters to students from Prep to Year 10; or children who can barely write to teenagers who think they are ready to drive. The nuns live a in a double-storey red brick gothic style convent beside the school. No student is ever allowed in the convent. There are lay teachers as well as nuns who teach, but it is the nuns who have the authority. There is Sister Ambrose, who later changes her name to Sister Nora when Rome allows women to take on a female name. The principal is Sister Maria, a large red-cheeked woman who is considered fair but strict by students. Many of the older boys are farmers' sons who are used to physical work, and who have long hair. The older girls also have long hair and suntans. There are fights in the 'burner yard' at lunch time; an open play area with patches of grass stranded amongst expanses of clay and gravel. Lunch time sports such as football, cricket and British Bulldog are either played in the burner yard or the top paddock. For another kind of competitive sport, the Year nine and ten boys slug it out, tearing at shirts, bloodying noses and trading blows until Sister Josephine comes out with a broom to shoo them off each other. She is half their size but her voice carries the air of authority. Soon after, the thwack of a strap hitting a bare hand can be heard from outside Sister Maria's office. However, this type of justice doesn't seem to deter some of the boy-men, whose reputations carry more weight than leather.

One of the lay teachers whose reputation precedes her is Mrs O'Connor, or Conny as we call her. She is a large, imposing woman in her sixties, with greying hair tied into a bun, glasses, wrinkled skin and a booming voice. She yells and rages at students in all classes and consequently, students behave themselves. She prowls the classroom, peering over students' shoulders with her raspy breaths, eyeballing any student who looks up. This is the era of rote learning, of repeating spelling words together as a class from the Level Speller. If one student misspells a word on the list, the whole class has to go back to the beginning of the list and repeat the words. Times tables are chanted like prayers. In Annie's classroom the bottom row of windows is white-washed by Conny because students are looking out the window instead of saying their times tables.

In grade three, Miss Hughson wants to know what we will be when we grow up. We have been warned about having to stand up in front of the class and speak for some days beforehand and I am feeling nervous and worried as I haven't been able to come up with anything. At home, I ask Mum what I should say and she says I should say what I want to say. But I don't know what I want to say. Each student walks up in turn, steps onto the wooden platform at the front of the class and announces to the silent throng what they will be. Naturally, there are several students who want to be farmers, nurses, and some teachers. My heart is thumping as I bump my way around desks to the front and announce in a quiet voice that I want to be a banker. Miss Hughson is supportive and smiles. I walk back to my chair blushing, trying to get used to the idea that this could actually happen. I don't know anybody who is a banker.

Most afternoons Mum drives the blue HR Holden from our farmhouse on Vickers Road up to Occupation Lane to pick us up after school. It is three kilometres from our farm to the bus stop. Sometimes we have to walk home along the gravel verge of the Princes Highway facing oncoming traffic before we turn left into the sanctuary of Vickers Road. Nobody else, besides the Monks and the milk tanker drive down Vickers Road. It is a gravel road of potholes bordered on the east by a line of towering cypress trees. An old wooden bridge with paint peeling from its rails crosses the shallow waters of Mt Emu Creek. It is a road that sends up clouds of dust whenever any car ventures down it. It is a road Theresa careered down, as her Torana skidded on a patch of worn blue metal stones. It is a road Jack rolled his car on, then rushed home to get his camera so that he could take photos with his mate hanging out of the car windows. It is a road that I know. The times when we do have to walk home Mum is usually helping in the dairy. These walks home from the school bus are times to daydream, look at the thistles in the paddocks, keep an eye out for snakes in the roadside grass and blackberry bushes. I walk home with my brothers and sisters trailing behind or ahead of me. We could be anywhere in the country, yet there is something known about this road that never leaves me. I walk home kicking stones and know that I am leaving an unknown world behind.

Growing up on a farm often means that we don't come into contact with many strangers. The people who visit our farm are neighbours, extended family, milk tanker drivers, the occasional farm machinery salesmen, locals from the football club and church. In some ways it is a sheltered world but without the strict moral teachings associated with some religions and their attitudes. One time, a man in his forties opens his car door for us when we are walking home along the highway. He has a large nose and a friendly smile. He says that he knows our parents and just wants us to get in and he will drive us home. Annie, Theresa, Mick and Kathryn and I are walking west and the driver is driving in an easterly direction. We are suspicious as we don't recognize this man who doesn't dress like a farmer. Annie shakes her head and we walk on with the man shouting at us to get in. Other cars pass by and the man drives off. When we tell our parents about the incident, Mum makes a greater effort to pick us up from the school bus.

The other occasion when our known world is infiltrated by the outside world is when I am at secondary school. By this stage, we have bikes and the ride home from the end of Vickers Road to our farmhouse takes little more than five minutes. Annie, Theresa Mick, Kathryn and I ride our bikes to the end of Vickers Road in the morning and leave the bikes under the lower branches of the cypress plantation at the end of the road. One day we hop off the school bus and step in under the cloying smell of the cypress branches and discover that our bikes have had their frames smashed in, by what looks like hammers and axes. The wheels, as well as the frames, are bent. The bikes are unrideable. We stand around gasping in disbelief at who would do this. There are no tyre marks on the gravel, or rubbish that might have been thrown from cars. Reluctantly, we push and carry our bikes home, crying and upset. It is an incident that is never resolved, or properly investigated and later on we put it down to people who are bored and who park down quiet back lanes to drink and pass the time. Our bikes are eventually replaced and we return to riding home from the school bus. There is never any damage to our new bikes again and we are left wondering about the casual violence that now seems to be a part of the world.

Inflated by memory

In 1976, The Sex Pistols release 'Anarchy in the U.K.' and I begin my secondary education at the Christian Brothers College in Warrnambool. When I step down from the Laang school bus and walk across Canterbury Road to the double-storey orange brick school building of the Junior School, I have butterflies in my stomach. There are boys everywhere, some hopping off buses from Port Fairy and Koroit, others walking up side-streets in their red blazers and grey trousers. There is a Brother wearing a long black gown over his black shirt and trousers and who stands out from the parents because he dresses like a priest. He is older than I had imagined the Brothers to be, about the same age as one of my uncles. Parents pull up in Holdens and Fords to drop off sons. School buses slowly lurch away. For a moment I have an idea that this is an important place. This school is somewhere to be. Canterbury Road has long been considered one of the best streets for houses in Warrnambool. One house opposite the school has a tennis court, others are Victorian or Federation style houses with wide manicured gardens, mature hedges and stone fences. My brother Mick is in year nine, and he is not so impressed with the surroundings. We cross Canterbury Road and he points me in the right direction. I fall into line with other students walking to the year seven classrooms. The only friend I have is Billy Nolan, son of Ray, whose farm runs along Occupation Lane. We have known each other since primary school, and although we are not close, we walk together on that first day.

The boys that I tend to hang around with in year seven are also from the country. We bond through our difference to the townies from Warrnambool. Some of us milk cows on weekends, each of us has left a small primary school to come to CBC. None of the boys I know listen to The Sex Pistols, The Jam or The Clash. Mostly, I keep my knowledge of punk music to myself.

With boys from the country, I play handjax each recess, our own version of downball, and sometimes in an undercroft below the school hall. Here we can be ourselves, invent nick names for each other, compete to be winners. The townies have their own groups, who they know from the different Warrnambool primary schools, and they rarely infiltrate ours in year seven.

A short distance west of CBC is St Ann's College, a convent school started by The Sisters of Mercy in 1872. Annie, Theresa, Kathryn and later on Rebecca all attend St Ann's. From a boy's perspective, St Ann's is a mysterious place of old stone buildings, nuns and lots of girls. When the Laang school bus stops outside St Ann's to pick up students for the bus ride home, I stare at the girls as if they are from another country. All day I have been surrounded by boys and to suddenly hear the chatter and laughter of girls on the bus relaxes me. However, I blush easily if any of the girls look my way. In my time as a student at CBC, the two schools have little to do with each other. There are year 12 socials, occasionally musicals, where male and female students are cast alongside each other, but generally the two schools operate independently from each other. Consequently, some of the boys at CBC become obsessive about girls, talking about them non-stop, but when they meet a girl they become tongue-tied and look to others to continue a conversation. Sometimes an image from *Playboy* is passed around the yard, and if ever a girl walks past the school she is wolf-whistled. I count myself lucky to have grown up in a family with four sisters, yet I still understand little about girls in year seven. From a Brother's perspective, girls are seen as a distraction to the more serious boys' education. It is unheard of that girls and boys should be in the same classroom together. The irony is that in 1991, St Ann's and CBC amalgamate to form Emmanuel College, a catholic co-educational school that exists to this day.

Part of the reason why my parents and no doubt other parents send their country sons to an all-boys school is to have their sons taught discipline and the value of learning. Not that these values couldn't be imparted at other schools. It is an accepted wisdom amongst my parents and their friends to send their wild sons to a catholic boys' school so they can be straightened out, taught how to respect others, in short to be controlled. However, CBC is much more relaxed than I imagine. Although there is an acknowledgement of the past achievements and values of Edmund Rice, founder of the Christian Brothers, there isn't an old school network or reliance on the achievements of the past. Corporal punishment is practised, more so by some teachers than others. Implements vary from a strap, to a hearth brush to a clip over the ear. Yelling at students is common as are threats and belittling of students. Brother Edward Dowlan, the convicted paedophile who taught briefly at CBC used to make boys put their hands up and stand beside their desks when they had a question to ask. There are disciplinary procedures of a kind that students know about but from a student's perspective these always seem to be ad hoc. The greatest discipline and measure of conformity comes from the students themselves.

Midway through year seven, I was involved in a minor classroom incident that would affect and haunt me for a long period of time. Paul Harrison was one of the tough boys in our class. He had the beginnings of a moustache, was tall, had a deep voice and possessed a confidence that set him apart from many other students. He had a group of followers who backed him up whenever an occasion warranted it. He was sitting behind my desk in class one day when he put his foot up on the back of my wooden seat and kicked me up the bum. I yelled out in surprise and turned around to see Harrison smirking at me. The teacher took him out of class and gave him the strap for upsetting the class. At the end of the day, word was going around that Harrison was out to get me. My face was flushed as I packed my bag and made a quick exit from the White House towards the school bus. The moment I stepped out onto the bitumen, Harrison spotted me and gave chase. An eternity seemed to pass as I ran across the playground, past junior school students playing basketball or handjax. Several students turned to look in surprise as I ran with my bag to escape Harrison's panting breaths. I had no idea what he would do to me, I just knew that I had to make it to the bus. Fortunately, Canterbury Road was quiet. Buses were waiting at the bus stops and a Brother was on bus duty. I ran across the road and threw myself at the waiting bus door. The driver closed the door and I turned back to see Harrison's fists pounding the door and sides of the bus. I walked down the aisle to the back seat to sit with Mick and his friends. I was out of breath, unable to speak. I sat down and turned away from Harrison's departing glare.

Looking back at this incident, as I have done over the years, memory has reduced and enlarged this experience which makes it difficult to write about truthfully. Not that truth is the only way to make sense of formative experiences. Once I was on the bus, I was already concealing or burying the incident, hoping that by the next day it would be forgotten about. But it couldn't be forgotten, and this formative experience, minor as it was, has remained with me as a type of marker of character, a fence post in a line for me, of not facing up to issues or events that I needed to. The next day I was too sick to go to school and spent much of the day in bed. I managed to convince Mum and Dad that I was sick for the rest of the week. Living on a farm made it difficult for Mum and Dad to drive into Warrnambool for a doctor. By the end of the week, Mum was becoming suspicious as I didn't have a temperature and I still had my appetite. I broke down crying one night and told her about Paul Harrison, and how he had wanted to fight me in front of his gang. The next day, I went to school under guard from Mick and his friends. I spent the time before classes browsing the shelves in the library hoping to avoid Harrison. Many of the novels were familiar to me and for a moment I could forget about what I was afraid of that day. One of Harrison's friends appeared, spotted me and came over to the shelves. 'Ryan, you've finally turned up. Harrison is going to get you.' He seemed to take particular pride in delivering the news to me, and stood there grinning, waiting for an answer. I turned away and began to shake and then headed for the toilet. However, Mick and his friends had hunted Harrison down that morning and roughed him up for threatening me. In turn, Harrison spread the word around the class that he was going to bring in his older brothers and cousins to the school to settle things. For the rest of the day, Harrison gave me dirty looks and each time I looked at him or his mates, I felt like something cornered. Harrison's brothers didn't turn up at the school and by the next week the incident was forgotten by some, but not my reputation within the class.

Harrison did keep his distance from me, but it was his gang who bullied and teased me for much of the year. It was their way of showing loyalty to the tougher bully. Throughout this time, I also suffered a lot from acne and often went to school with pimples on my face. Treatment for pimples was not widespread in the 1970s, and no matter how much Clearasil I pasted onto my face in the morning, I still trudged out the door with red blotches around my chin and nose. Whether the pimples were brought on by anxiety as well as hormones, I am not sure. Some of the names I was called varied from 'dot-to-dot face', 'your face is a mess' to 'gutless wonder'. The teasing was something I simply had to endure. It didn't really occur in front of my friends, but when I was walking to class, was on my own for short periods at lunch times, or when I was forced to sit beside one of the bullies in class. I kept my head down and looked to the ground so that I might blend in with the crowd. Punching and pushing were a regular occurrence at the school, and often it was as a joke as boys passed each other. A punch in the arm was how friends communicated, a reminder of who was toughest. Sometimes boys would punch each other in the balls, as a joke, other times more seriously to make someone suffer. In the time between classes, when boys thundered down the White House steps for another class or to lunch, boys punched me in the arm, sneered or stared me down. At other times, if I was on my own, some boys spat at me. I see myself then as a shy, nervous student who lacked the confidence to speak up for himself or to come back with the winning comment. I blushed too easily. Inside I was a fury of anger, sickness and shaking and unable to express how I was feeling. I turned away when boys pushed and goaded me into a fight. I couldn't bring myself to fight back for the fear of failure paralysed me. Easily taken advantage of by more confident boys, I was relegated to the outside of the popular groups. The Brothers went about their business of teaching, their presumptions that if we all love God then God will have a special place in his heart for each of us. They had no idea of the trouble and anxiety I was experiencing, as I presume they did with other students. Many students created a front or a façade with which they dealt with the daily pressures of school and of being accepted within a class. It was a coping mechanism that every student looked for.

I struggled through year seven pretending to the outside world that everything was fine. In time, it became easier for me to separate my life into sections and to hide the parts of my days that I didn't want to talk about. Any activity that took my mind away from Harrison and his gang helped me to think that school wasn't that bad. I milked the cows on weekends and began playing football for the Under 17 Panmure side. At night I lay on my bed staring up at posters of Black Sabbath and the Rolling Stones, listening to music with Mick in our bedroom. Farm jobs such as harrowing, chasing after cows and calves, or feeding out hay to the milkers also kept my weekends busy. However, when I returned to school, I had to put up my guard and watch out for who could suddenly appear around the next corner. Just looking at other students could affect how I was going to get through the next class. I kept my head down and hoped that somehow the year would pass.

Fortunately, I didn't have any direct dealings with convicted paedophile Brother Dowlan, although I can remember two incidents at CBC that stand out as examples of the type of person he was. Both of these incidents occurred when I was in year seven. A short walk from the school grounds, past the Botanic Gardens were two large sporting ovals. Students would walk down Ardlie St to the ovals whenever they had sport or there were school athletics days. One day I was on the oval playing cricket with my class when one of the boys was hit in the groin by a cricket ball. He screamed in pain and students ran over to him. Dowlan also ran over to the boy and put his hand down the boy's trousers to massage his balls. Understandably, many boys turned away when this was happening and the boys were directed to return to the game while Dowlan comforted the boy. I can still remember the boy whimpering and Dowlan with his hand down the boy's trousers gently massaging him in front of other students. A short while later, the boy was able to stand up and walk around. On our way back to class, we were talking about what Dowlan did and shaking our heads in disbelief. We couldn't talk about it to another teacher, nor could I talk about it to Mum and Dad.

On another occasion, I was with a group of year seven students who were caught wagging down the street. We were not the first CBC boys to wag and we really didn't give much thought to what we were going to do down the street. It was simply a case of wanting to skip Latin and do something different to our expected routine. We walked into a milk bar on Fairy Street, a short distance from the school, and started to browse for chocolates. Pretty soon we were stuffing chocolate bars down our pants and into our pockets. The shop owner looked at us suspiciously. Somebody did the honourable thing and paid for one chocolate, while the rest of us ran out of the shop laughing with more chocolate in our pockets and down our pants. What to do now? Rather than continue down the street and risk being spotted by a parent, we walked back to school and made up stories as to why we were late to our classes. The next day, we were told to wait on the stairwell outside Dowlan's classroom at recess. The harsh crack of a strap on a boy's hand let each of us know what we were in for. A boy walked out, red-faced and embarrassed and another one of our group walked in. We waited for the repeat of the strap but the room was silent except for a quiet murmuring. Anthony Mahoney and I were waiting outside the double French-style doors of the classroom and moved closer to look inside. We pulled the doors slightly ajar and saw Dowlan with his arms around the boy's shoulders, pulling him close to him, in an embrace and talking quietly. We looked at each other and skedaddled back down the steps vowing never to return. Neither of us wanted to be hugged by Dowlan. The strange thing was that neither of us was called up by Dowlan the following day. He may not have known that we were involved, however I am sure that he would have been given a list of the boys who wagged from the school. Waiting on the stairwell outside the classroom, hearing a low murmur from inside with the expectation that whatever was happening inside, both of us would soon be experiencing, is a moment that has remained with me.

Although CBC had a reputation in the community for being strict and pushing students to excel academically, it was a reputation based on stereotypes and a perception that parents wished to be a reality. There were Brothers who controlled their classes by yelling and mocking students as well as giving backhanders over the head as they walked past a row of desks or tables. I can never forget the time a lay teacher, Mr Polnik gave me a lecture in front of my friends. Polnik was a science teacher who liked to quote statistics such as by the time this class leaves school at the end of year 12, 25% of you will be unemployed. A short, squat man with dark thick-rimmed glasses and a steady gaze that he would fix on you in class, he'd challenge students with, 'And Ryan, what do you have to say for yourself?' His small stature was obviously an impediment that he countered by his steely gaze and the authority of his pronouncements. A group of my friends were laughing and pushing each other in the hallway outside a class room where Polnik was supervising students who had been kept in during lunch. He came out into the hallway, yelled at us to stop, seized upon the first student that he saw, who was myself and demanded that I kneel down and apologise to him for making such noise. At first, I thought he was joking, but his glare became more concentrated and his voice louder. Reluctantly, I knelt down on the polished lino tiles, in front of my friends and apologized to him for making the noise. He turned to eyeball each of my friends, remaining silent and then returned to the classroom. I stood up, blushing and swearing under my breath. None of us could believe he had made me do it. It was a minor incident and yet, it is a memory that I have returned to, perhaps inflated, often when I associate particular places within the school with a moment that has over time grown into an experience.

School mornings were a mad rush in our farmhouse with breakfasts being scoffed, sandwiches hurriedly made before the magic time of 7:45. The radio was always on with the 3YB announcers cheerfully relaying local news and playing hits of the 60s and 70s. Our farmhouse was unheated and there wasn't enough time to light a fire in the fireplace to warm up the kitchen. A two bar radiator was produced in winter, but all it did was make my brothers and sisters and I fight over who could warm their ankles before the two glowing red bars. Mum had two drop-offs to do in the car, while Dad put the milkers through the bails in the dairy. When we were younger, Mum often helped Dad milk the first 100 or so cows until it was time to get us out of bed and ready for school. We scrambled for blazers, lunch boxes, home work and ran out to the smell of the paddocks and the roar of the dairy's engine and hopped into the car. If we were early enough, we rode our bikes two kilometres to the bus stop at the end of Vickers Road. Mum was not a confident driver, even when we bought our first brand new car – a lime yellow automatic Valiant station wagon. Due to its colour, the car quickly became recognizable to locals at Mass as the Ryan car. No longer did Mum have to crunch the gears on the column shift as she did in the old blue HR Holden. The Valiant was spacious inside, wide enough to fit two adults and two children in the front bench seat and Mum's feet barely touched the pedals. She shuffled her hands around the tan steering wheel as she turned right out of Vickers Road and onto the Princes Highway to drop off Mick, Annie, Theresa and myself. After this, she drove half a mile up the highway, past Boo-Boo Clarks to the intersection of Occupation Lane and the Princes Highway to drop off Kathryn, Jack, David, Philip, Kieran and Rebecca who all attended St Thomas' Primary School in Terang.

Sometimes we waited in the car with Mum at the end of Vickers Lane, other times if Mum had to milk in the morning with Dad, we stood on the edge of the highway facing into the cold and the wind until the bus arrived. We were not often early. The bus ride into Warrnambool took an hour. After picking us up, the bus continued east along the Princes Highway and then south through the districts of Garvoc, Laang then west through Panmure, Cudgee, and Allansford and on to Warrnambool. In many ways, sitting up the back seat of the bus and travelling into and out of Warrnambool each day was more of an education for me, than sitting in a classroom.

We were the first family on the bus in the morning and the next stop was one kilometre away where the Nolans stepped on. Billy and I usually sat together. The bus driver worked through the gears and looking out the windows I could see trails of cows spilling out from the dairies that we passed. Two families of Meades were picked up before the bus turned right into Sampson's Ford Road. The Lenehan girls were often standing and shivering at the corner. Phil O'Keefe sat behind Caroline Lenehan and often serenaded her with 'Sweet Caroline'. She was slim, had long dark hair and occasionally played the organ at Mass in Garvoc. She was not impressed with Phil and did her best to ignore him. Later on, after he completed form three at CBC, Phil was sent to the much stricter St Pat's College, a boarding school, two hours away at Ballarat. Throughout my schooling years, I carry a fear that I might be sent to this boarding school I have heard so much about: the beatings, the strict rules, having to live away from home for much of the year.

The bus heads south from the highway and into the wilds of Laang. Sampson's Ford Road barely deviates as it passes over a railway line, ferns and blackberry by the side of the road, down the steep hill into the river flats of Mt Emu Creek, over the narrow bridge, cypress hedges in the paddocks, past dairies and tin machinery sheds, stands of bush and isolated farmhouses. I watch the kids I don't know take their seats further up the front of the bus. Steven Mugavin entertains us by turning around and taking out his glass eye, showing us the folds of skin beneath. Tony Morrison is known for blowing smoke rings so perfect that each ring slips through the ring of another smoke ring.

After a left turn near Morrison's white weatherboard farmhouse at the T intersection with the Heathmarsh Road the bus continues past Edge's weatherboard house and dairy. Their paddocks in the flats before a slight incline always seem to be waterlogged. We pass yellow roadwork signs for Soft Edges and immediately use the name to describe the Edge girls. We turn right at a signpost signaling the Garvoc Laang Road, then head south past Campbell's dairy that fronts the road, old car wrecks are scattered in nearby paddocks. The road has been widened. We pass an old quarry down a dirt lane that I used to swim in on hot summer afternoons during the school holidays. The bus slows down for the mostly abandoned houses in the bush that make up the township of Laang. A weatherboard hall and tin roofed fire brigade shed still exist and a family now lives in the old school building. The tennis courts are used throughout my years on the bus but the white lines have since faded and grass grows on the courts. We turn right into the Panmure Laang Road that winds its way through more farms and stands of bush. We pick up Sarah Moloney, my first girl friend, a girl I spend many bus rides home with in Year 9 and 10, up the back seat of the bus, kissing and fondling, We pick up the Cockaynes, Trevor Wright, the Clarke sisters and as we drive into Panmure the bush thickens. We pass the overgrown hedges of the McLaren brothers. There are signs around the house written on tin and scraps of wood: *Keep Out Wild Dogs, Trespassers Prosecuted.* There are car wrecks and rusting machinery in the paddocks. Who are these people who want to keep the world at bay with their signs and anger?

Year nine was where I learned the value in knowing certain song lyrics as I flirted with girls on the bus. Some of the boys were stoic and refused to sing along to *Paradise by the Dashboard Light.* Other students knew that whatever they did, they could never be accepted in the bus' pecking order. They were overweight, plain looking or lacked the confidence to smile openly. Many students had their designated seats and so stared out the window at the gum trees and paddocks while the rowdy lot up the back sang and shouted. At home, I listened to punk music and Midnight Oil while on the bus I sang along to Olivia Newton John and John Travolta in 'Grease.' The girls on the bus pleaded and giggled as they sang into each other's eyes. *Greased Lightning* had us all singing and acting out the actions. Part of me felt silly, but I couldn't help being swept up by the fun of the songs. It was so different to what I went through at school. Nobody on the bus from other schools knew about the name calling and teasing I suffered through on a daily basis. The kids on the bus knew me from Panmure, from playing football or from knowing our family. I wanted to be part of the action on the school bus, the fun of singing along, of knowing the words to the songs because to me that's what really mattered.

Outside of socializing at the weekly football games, there wasn't a lot for younger people to do in Panmure. There was the pub for adults and two milk bars where some of us used to hang outside on weekends with our push bikes, drinking Big Ms and watching the cars pass on the Princes Highway. In summer, we rode to the Big Hole, a deep swimming hole on a bend in Mt Emu Creek at the edge of the township. Nights were quiet, star-filled and seemingly endless to a teenager. Disco music was taking off around the world. I watched it on 'Countdown', listened to it on the tape recorders of other students on the school bus, but there was nowhere in Panmure to go and dance. Even though I still listened to punk and new wave music at home with Mick, I sensed the intimacy that disco could bring me closer to girls. Kathryn and I started badgering Mum and Dad to hold a disco in Panmure. We had heard of Blue Light Discos run by the police in Warrnambool, but Warrnambool was too far away at night and there weren't any buses that would take us to them. Mum and Dad were too busy from milking or too tired to drive us into Warrnambool. We recruited some friends to help us organize a Dj and eventually Mum and Dad agreed to the idea of having a disco at the Panmure Mechanics Institute, or the Hall as we referred to it. The only catch was Dad insisted on being on the door to make sure that people stayed inside the hall.

The first disco was a great success with teenagers being driven from Warrnambool and across the district to dance to the music of Ami Stewart, John Travolta and The Bee Gees. Strobe lights passed over World War Honour rolls, coloured streamers hung from the walls. Dad sat on a chair on the stage with his friend, Harry Hastings watching the dancers and making sure nobody went outside. I stood around in the darkened corners with friends until I found a girl to kiss who I wouldn't see again.

After organizing three discos and coordinating them successfully, the work involved in publicizing the discos and finding a suitable Dj had become too difficult. However, we had started something in Panmure, a place where hardly anything happened, and had seen what was possible at a time when teenagers would do anything to be able to go out and dance. For a short time, our social lives consisted of more than being roped into old-time dancing at kitchen teas and cabaret balls. For a short time we were able to meet other young people and see ourselves as being part of a larger like-minded group. Some of the older teenagers were drinking before the discos and so came into the hall with grins and mad-cap energy. Others drank slyly in the dark from stubbies hidden inside coat pockets. Watching other people from Panmure dance to Barry White was a revelation to me, as I had never imagined some of the farmer's sons and daughters knowing about such music. But disco smoothed our edges and gave our bodies the curves necessary for flirtation. The rays from the strobe light ricocheted around the room and we were transformed into teenagers with attitude. It wasn't quite New York, but for a night it was more than what Panmure could ever be. We danced in groups, with partners, or alone. It didn't matter with whom we danced. We were dancing in a hall that had never seen disco before.

An incident that year that had an effect on who I was, and in turn, would affect how long I remained at school, occurred in year nine. My R.E. class was doing group work and so there were students walking around the classroom or working loudly in groups. Scunger Ward was a middle-aged Brother who wore thick-rimmed glasses and who was virtually bald. A genial man with a ready smile, on this particular day he was sitting at his desk talking to a group of students. A boy new to the school who was still trying to prove himself challenged me to a fight in class. Tony was Italian and at the time there were few Italian students at the school. I laughed off his challenge and made to walk away when out of the blue, he punched me in the face, knocking me to the ground, bloodying my nose. I was surprised as anyone, least of all Scunger, who gradually woke up to what was happening in his class. The rest of the boys began circling and chanting 'fight, fight, fight'. Scunger stood up and told us to settle down. I went downstairs to the toilet, cleaned myself up, returned to class and tried to pretend nothing happened. Scunger called me over to ask what had happened. 'No problem sir,' I replied. 'Just a misunderstanding.' I glanced over to Tony and his mates who were smirking back at me. I knew what was going to happen and an old queasy feeling returned to my stomach. It was organized that I would fight Tony after school and settle the problem then. He was much smaller than myself, outspoken, and rough in his way of talking. He wasn't popular amongst the townies, possibly because he was so different to them. Still, I had a bus to catch after school and so the fight was postponed. However, I couldn't bring myself to fight him the next day. I thought and brooded about the possibility of losing, of having Tony beat me in front of my friends. I couldn't live with the image of failure, of being whacked by an ugly upstart who nobody really liked. Naturally, Tony kept goading me and recruited his friends to do likewise. They would catch me in other group situations in class, calling me names such as bog, shit, shit Ryan, bog Ryan, all suggesting I was shit-scared of him. They stopped whenever any of my friends were present and relied upon catching me alone, walking to class or out in the yard at lunch time. My friends couldn't see why I was putting up with it, and out of frustration they would push Tony around to get him off my back.

Just like in year seven, school became a place that I had to endure, of deciding where to be at lunch and recess, somewhere away from Tony and his friends. If I saw them from a distance in the yard, I walked away. I spent a lot of time in the library, browsing and reading, sometimes with friends, often with the boys who didn't have friends. I was surprised by how many other boys there were sitting at the brown laminex tables reading or talking quietly with other loner-types. I was as confused as anyone as to why I didn't just walk up to Tony and smack him. I had imagined myself doing this countless times on the bus home or at night when I was trying to sleep. However, each of these imaginary fights always ended with me being beaten and feeling the shame of being beaten. I could never live with myself if I was beaten up by Tony in a fight in front of his friends. Some days I imagined that I got along with Tony and that there wasn't a problem. It was all a drama that I had made up. Tony was my friend, until he saw me and goaded me again with his fists across the class room. Ultimately, I relied upon time to win the battle for me. In time, Tony would forget about it, I would forget about it and school could partially return to a place of learning and fun. In year ten, this became the case where gradually, Tony's power and influence over me became less as my friendships with other more confident boys became stronger. He would still try to catch me out in class by shoving a fist into my face when I was sitting at my table, or catch my eye across the room and grin, but he too was wary of my friends. Most other boys in the class called me by my surname as a nick name. Only Tony and his one or two friends called me shit or bog, names that I was deeply embarrassed by. By the end of year ten, Tony had left the school and for a while it seemed that what I had endured throughout those two years was finally over. It wasn't me but time that had won the fight.

In year ten, Brother Moloney my homeroom teacher, taught me history and English. He had a square-shaped head, short graying hair, wore glasses and had the trace of an Irish accent. He was strict, often bellowed at students to pay attention, threw chalk at them if they were talking and he had a habit of squinting as he repeated students' questions before he answered them. 'You want to know why Caesar died son?' He wore a long black tunic that brushed the wooden platform he strode across as he talked to the class and wrote on the blackboard. Some days his tunic would be smudged with chalk as he wrote so much on the board, wiping out his mistakes with his hand as he went rather than using a duster. Those were the days of copying paragraphs from the board into the ruled pages of our workbooks. One side of the blackboard was filled with words from a book, then the other side was filled, and finally both sides of the blackboard were wiped clear by a student and more lines of white words were written to cover the black spaces. We learnt about the British presence in India and I can remember the blackboard being filled with writing about the origin of the word juggernaut, Ghandi and the meaning of 'Only Mad Englishmen go out in the midday sun.' It was a light-filled classroom with rows of windows on the northern side of the room. Afternoons passed to the sound of pens completing pages in workbooks. Despite Moloney's over-the-top manner, I was able to concentrate in his classes and momentarily forget what happened when I was out in the yard.

Towards the end of 1979, I had to choose subjects for year eleven and twelve. I wasn't sure of what I wanted to do after school but I had a vague notion that I would complete year twelve. I enjoyed English, history and sports but I was lousy at maths and science. We didn't have much in the way of careers counseling at the school other than some brochures in an office and a teacher who didn't seem to know the details about the courses at university. Mum and Dad were encouraging me to complete year twelve and part of the thinking in those days was to study challenging subjects in year eleven and twelve which would make it easier to choose university courses. The harder the subjects I studied at school, the greater the chance I would have to go to university. Mum and Dad arranged an interview with Brother Moloney at school to try to discover if he thought I was capable of going to university, and secondly what subjects I should choose. Before the interview, I had decided that I would study maths one and maths two as well as a science subject that would assure my entry to university. I was nervous about studying subjects that I hadn't done well in before, yet I really wanted to leave the farm and try university.

The interview was conducted in a large study within the Brother's house, a double-storey, white Spanish Mission style building I hadn't been allowed into before as a student. Moloney sat behind a wide, imposing desk in his black tunic and talked at length to my parents about my prospects. As was his nature, he soon became opinionated and rhetorical. He wasn't impressed with my friendship with Mahoney and said that 'we both lead with our chins'. In other words, we don't see the trouble we are getting ourselves into when we muck around in class. He then went on to state that I was just an average student who was capable of more, but he didn't think I would go on to university. He didn't think I would make it. Mum and Dad thanked him for his time and walked out quietly. On the way back to the car, Dad shook his head at what Moloney had been saying and Mum was quiet. I could sense that they weren't happy. Nothing much more was said over the next few days until they both told me to do what I wanted to do and to disregard what that mad Brother had said. It was one of the first times I felt an affinity with my parents against the authoritarians of the school. Duly, I chose maths one and two, chemistry and accounting as well as the mandatory English and religion for year eleven. I had chosen the subjects I thought would take me out of the district and to university.

Yet by the end of year eleven, I had decided to leave school. My report wasn't good. I had failed both maths subjects, had received a D for Chemistry and had been lucky to pass other subjects. In fact the school gave me a compensatory pass for year eleven. The Sex Pistols broke up in 1977 and punk music had evolved into New Wave and New Romantic music. With little prospect of ever going to university, I spent the summer of 1980 going out to pubs and parties listening to The Angels and Duran Duran while my school mates considered studying for form six. For a while it seemed, Moloney had been right after all.

My parents currently live a short distance from CBC and the Botanical Gardens. Sometimes I walk along Canterbury Road, past the orange brick buildings of the school, the white stone wall that runs around the perimeter of the grounds and I have to remind myself that this was the school that greeted me on that morning in 1976. So much of the physical size of the school has been exaggerated in my mind. The grounds are much smaller than I imagine, yet there are still spaces such as a patch of concrete outside the senior years' classrooms that are keys to those formative experiences. For many years, I have wanted to put CBC behind me, to forget about it, even to imagine that it didn't exist. I left the school at the end of year eleven, happy to have escaped the Brothers, the rules, the conformity, the uniform. How could I have ever known what lay ahead of me that morning as a new year seven student, eager and nervous to take my place at the school that Mick went to?

After I left the Western District, I was very guarded about telling people that I had attended CBC. I was embarrassed by some of the experiences that I had struggled with there, and I discovered it was also a revelation for many people that I didn't complete year twelve. Even as a secondary teacher now, I am continually surprised by the assumed expectations people have of each other regarding finishing school.

For many people who move to the city from the country, the experience of moving allows for a certain amount of fictionalizing of identity. When I moved to Melbourne, I knew far fewer people than I did in Warrnambool, and the people in bars who I gravitated towards seemed to be more interested in Melbourne schools rather than country schools. In order to fit in with the students from private schools who I was meeting in St Kilda I made things up about myself, partially to be accepted, but also because I didn't want to have to explain where I came from. People didn't know my past or history, unless they too were from the Western District. The freedom I attained from making things up about the schools I went to or even some of my experiences made it easier to have conversations in the short term and easier to believe in the past I was creating for myself. It was a past that, at the time, made sense. It has only been when I have confronted those memories through writing that I have been able to face up to the experiences that I call my own. When I walk along Canterbury Road now, I often pause to consider the memories of those spaces within the school where I was with friends mucking around, playing handjax, wagging a period with Mahoney in the gym change rooms and laughing at other students walking to class. Another part of me keeps walking though, knowing that something more than skin was shed behind these white stone walls, all those years ago. Eventually, I did go to university and study, but that too was a chequered pathway of moving through different universities and completing courses over a number of years to become a teacher and a writer. The Brothers at CBC stamped me with their authority and like many catholic boys, I was free to go.

Centre of the world

Football has always been a family passion, even more so, for a family with ten children. Family footy matches were played in our front garden paddock that sloped down to Vickers Road. My sisters kicked the footy until my brothers and I grew older, tackled harder and put knees into backs to take marks. In these matches, we fantasized about taking Jezza speccys or kicking McKenna goals. My brother Dave, who had a long and successful footy career, playing with the Brisbane Bears Reserves for two years and then winning the Hampden League best and fairest, would often be kicking and running around imaginary opponents well into the dark before tea. When Dad kicked with us, it was special, even more so, when Mum had a kick. Dad's claim to footy fame was limited to running out for Garvoc and Tower Hill in the 1950s. He could kick a ball, but we liked to take marks over his shoulders and wear him out. Despite the twice-daily pull to milk cows, there was always time to play kick to kick.

Dad barracked for Carlton and so did the majority of my brothers and sisters. Mum took on the long-suffering mantle of St Kilda because she liked Cowboy Neale who grew up nearby at Garvoc. I barracked for Collingwood. I'm not sure of the exact reason why, but it may have been the success of Peter McKenna who was regularly kicking over 100 goals a season. He was also cast as an early football celebrity; releasing a record, and having books published about him. This decision to go against the rest of the family may also have been connected to an innate need of mine to adopt a different point of view. I wasn't a contrary child, but I just couldn't bring myself to barrack for Big Nick and Carlton. Consequently, I suffered throughout the many grand finals between Collingwood and Carlton in the 1970s and 1980s. I can still remember crying at the end of the 1970 Grand Final when Carlton overran Collingwood after we had been up by 44 points at half time.

Football was not just a statement about my family; it also helped to teach me geography and to understand the importance of place. I learnt to understand the places of the Western District by the distance between teams I played against in the Mount Noorat League. The travelling distances to different footy grounds varied from twenty to sixty minutes, and often involved driving along back roads through pockets of bush, or travelling north into the flatlands of the Western District. A number of teams were located around or near the extinct volcano of Noorat, a short distance north of Terang. This is the town where Alan Marshall's memoir, *I Can Jump Puddles* was set. To the outsider, Noorat is a town to pass through, but to the Conheady, Moloney, Clarke families, among others who played for Noorat throughout those years, the town had the best football ground in the league.

We travelled to football grounds along chipped, potholed roads that stretched like frayed ribbons into unnamable distances. To familiarize ourselves with this different country we looked for landmarks: weatherboard farmhouses, particular dead trees or where the narrow lanes might occasionally curve and then stretch into the distance. One sheep farm became synonymous with a trip to Worndoo because the owners had a dam wall that was two metres high and 200 metres in length. Whenever we reached the dam, we knew that we were out of dairy farming territory. We were travelling to a different world. Hexham was fifty kilometres away; Woorndoo sixty kilometres. This was flat-paddocked sheep country with 200 acre paddocks. When we arrived at the Worndoo Football Ground, the players seemed bigger and tougher. They were graziers' sons, men who seemed to be hardened by hours in the sun. Here was a social world we knew nothing about.

Travelling to these small townships was like travelling to the outer circles of my existence. What happened on the other side of Worndoo didn't interest me. I knew this country by the roads I travelled on, and by the names of people I heard announced in the footy teams on the radio each Friday night. These teams were like beacons in the Western District night, lighting up the darkness outside our farmhouse. Whoever was picked to be in a team often affected how we thought over the next two days, especially so when I was playing for Panmure. To me, this country within the boundaries of the League was known land. Travelling to each Saturday's game became a pilgrimage to renew myself with the paddocks and roads of the country I knew.

The Panmure football ground in the 1970s and early '80s was often a quagmire. The oval was small and poorly drained. I remember training on Tuesday and Thursday nights, doing circle work and crocodile laps with the mud on my footy boots weighing me down. Often I would have to slide along the ground to grab the ball with pools of water rushing up under my jumper. There was one light for the ground, which meant that the outer flanks were in darkness. We trained close to the sheds, which also made that part of the ground muddier. The change-room sheds consisted of two corrugated iron sheds with shearing shed-style slats on the floor. The cold air always seemed to whinny through the slats when we were getting changed. Players hung their clothes on nails hammered into the wooden studs of the walls. The showers were often cold and players had to step down into a dark pit to wash themselves. There was poor drainage in the showers and so the dirty water often pooled up around players ankles and shins. The smells in the footy sheds were like many other clubrooms: chewing gum, training oil, mud, deodorant, and in those days cigarette smoke. When the teams were on their feet warming up, the stops on their boots made an urgent, clattering sound on the wooden boards. The noise of coaches' addresses, of players shouting and urging each other on became deafening. There was always hope in the sheds before a game.

I was only twelve when I badgered my parents to let me join Mick in the under-seventeens. Each Tuesday and Thursday afternoon, my bag was packed for training. The older players humoured me because of my size and age. I did all the training that the players did; the main difference being that when I kicked the ball, it went for about ten metres. I was often the 'drinks boy', or I carried out the cut-up oranges at quarter time. I didn't mind. I was connected to the team. At night, I slept with a football because our coach, Neil Clarke, had told us to.

Each Saturday I packed my footy bag and took it to the ground just in case a player didn't turn up. One Saturday, Neil Clarke took me aside and asked me to fetch my bag and get changed. His son Phil, who was a bit wayward, hadn't turned up to play. The team was one player short. Elated, I ran to our car, grabbed my bag and returned to the sheds to change. Meanwhile, the team had run onto the ground. I would be twentieth man, on the bench, and if I were lucky I might be given a run in the last quarter. Neil found an oversized footy jumper for me and I put it on. It was an old-style woollen jumper, two sizes too big and it smelt of mothballs. Just as I was about to walk out of the sheds, Phil Clarke rushed in with his footy bag. He smiled and winked at me. Neil turned to give me the bad news. I retreated to the bench to unlace my footy boots. After Neil and Phil had gone on to the ground, I sat in the sheds quietly crying at my missed opportunity.

One of the traditions that locals followed as soon as they had their licence was to buy a car, hot it up with a V8, mags, extractors, bucket seats and drag each other off around the back roads of Panmure and Laang. Motorbikes were also popular, and in the 1970s, riders on P plates could drive high-powered 750s. Some of the players from the under 18s side used to gun their bikes around the district with a carefree, wild conviction. They wore their hair long and rode fast, so fast that I often heard them a minute before I saw them barreling down the road. In one year, three of these locals were killed in separate motorbike accidents. Some years later another footballer from that same team was killed when his bike collided with a sheep a short distance from his family farm. The deaths of the three footballers within a year of each other affected many people in the Panmure and wider community. One death was bad enough, but to have three friends die in horrific accidents results in a prolonged period of disbelief and remembering. It was the first time that the suddenness of death had been brought home to me. I realized that this is how people can die. These cool, long-haired country men who I looked up to, who I saw get into fights on the footy field, who played solid games in defence – they had no answer for death. Dying too early spoke for them, and to me. I never rode a high-powered motorbike and like many people in the district the impact of their deaths rippled out into the type of memories that seem to take hold of particular back roads in the country.

After I had left school at the end of year eleven I worked on our farm when the milking season was in full swing and at the Kraft cheese factory during the summer and autumn months. For a short while, it seemed that my destiny was complete. I would be working and remaining in the district; living at home rent-free and spending whatever I earned. One of my jobs on the farm was to pick up my younger brothers and sisters from the school bus. This particular day I was in farm clothes and rubber boots. I had brought the cows in and was about to begin milking. I pulled out onto the highway, saw no cars approaching and swung my HQ Holden around to complete the u-turn. It was just when the front wheels were on the white lines of the highway that I heard a horn. I looked up to the left and saw a police car hurtling toward me. I slammed on the brakes and stopped. There was still part of the highway and the entrance to Vickers Road for the police to steer around. But they were travelling too fast. The front driver's side of the police car collided with my passenger side, just in front of the front wheel. The force of the impact spun my car around in the opposite direction. I was flung across the front seat, hitting my head on the passenger door. For a moment, I was stunned and couldn't believe what had happened. Four policemen climbed out from their car and walked toward me, one of them was the Commissioner of Police for the Corangamite District. It was my luck to run into the most senior policeman in the district. They asked did I see them coming, but they weren't admitting anything. Steam billowed from the radiator of my HQ. I couldn't see the front of the car. I opened the door and looked over the wreckage of the front end. The bumper, grille, and front guards were mangled and pushed back almost beneath the engine. My beloved HQ was a write-off. I escaped without serious injury. Apart from a sore neck, I felt ok. The next day I played footy for the Panmure seniors, kicked four goals, and played one of my best games for the club. Nothing like a car accident to motivate a player. I was on four charges from the accident but managed to get off by pleading my case to a local magistrate. I was lucky but it would cost me over two thousand dollars to fix the HQ.

Although there has been significant change within football clubs as far as the involvement of women as managers, players, trainers etc at a national level and at a regional level, the inner sanctum of smaller country football clubs is still often driven by men. Apart from the players themselves, the coaches, trainers, club officials are invariably male, and so the assumption of men thinking alike in terms of a football club is often taken for granted. This was always the case when I played football, and so being in a room of men before and after a game often showed me the best and sometimes the worst in men's behaviour. One year after Panmure won the league premiership, a large crowd packed into the football shed to witness the triumphant team prepare for the unveiling of the premiership flag and their first game of the year as reigning premiers. There had been a number of players retire from the previous year's team and a full-forward was seeking a transfer to another league, a transfer that wasn't being allowed. I was sixteen, playing in the under 18 team and I was in the clubrooms before the senior match watching the seniors warm up and feeling the energy in the room rise. Smells of training oil, chewing gum, and towards the back of the crowd, cigarette smoke infected the air of the clubrooms that had been transformed from the former Illowa Primary School classrooms. Players were handballing to each other, shouting, running on the spot, occasionally knocking into each other. Suddenly a fight broke out between the club president and the full-forward. Both were tall, burly men and they traded blows to the face. I was shocked as the president was a dairy farmer who lived a short distance from our farm. I had never seen him throw a punch before. Other players jumped in to defend the president and quickly the fight broke into a melee of swinging fists, shouting and pushing. I was shaking and heartbroken that the team that won the premiership the year before could descend into a rabble of men fighting each other. That day I saw what grown men were capable of and how the glory of a premiership team could be so quickly dismantled. The fight was a way for the men to sort things out, and for much longer, for recriminations and silences to continue.

The anticipation of playing in the finals, the celebration of a premiership continued to be the lures a country football team chased. A premiership in a small country town could lift the spirits and moods of a district, especially when many players or family members were unemployed. Every year former VFL players and motivational speakers toured country towns to speak at clubs. In the lead up to the finals of one year, Panmure held a pie night and a motivational speaker was booked to speak to the team and to try and rev us up for the finals. After the speaker had finished and the team had been announced to the playing squad, some 'light entertainment' was provided. The entertainment was watching a porno film on video in the pub's lounge. This was before the availability of porn on the internet; a time when porno films were either bought by video, pirated amongst friends or bought from overseas. The illegal and illicit nature of the film quietened some players, while others burst out laughing at the images of naked men and women. I could hardly believe that the players and officials had to sit down and watch a porno film for motivation. I had heard that some footballers even spoke about abstaining from sex before a game as they wanted to remain mean and focused before they were to play, as if sex would dilute their masculinity or hard ball get. For others, on that night in the back lounge of the pub with its dimmed lighting and older male officials hovering near doors, the sight of naked bodies and women's breasts was the kind of motivation they seemed to need. I watched some of the older men standing up taking it all in, not laughing or smiling, just swaying there with their hands in their pockets, and I wondered if they had seen such images before. Some of the younger players were laughing and cheering, occasionally punching each other playfully in the ribs and shoulders. After a while, I had seen enough and asked if I could go home. I wasn't sure how the porno film would motivate me to take a mark or kick a goal. I had heard that it was a common practice at a number of clubs, but mainly for the end of year celebrations, not as motivation for a final. I remember that there weren't any women in the room.

Through the influence of Mick, I eventually left the district and pursued my interest in punk music and alternative fashions. Instead of footballers, I hung out with the artists and the unemployed who could then afford to live in St Kilda. I had moved to Melbourne, to be of all things, a Dj, and I was enrolled in a Dj course – at the Gary Mac School of Radio – while I attempted to start a radio career. St Kilda offered nightlife, but by day was I labouring anonymously in timber yards in Port Melbourne. I missed the wide spaces of the country, my family and the people with whom I had grown up, so I decided to try for another year with Panmure.

I trained during the week in Elsternwick and drove three hours each weekend to play for Panmure. By this stage I was wearing 'Nick Cave' jackets, torn jeans and colourful shirts; not quite Mt Noorat League attire. While new wave fashions certainly set me apart from locals at the footy grounds and in the pubs of Warrnambool, I don't remember too many adverse reactions. I was beaten up in a toilet in Warrnambool, but that wasn't because of my clothes; it was just the done thing at that particular pub.

Whether it was my emerging diversions, or the fact that I had mislaid my football talent, I found it hard to maintain a game in the senior team and was dropped before the finals that year. I continued to train in Melbourne and drive three hours to support the club, but at the end of the season I decided to give football a rest. Had I been a player essential to the team's success, it might have been different. I was twenty-two and could have played for many years if I had really wanted to. Instead, I played many games in my dreams; kicking goals from impossible angles, taking strong marks in defence, winning the game off my own boot, only to wake with a powerful sense of loss.

Not all the dreams were as positive or heroic. In some dreams I would be running onto the ground but I would be the only player who couldn't find the gate in the fence to run onto the ground. In other dreams I would be looking for a footy jumper to put on, only to find that all the jumpers had been taken. I would wake up in shared houses in St Kilda and Fitzroy wondering why I was still dreaming of playing footy for Panmure. I was too embarrassed to tell my housemates, none of whom liked football. Just as I have kept returning to the Western District for family visits, these football dreams have persisted into my married life. My wife has become familiar with 'another football dream morning'. Only in my dreams could I find a place to be recognized within a footy team, or travel those back roads to Kolora, Ecklin and Woorndoo as if they were still the centre of my world.

Man on the gate

Oilskin keeping out the cold
the muscles in his legs wearing down
through the under 12s, netball, under 14s
under 18s, reserves and finally seniors around two.
A job we all expect somebody to do.
A man who complements the scene of cars nosed up to
the boundary fence,
kids walking around with a piece of cardboard
displaying the winning raffle ticket.
Panicked voices rifling through the air –
Kick it Moorey. The crowd by the clubrooms
groaning like an ancient ship – red faces, stubbie holders,
club jackets sponsored by local businesses,
A gathering necessary as a pie from the canteen.
Certain women cheerfully handing over Cherry Ripes,
polystyrene cups with scalding tea. Each person
connected through marriage, kinder, school
or just plain proximity. Generations of neighbours
realizing their duty, lives flowing through moments
of a job – somebody has to blow the siren,
somebody has to cut up oranges into quarters,
somebody has to collect the footy after it sails
over Monk's barbed wire fence,
somebody has to sit in a car with kids climbing over seats.
It is a scene that swells through the afternoon
like the feet of the man on the gate
shifting his weight on the gravel,
puffy, arthritic fingers fumbling
with the texture of crisp notes.
A small town's investment in belief.
A community finding something to do.
Each year, he says, will be the last.

Ash Wednesday; a memorial

One week before the Ash Wednesday bushfires of 16 February, 1983 a dust storm swept across Victoria. As a cruel feature of the 1982 drought which had claimed much of the land north of the Great Dividing Range, the wind scooped up topsoil from the Western District, Wimmera and Mallee regions and carried it east, blanketing Melbourne in early afternoon darkness. The division between sky and earth became a rolling wall of dust and twigs. Melbournians have since told me how night fell early that day; streetlights blinked on in the afternoon, car headlights were used. The topsoil of Victoria dirtied eyelids, lips and doorsills. I remember trying to feed hay to the cows on our farm at Panmure, three hours west of Melbourne, hayseeds and pieces of straw hitting me like spears as they flew into my face and ears. It wasn't one mighty gust of wind that did the damage; it was that the wind didn't let up for the whole day. The afternoon darkening on our farm upset the rituals of our milkers. At two pm, the cows began filing toward the dairy. They waited on the track with their heads down, flicking flies with the stumps of their tails, expecting to be let into the yard to be milked. Our lives on the farm have always been dictated by the rhythms of cows; milking morning and evening, checking them each night with a spottie from the porch when they were calving in the paddock beside the house. We had little choice but to milk early that afternoon, with the lights on, aware that the cows would be too upset to give any decent amount of milk. The vat would be down, but it was often down on hot days when the cows were unsettled by the weather. It is easy to see now how that day was a foreshadowing of things to come. Not that I would have known. I was nineteen. The summer had been dragging on. Windy days were a regular part of my life growing up in the southwest. As a farmer's son, I carried a deadpan maxim in my head. *The world may change but the cows still have to be milked the next day.*

On the morning of 16 February, I was walking around the house in shorts, listless and irritated by the north wind which had begun blowing at 10. It was a day of total fire bans. The temperature had been forecast for the high 30s. I tried to make sure that I had all the jobs around the farm finished by lunchtime. Around midday, the temperature began to rise quickly. Each time I stepped outside our back door, the heat was like a furnace. It was stifling. Our Hills Hoist was spinning in a mad frenzy. Already I could sense that this was not a normal day. The intense heat and gusting wind were determining my thoughts and actions. Mum and Dad had planned to go shopping for groceries in Warrnambool as they did each Wednesday. The fire spotter on nearby Mt Warrnambool had been kept busy all morning informing brigades of minor grass fires outside our brigade region. Dad had been captain of the Panmure fire brigade for ten years, and his unusually quiet manner suggested he knew this day would be different to others. While the wind swept the dust from the back door, we sat in the kitchen listening to the weather forecast and wind directions from the Listening Set.

Finally, Dad decided that the wind was too strong for him and Mum to go shopping, not until it died down would he relax. It was one of the most important decisions he had made. Had he not been at home at the time we were notified of a grass fire approximately 10 kilometres west of Panmure the response to the fire would not have been so swift and coordinated. As it turned out, there were still mistakes made in regards to notification of the fire.

In November 1982, the Panmure fire brigade purchased a Listening Set as part of its equipment upgrade. By then I was secretary of the brigade and so I managed the payment. The main benefit of the Listening Set was that it enabled a person to listen to directions from fire spotters and other brigades. It was somewhere between a two way radio and a CB radio, although we could not use the device to speak directly to other brigades. The Listening Set was positioned in the kitchen, beside our radio and underneath the television, which sat on a table that

I had made for my parents in year 10 Woodwork. This was our technology corner. It was strange to listen to the flat drawl of the CFA firemen as they 'came in' beside the rehearsed tones of the radio DJs. This would happen during the hot days when we left the Listening Set on to monitor any fire activity around us. The tone of the fire fighter's voices was more direct, even when they were speaking in roundabout ways. Their voices were local, rough, unassuming, and barely aware of an audience. They brought the characters of the people into our kitchen, mainly because we recognised the people behind the voices, but also because they lacked the uniformity and received style of the DJs' tone of voice.

Apart from the Listening Set, the brigade also had an emergency fire number that people in the township of Panmure could ring if a fire was known or seen. When the fire number was rung, the phones of other brigade members would also ring. This interconnecting phone service saved a lot of time in ringing people and repeating instructions. Brigade members would simply listen for directions, usually from Dad and proceed to where they were told to go. A siren was activated at the fire station each time the fire number was rung. This caused a few problems, when people rang the fire number by mistake and the siren blasted throughout the town on false alerts. As a consequence, the fire alarm was turned off.

Much of Dad's time as brigade captain was spent delivering water in the summer months to people whose rainwater tanks had dried up. It was a job that he had no hesitation in doing, as we were also dependent on rain for our water supply. With ten children in our family, water was a valued commodity to be used wisely for cooking and washing. Often we were allowed to accompany him on his deliveries to neighbours and afterward he would bring a truckload of water home for us. Emptying water from the fire truck was usually a job for the boys. Dad would twist and turn the heavy red lid from the top of the fire truck's tank, and I would peer into the darkness, wondering what it would be like to fall in. I remember the smell of the rubber fire hose as I held it in position and watched water cascade into the two corrugated iron tanks beside our house. It was an important job. It meant that we could have a bath that night. My brothers and I always competed for the jobs our father gave us.

There were also grass fires for Dad to attend to; hay stacks that self-combusted after the hay was pressed too green, and the occasional house fire. Not one of these fires had taken Dad away from us for more than a few hours at a time. A phone call would come through and he would drop whatever he was doing and race up the gravel road, clouds of dust behind him, towards the fire station in Panmure. Sometimes a call would come through as we were milking. Dad would quickly wash his hands, give my brother and I directions and we would finish milking the cows ourselves. When we were fourteen and twelve, Mick and I were considered old enough to handle 180 cows on our own. If a fire call had come through when we were younger, then Mum would stop cooking and come over to help us finish the herd. At other times, Dad might be sitting down to dinner when the call came. It was an announcement that quickly silenced our shouts and teasing. Each of us stopped to consider the possibility of what a fire meant. For us, it was a word attached to drama, action, energy and associated with the seriousness of Mum's face and Dad's willingness to give himself up to the call. He was the brigade captain and he had a duty to carry out. After he had left, my brothers and sisters and I returned to our games and squabbling. Our lives were consumed by whatever was happening at the moment. Later, when he opened the back screen door and sat at the red laminex table, exhausted, with his hair out of place, his face stained by dirt and sweat we all pestered him with questions. Where was it? Was anybody hurt? How big was it? Mostly, he smiled and laughed with us until Mum shooed us outside so that they could have a few moments of peace together.

A phone call came through at approximately 1:30pm on 16 February. A small grass fire was burning out of control on Bob Harrington's farm west of Panmure. Bob was tall and wore a dark, bushy beard. He played football, briefly for Panmure in the 1970s. The Harrington farm was in rocky country with gullies and stone outcrops dividing it. The farm bordered Brucknell Creek to the south.

Dad and I left the house in a hurry. This was the first fire I had fought as secretary of the brigade. While I had undergone some CFA training, my experience with the fire truck was largely confined to helping Dad cart water. As Dad sped along the gravel road toward the fire I was curious as to what it would be like to fight a fire with him. I imagined that we were going off to fight a battle, that something about the afternoon would be a test for both of us. I also felt safe, protected by Dad's fire fighting experience and was expecting him to organise the other brigade members with his common sense directions. I remember the sense of urgency that seemed to grip him as he drove our yellow Valiant up Vickers' Road. Several times, I thought that he was going to take us into a skid. This reckless speeding on loose gravel was so different to the way he normally drove. We didn't say much to each other. I could see that he was thinking about the fire, planning a strategy, perhaps trying to visualise the extent of it.

When we arrived, we could see a thin column of smoke rising from a paddock well inside Harrington's farm. The wind had increased in strength and the temperature was now in the 40s. All morning I had been wearing shorts and a singlet. Now I was made to wear heavy yellow overalls. While I protested, I could also see that Dad wasn't in a mood to tolerate disagreements.

We looked for our truck amongst the other fire trucks that had arrived at the farm simultaneously. Dad swore as he saw it with its flashing light racing over the paddocks toward the fire's front which was burning in a southerly direction. He drove after the truck, our Valiant thumping into ditches, its exhaust scraping on rocky mounds along the way, until we pulled up alongside the truck. He exchanged heated words with the driver and told him to go back and fight the fire from the eastern flank; otherwise the truck would be in the path of the fire. This lack of fire sense was common amongst some brigades in 1983. Volunteers were keen to help out in the case of bushfires, but their lack of appropriate training also hindered their fire fighting efforts.

The fire was in the pit of a rocky gully. It was a small grass fire protected by the gully walls, a natural amphitheatre enclosing it from the prevailing wind. At this stage, we didn't know that the fire had been caused by clashing power lines. It was simply there when we arrived. Dad quickly reversed the truck into a position from where we could train our hoses onto the flames. I was sweating beneath the over-sized yellow overalls. Across the ridge, several other brigades could be seen: Cudgee, Allansford, and Naringal. I noticed friends holding hoses, most of whom had little experience with fighting bushfires. We all wore the yellow overalls, and some of us wore brightly coloured hats, but we were largely unaware of standard fire fighting practices. We knew how to hold a hose, but to choose the right spray and to protect a fellow fire fighter was entirely different. Many of us appeared clumsy and awkward as we grappled with hoses snaking around our legs and catching on rocks and thistles. We remained at this position for approximately 15 minutes, pouring water into the gully, and it looked as though the fire would soon be out. Then a strong gust of wind blew into the gully and literally lifted the fire out and dropped it onto the paddock beside us. Before we could put it out, the fire was racing south over dry paddocks towards Brucknell Creek. Trucks were started and the race began.

While other brigades were moving away from the gully, our truck stalled on the ascent of a small hill. The heat had seized the engine or vapourised the diesel in the fuel line. Dad was at the wheel, desperately trying to re-start it, pushing the over-ride button that was designed for such occasions. Meanwhile, the fire was advancing up the hill behind the truck. I was spraying water onto the approaching flames with other brigade members. The sky was darkening around us as the smoke blocked out the sun. The flames were rising in height and being whipped into a frenzy by the northerly wind. If Dad didn't get the truck started soon we might have to abandon it. We were about to turn off the hoses and leap from the truck when he managed to turn the engine over and it took off, dragging our hoses behind it. In his haste, Dad ruptured the fuel tank on some rocks. The hole in the tank was small enough for him to drive the truck to a nearby mechanic. The brigade members were transferred to other trucks. Dad sent me to check on our farm and to shift the cows on to a ploughed paddock that we were preparing to sew for rape and turnips. Meanwhile, we had heard about a second fire at Ballangeigh, 20 kilometres to the north and travelling south towards Panmure.

Before I returned to our farm, I was to drive up to Occupation Lane, see where the fire was, and ask if the Kellys needed any help. Occupation Lane is four kilometres north of our farm and the Kelly farm is another two kilometres further north. From the hill near their farm, I thought I should be able to see how close the fire was to our own, and so calculate how much time I would have to move our milkers on to the ploughed paddock. Thinking about this decision now, it seems foolish for Dad to have given me directions to drive around looking for the fire, when I could easily have been putting my life in danger by driving straight towards it. And yet, it turned out to be a life-saving decision.

The Princes Highway was relatively quiet as the police had blocked the highway between Panmure and Garvoc. Only emergency vehicles and local cars were being allowed through. I turned left up the hill toward the Kelly farm, the acrid closeness of the fire becoming stronger. There was smoke rising above paddocks to the west. I looked across a large valley that had once been a lake toward Mt Warrnambool. Although flames were rising along its eastern ridge, the mountain was another kilometre away. Safe for now I thought. I slowed down as

I approached the Kelly farmhouse. The sky was suddenly darkened. Another fire front had 'risen up' and was attacking the property across the road. The sound of the flames was like thunder, an uncontrollable roar coming from deep within the earth. The Kelly's original weatherboard farmhouse was across the road from the 60s-style conite house that they currently lived in. A local family rented the old farmhouse from the Kellys. The mother, Mrs. Conroy, stood on the front lawn crying with her children. Pat Kelly, who was two years older than myself, came running up and asked me to take Mrs. Conroy and her children down to Panmure. He was panicky, running as he was talking. He was going to shift cattle onto a ploughed paddock before he too left. The fire had engulfed the hayshed beside the old house. The flames were 20 metres high, and writhing around a cypress plantation between the house and the hayshed. In a matter of minutes the house would be gone. I pleaded for Mrs. Conroy and her children to get in the car quickly. She didn't want to leave the house and her possessions. I was worried about getting back out past the fire. I turned our Valiant around. Plumes of black smoke were blowing across the bitumen. Twigs, branches and dust blocked out the sky. The family scrambled in and I took off, but I was driving into a whiteout. I couldn't see where I was driving. The children were crying. One of them asked their mother, 'Mum, are we going to die?' I drove slowly, trying to feel the road beneath the tyres, listening for that faint pummelling sound. Two or three times the left wheels hit grass. I prayed that we would not run into a car coming in the opposite direction. I was also worried about falling power lines, and how long the tyres might last in the heat before they melted. These people who I was rescuing were virtual strangers to me; people I knew who simply lived up the road. If I was to die, I wanted to die among friends. Embers and smoke whooshed around us. The car shook in the wind. Its unearthly roar seemed to take us into another world. I had no idea how long we would have to drive for, or when the flames would be on top off us. And then suddenly we were through, into daylight. Everybody in the car cheered and cried. Somehow, we had survived the front of the fire. We had driven for little over 400 metres through thick smoke and embers, and yet at the time it had seemed an eternity. We drove back to Panmure triumphant. I dropped Mrs. Conroy and her family off at the Hall. I ran into my school friend, Anthony Mahoney who was overjoyed to see me. He said that I had been reported missing and he thought that I had died. I found it hard to believe that people had raced to such a conclusion. After reporting myself alive to the CFA personnel, I drove out to our farm to shift the cows onto safer ground. Nobody tried to stop me.

While Dad and I were away fighting the fire, Mum had been picked up by a neighbour and driven down to Panmure, where she would remain for the rest of the day, either helping out at the Hall or waiting under cypress trees with other women and children at the local swimming hole – The Big Hole. My brother, Jack, who was fourteen at the time and had been kept home for a dental appointment, drove my car down to Panmure. My other brothers and sisters became isolated by the fires. Those who went to school in Warrnambool had to stay the night at their school, while others who went to school in Terang, were put up by local families. All the while, Mum was told to wait at The Big Hole, until it was safe for her to return home. That night she didn't know where the remainder of her children might be, how safe they were, or how long it would be before she saw them again.

As I drove home along Vickers Road, I was reminded of how dry the paddocks were. Wispy remnants of bleached grass, paddocks bitten down to the dirt. The roadside verges were bare. A fire could scoot across these paddocks in minutes. A large plume of smoke now rose from Mt Warrnambool. With a strong north wind blowing the fire south, it could be licking our farm boundary within 20 minutes. I walked into our empty house. There were dishes in the sink, some dirty plates on the table. It looked as though Mum had left in a hurry. The eeriness of the house was accentuated by strange, discordant voices coming from the Listening Set in the kitchen corner. Brigade captains were calling for more back-up, describing the size of burning trees that had fallen, hay sheds and houses that were alight. There was a palpable sense of urgency in their voices, of people in the moment, fighting the fire, making quick decisions. I stood in the kitchen transfixed by the reality of their situations and the silence of the house. It felt as though I had been taken back in time, away from the fires. No power, and our house seemed like a refuge from the flames I had seen. Could I just stay in it and forget about the prospect of fire? I walked into the lounge, remembered what I was supposed to be doing and raced around the house looking for rags to clog the spouting. I kept thinking about what I should take if the house became endangered: photos, the TV? We didn't have a fire plan. I turned left into Mum and Dad's bedroom and stood there, almost hoping for an answer. The dilemma was too great. I hurried outside and started spraying water on the walls of the house. It seemed like a useless exercise as the house wasn't burning. I felt as if I was practising for the real thing. I can still remember the confusion of this period when I couldn't think straight, nor do what I was supposed to be doing – shifting the cows on to ploughed ground. I was caught in the emotional upsurge from what I had seen of the fire. I remember the fire as a ribbon of orange flame hovering on the mountain's ridge before racing down through paddocks toward our farm. There appeared to be two fires burning at once; one on the ground that burnt grass and understory, and another which sailed from tree to tree and sent embers ahead to burn more grass. The fire was being blown south at a steady speed. It seemed inevitable that our farm would be burnt.

    I ran over to the machinery shed to start the motorbike. The fire was about to leap the river, which was no more than half a mile away. A line of red gums that bordered the river would slow the fire down but not for long. The wooden bridge would probably go as well. I realised that for the first time in my life I was fighting a fire that was out of control, chaotic and unpredictable. I could die. I unchained the dog, noting that the chooks beside him in their pen were screeching, running back and forward beside their chicken wire fence. I was unsure of their fate, but thought that they would be safer inside the pen. I was running out of time.

I sped down the dirt lane to the paddock where the milkers had been feeding. There were about two hundred of them, bunched up around the gate, waiting to escape. I could see the fear in their startled eyes. They reminded me of dogs in a storm wanting to come inside the house. Something in nature had gone awry. I stood back as they bolted through the gate and kept on running. All the gates along the lane were open for them to run across to the ploughed paddock on the western side of the farm. I thought that I had better check for any cows sheltering underneath the pine trees that hung over our boundary fence. But for once, all the cows had stayed together; so keen were they to escape the roar of the fire. As I rode back toward the gate, it was the sound which made me stop and turn around. A fire front had rushed up behind the pine trees. I couldn't move. My eyes were transfixed by the flames shooting up the length of their trunks. The trees, over 20 metres high, were sheeted in flame. Sparks flew onto the grass and the fire surged forward. I kicked the engine over and rode off toward the cloud of dust the cows had left hanging in the air. The fire was now a speeding wall of flame moving south across the paddock I had just rode out of. It scorched 40 acres in under a minute, the flames maintaining their height of 20 metres right across the paddock. This wall of flame exploded across the paddock like continuous claps of thunder. Only when the advancing fireballs reached a thin line of bush was its progress slowed by the dense ground fuel of ferns and fallen trees. Our farm was on fire and there wasn't anything I could do about it.

I followed the cows across the road toward the ploughed paddock. A fire truck sped down the hill past our farm towards our neighbour's house, and shortly after, returned. It was Dad and his long-time friend, Harry Hastings. The neighbour's house was untouched. They had returned to fight a small fire front that had been blown back toward our house. Dad was a changed man. He was in a mad hurry. I followed him into the house. Words were being thrown at each other; questions and orders were unformed. The bare essentials were all that time allowed: *hose, spouting, shut all the windows, water the walls.* And then he and Harry were gone, abrupt as ghosts, leaving me with the eerie stillness of the house.

I grabbed a ladder and began stuffing tennis balls in the spouting corners. When I ran out of tennis balls, I used wet rags. I kept looking back to where Dad and Harry had disappeared in the truck. They had had to cut a fence with wire cutters to get into what we called our 'bull paddock'. Cutting a fence on your own farm is sacrilege; a blow against the hard work it took to erect the fence. It is also an act of disorder, vandalism. However, this was a day out of the ordinary when much of the order that we lived by, religious or farm work, had been cast aside.

A thick cloud of white smoke was rolling toward the house, reducing visibility to 20 metres. I had no idea if there were flames behind the smoke or not. I couldn't see the truck and felt that it was pointless to scream out. They wouldn't hear me. Suddenly, a figure stumbled forward, waving his hand and coughing. It was Harry. He was hyperventilating. I rushed him inside to the bathroom, washed his face and tried to calm him down so that he could speak. Somehow, he had become separated from Dad in the smoke. I looked outside. Dad was somewhere beyond the white fog that burned my eyes. I stood waiting for a sign, a sound of the engine. Could he be lost? Should I go and see where he was? Then I saw the red bonnet of the truck as it charged through the smoke, down through a drain and uphill toward the house. The wind had paused and it seemed to be changing direction. We ran out to meet him. He was coughing as well. He had a serious, determined look on his face, as if he had just been somewhere he had not wanted to be. The wind had swung around to the southwest. Dad and Harry returned to the paddock and put out the small grass fire that only minutes before had been threatening our house. Such fortuitous changes in wind speed and direction happened at random that day. We were lucky; our house was still standing.

After they had extinguished the fire, Dad and Harry drove off to fill the tanker up with diesel. I was to return to Panmure and see if other brigades needed help while our truck was out of action. The three of us had been fighting the fire for three hours, and the experience had moved into something greater than I could have imagined. My life experiences of growing up on a farm had brought me close to nature. Storms, blustery rains, endless hot afternoons were imprinted on my psyche. The land that I grew up on was synonymous with wind. Yet, I had not experienced changes within nature on this scale. I had become used to gradual change, where three days of rain were followed by a fine day, or a cold day before more showers passed over us.

When I returned to Panmure, the Mechanic's Institute or 'the hall' as we referred to it was busy with fire fighters and CFA personnel. It had become the nerve centre from where directions were given by the CFA Operations Manager, Bruce Furnell, to the many brigades fighting the fires. Whiteboards, two-way radios with leads snaking across the hall, firefighters in smoke stained yellow overalls, CFA management and visiting parliamentarians, including then Prime Minister Malcolm Fraser, all helped to give the hall a vital role in combating the fire. It was difficult for locals such as myself to comprehend. We only went into the hall when there was something to celebrate like a marriage, the wake after a death, or a football Grand Final. The kitchen at the rear was crowded with women preparing cups of tea and sandwiches. Donated clothing piled up in corners where previously farmers had scuffed their shoes in the dust of cabaret balls. Camp stretchers were set up against the walls for homeless families. Beneath the Honour Rolls, the room was buzzing with news about who had just lost their house, where the fire was, of people who had been lost and found. Suddenly our town was 'on the map', our unknown lives were being touched by the business of the outside world. Drinks and dishes of cool water were laid out on trestle tables for weary fighters to cleanse smoke-stained eyes. Some of these men lay down exhausted staring at the dirt, tracing patterns in the dry soil with twigs their fingers had chanced upon. Others sat around in their dirty ill-fitting overalls, smoking and telling stories of their most recent battle with the fire. They spoke of farms reduced to ash and of the wind, its speed and gusting pressure. It was a wind they hadn't experienced before. Yet despite the trauma of the day, some divisions between men remained. Men who were not thought of highly had to ask around for brigade captains to let them help out on their trucks. Friends tended to stick together. The firefighters worked shifts on different trucks throughout the day and night. Those fire fighters local to the area helped out on visiting brigade trucks. The fire had assumed such mythic proportions in my mind, my daily life had to be put on hold. I couldn't talk about footy, the weekend, girlfriends or family. They all seemed to be remote and distant from this reality that I was experiencing. It was a Wednesday, a mid-week working day. Each of us was caught up within the unreality of events, and by its very strange nature, the fire was bringing us together, uniting some of us in ways that we would not normally experience.

■

The remainder of that Wednesday has become a blur for me. The passing of time and emotion has rendered the experience as a series of vignettes, or snapshots as seen from a passing car. The fire was brought under control with a wind change and rain falling at approximately seven pm. There was still a lot of mopping up to do, spot fires and smouldering logs would continue to burn for another three weeks. There had been tragedies on the day. A man whom I had played football against died when his car was engulfed by flames five kilometres from our farm. The heat inside the car was so intense that the wheel rims melted into the bitumen. His father and two other men also perished in the car. Several other people had died in similarly horrific circumstances short distances from our farm. A farmer died after he was thrown from his horse when he was rounding up cattle. A mother died when she fled a car trapped by fire on a back road. A short time later a man ran up to the burning car and carried her badly burnt son to safety along a road where the bitumen was like a river of fire. The only thing protecting the man and stopping him from slipping were his workboots. In the process of rescuing the boy, parts of the rescuer's hands were burnt. He managed to reach a car at a nearby roadblock and the boy was rushed to hospital. However, this car was involved in a collision a short time later due to poor visibility from thick smoke. The sad irony was that the man who came to help at the car crash was the boy's father, who could only recognize his badly burnt son by the sound of his voice when he said 'Its me, Dad.' His son died a short time later before they could reach the hospital. Each of these deaths took this day into another existence, another realm.

I spent the night putting out spot fires on different brigade trucks. There were many scary experiences: aiming hoses at 20 metre trees being scorched by fire, riding in trucks with burning trees falling across the road behind us. In some of the trucks, the volunteers were drinking stubbies. It had been a long day for everyone. The Panmure Hotel was giving away beer to fire fighters who needed something to help them cope with what they saw. It was standing room only in the front bar of the hotel. Dad drove me home around 2am. I wanted to keep mopping up with him through the night but he insisted that I sleep. I remember trying to sleep and seeing paddocks of burning trees close-up behind my eyelids. The fire was imprinted upon me like a tattoo. I would carry this vision of the fires with me each night before I slept for another week.

Dad didn't sleep that night. He arrived home the next day for a few hours sleep and breakfast before returning to mop up the fires. Our electricity had been cut off. For once, the cows were not milked. Our worldly sense of order had been broken. A large part of our farm had been burnt. We lost several kilometres of fencing but suffered no stock losses. As captain of the brigade,

Dad assumed his responsibilities. He knew the local area well and was helping to coordinate mopping up operations for the many brigades who had arrived to offer assistance. Two days later, a police car brought him home. He had collapsed with exhaustion and had been sent home for rest. My mother, brothers and sisters and I rushed out of the house to see what the matter was as the police car pulled up in our driveway. Dad slowly eased himself out of the car, but he could barely speak. He was crying. The policeman told us that he needed rest and soon after drove off. Dad backed himself up against the wall of the house and stood there panting and crying, unable to speak. I had never seen him like this before. Mum was distraught. 'Are you alright, Dad? What's the matter? Go away, kids!' She sent us inside the house to let him get his breath back. We had always depended upon our father to carry us through, to be the strong one, to show us how to act. Now he was weakened, defeated by a bush fire. It was a shock to my thinking. I found myself sinking back from my brothers and sisters, watching Dad panting against the wall of the house. He was weaker than I had thought. Finally I had seen his limitations. It was in this moment where he was struggling to regain his breath that I thought he had never been so human. In retrospect, he has never looked so vulnerable as when he stood there with his back against the wall, as if he was asking the house for strength, or wanting something secure to lean against, to depend upon. Several minutes later, he had calmed down enough to come inside. Nine people died in the Cudgee-Ballangeigh fire. 50,000 hectares were burnt and over 7000 kilometres of fencing was lost.

After a lengthy enquiry, the fire was narrowed down to two causes. Clashing power lines were found to have started the fire at Bob Harrington's farm at Cudgee. The spark from a council roller was thought to have ignited the fire at Ballangeigh. Both the council and the then S.E.C. were liable for damages and the losses incurred in the fires. People had waited a long time throughout the enquiry for a cause to be found, and although money was eventually paid out, it was a pittance compared to the hardships that survivors had endured after the fires.

■

Writing about my experiences in the Ash Wednesday bushfires has become a recurring motivation for me. In some ways, it is like a dream that I continually return to, in order to make sense of the experience, perhaps because I have never been able to get a description of the fires right. Although I have written a story, a number of poems and an essay about the fires, the very nature of the event continues to haunt me. Perhaps I have failed to engage with the emotional intensity of the event and have written around what I have been trying to say. Perhaps by writing about the fires I only ignite old feelings and fears that others have managed to forget. Perhaps it is due to my nature, which is to dwell and reflect on things, rather than to accept that the events in the past are behind me, or that the past doesn't exist. Experience may shape us, yet it is often memories which fragment the experience. In the end, what do we trust? As Patrick White says, once you look into the fire, and have seen what you see there, you can rearrange your life. Each summer, bushfires rearrange lives throughout Australia. Even with the amount of relief money, trauma counseling and community support available today, it is not easy for people to achieve 'closure' or 'move on'. Several weeks after the fires, Dad and I were offered counseling from a group of people who turned up unannounced at our farm. Dad knew some of the people and we thanked them for their assistance. At the time we were busy repairing fences with help from volunteers. It hadn't occurred to me that I might want to talk to someone about what I had experienced. In some ways I was able to forget about the fires through the work involved in feeding out donated hay to cows, clearing up broken fences and rebuilding new ones. It took most of 1983 to rebuild the fences on our farm, which became a process in itself of moving on from the fires.

The fires have not been forgotten. Official memory of the fires; documents, committees set up to improve fire reduction, fire training and fire awareness in the community ensure that Australians cannot forget the legacy of bush fires. However, in the days after the Ash Wednesday fires when the metropolitan media were concentrating on reporting those fires closest to Melbourne – Mt Macedon, Cockatoo and Airey's Inlet – many people in the Western District thought that their suffering had been forgotten. Apart from extensive coverage in *The Warrnambool Standard*, city newspapers such as *The Herald Sun* and *The Age* gave very little coverage to the damage inflicted by the Cudgee-Ballangeigh fire. The phrase that many local people created at the time to describe the fires was: 'The Forgotten Fires'. While such a phrase invites a certain amount of self-pity, it is also one which emanates from the long-held division between country people and their views of people who live in the city. The perception that the city doesn't care about you the further you are away from it was borne out by the reluctance of metropolitan journalists to travel further than an hour from the city to report the fires. I have also been made aware of the lack of knowledge people have of the Cudgee- Ballangeigh fires through conversations with people over the ensuing years. More often than not, people can recall the horror of CFA members being trapped in their truck by the flames at Cockatoo, the fires at Macedon or what they were doing on the day when a huge cloud of ash descended upon the city. Nine people died in the Cudgee-Ballangeigh fires, yet their lives were assured anonymity by a metropolitan media reluctant to report the lives of people living more than three hours from Melbourne.

For many locals, it is the physical reminders of the fires on farms and in towns that ensures that they will not be forgotten. Around Panmure, where the Cudgee-Ballangeigh fires raged, there are several physical reminders. On the east side of Vickers Road, which abuts the Princes Highway five kilometres east of Panmure, is a line of dead cypress trees. The trees died as a result of being scorched in the fire. Several trees have fallen over or have been split down the middle of their grey trunks. I have a close association with these trees as I used to walk past them on my way home after being dropped off from the school bus. The branches would shudder and creak, lift and sway as a gust of wind scuttled through. The trees gave my brothers and sisters shelter from heat and rain. We used to store our bikes under the branches of the corner tree. Here in the darkened recesses where our bikes lay, I would sometimes see a cow's porcelain skull or bones partly submerged in the dark soft dirt. The wind moaned beneath the trees as if it bore their weight. The fires destroyed this line of cypress trees that I had been looking at my whole life. While the landscape has been changed by the trees collapsing in on themselves, it was their grey spindly branches spiking the sky like withered arms that affected me the most. It was as if I was made to watch the trees suffer. Months after the fires, new growth sprouted on other trees, and eventually the paddocks developed a thin sheet of grass, barely concealing the blackness beneath. My way of looking at the landscape had been changed by the burning of this row of cypress trees. No longer could I look up Vickers Road and see dust from the milk tanker coating the branches. The stability of a world that I took for granted crumbled. Each time I return to the District, I look to these trees to see if there have been further changes in their decline. New cypresses have grown around the old, but a glance at what's left of the old trees is enough to bring back the smell of ash and burnt wood.

    There are two sites of memory that still send shudders through me whenever I drive past them. These sites are not visible to the human eye. Some people would think that they do not exist, that they are nothing but a figment of my imagination. They are burial pits for burnt cows. One is on the corner of the Cobden-Warrnambool Road and the Panmure-Ayrford Road. On the surface, the paddock is green like any other paddock nearby, but beneath the ground are the corpses of cows I saw being lifted by front-end loader and dropped into the pit. It is an image that I can't get out of my head. For a farmer to see his or her cows being buried in the ground is similar to witnessing a mass burial of people. The cows are more than the farmer's livelihood; they are the animals that the farmer understands the most. I also saw cows being bulldozed into a pit on my neighbour's farm. The morning after the fires, I stood in a burnt paddock with Dad watching the front-end loader driver methodically going about his work. An eerie silence pervaded. Neither of us could speak about what we were witnessing. Some years after the fires I wrote a series of poems where I tried to understand the images that I saw in my head.

Morning after

I stand with my father
in the tyre marks of fire trucks
looking across burnt paddocks.
Paddocks he has walked in his head, in his dreams.
The same paddocks we have talked into arguments.

The past is scorched, but its heat
rises through my workboots.
My father shakes his head
scuffs his boots in the ashes of a fence post,
'You wouldn't credit it.'

A skinless calf hobbles from a drain.
Whispering beneath tangled fencing wire
the husk of a strainer post.
The strip of bush I explored as a child
has been left in black slivers.

There is a cemetery quiet my father
won't admit. He spits, rattles change
in his pockets as smoke enters our clothes, skin

       a bulldozer fills a pit with burnt cows.
       Their skin has been toasted the same grey colour,
       are they Jersey, Friesian, or Hereford?

       They fall from the bulldozer's bucket in clumps
       ten at a time, sideways, headfirst thudding
       into place amongst the flies.
            Some cows miss the hole
       and land broken-necked, half-in
       half-out, forcing the operator
       to scoop them up and start over again.

       A siren wails through charred gum trees
       lining Heathmarsh Road.
       Beneath the dirt, tree roots and peat bogs
       smoulder and glow. Everything
       we've ever leant against
       has been shelled and scattered.

Fire regenerates. It helps to produce new grasses and flowers. Aborigines have a long history of using fire as a tool for their survival. Yet the immediate aftermath of a bushfire is a period of shock for many people. The shock of unremitting change; of lives being taken away. The world becomes divided between life before and after the fires. They are bleak moments when you look at the paddocks that you have loved and grown up with. Charred and desolate, no longer productive, the paddocks have been knocked around and battered. Skeletal trees and smoke whispering from logs. The farm is like a giant ash tray. You walk on and your boot prints are left behind. It is as if your disbelief is being recorded by the circles you walk in, the birdless world you are now a part of. It is like standing on the edge of a new world after a bomb has been dropped.

Farm boys

After I had left CBC at the close of year eleven, I spent much of my spare time drinking underage in Warrnambool pubs. I had left school and was working on our farm until I decided what I might do in the future. Mick and other friends gave me lifts into the Warrnambool pubs such as The Lady Bay, The Cri or The Macs. Crowds flocked to the pubs that booked cover bands to play easy listening hits to well-dressed country crowds. The Cri and The Lady Bay had big name bands such as Goanna, The Models and Brian Cadd playing to full houses. Many of the country men wore neat pastel-coloured shirts and pale trousers and pretty soon I was as well, assuming that this was the way to meet girls. Drinks were cheap and the crowds were drunk by closing time. The Lady Bay employed bouncers who were renowned for their violent thuggery. Once I saw two bouncers punching a drunk repeatedly in the face and then throw him out, face-first onto the footpath. The bouncers were overweight, unsmiling and they took jokes personally. They watched us like hawks as we shuffled inside. Underage drinking was common yet it seemed to be accepted at the Lady Bay. There were blitzes every now and then, but this was before the era of photo I.D, and so many older siblings licenses were flashed if a check of underage drinking was carried out. I had a cousin who served behind the bar and she slipped me Bacardi and Cokes when nobody was looking.

Some nights I missed out on a ride home from the Warrnambool pubs and ended up walking in the direction of Panmure. If I was lucky, I was able to hitch a ride with a passing friend, but more often than not, I had to walk most if not all of the thirty kilometres home to Panmure. Despite the distance ahead of me, I didn't mind walking at night and thinking about the girls I had failed to chat up or the people I had seen in the Lady Bay. I couldn't ring my parents to come and get me and so I was left with little alternative but to fall into the rhythm of my own walking or the slurred thinking that the beer had left me with.

The Princes Highway was always quiet at 4am, save for the occasional truck barreling through to Melbourne. I trudged through my drunkenness to the breaking dawn, smells of dairies and cows around me. Dawn's chill replaced the warmth of the night. Once or twice I fell down embankments and drains as I lost my way in the dark. One time a police car pulled up near Cudgee and the copper gave me a lift home, no questions asked. He knew my father. Mum got the fright of her life when she saw me hopping out the front door of a police car. She had feared the worst. On these mornings when I did walk home, my feet were aching by the time I rounded the bend of Mt Emu Creek's 'big hole' in Panmure. With two miles to go along the Heathmarsh Road, I could look forward to a soft bed and sleeping in until after midday. Walking home from Warrnambool had been some sort of achievement I could start the day with. However, if it was my turn to milk, I'd have to change out of my beer-smelling pastel clothes into my milking clothes, and mumble a greeting to Dad as I put the machines on the first run of cows.

Farm boys

You can see their utes pulling dust toward the highway
smell the Brut, blue jeans
pressed by their mother
the night's milking shadowing their palms.

You can tell by the way they arrive
at a decent hour
support the bar with steady conversations,
add weight to the walls
watching girls they cannot talk to.

You can tell by the way they drink
without getting their lips wet
how they listen after a handshake,
study their boots as a woman passes
and five beers later, stories of their father.

You might remember them at the hamburger van
tall as hay sheds, still listening
to your opinions, the note
of your girlfriend's car they will memorise
until the sound of their tyres punishing gravel
becomes the night,
driving itself home.

The boundaries of a fruit picker

As a way to escape my future working at the local Kraft cheese factory, I persuaded some friends to catch the train to Mildura with me and to try our luck picking grapes. Jack, Steve and I were given a lift by some older fruit pickers to a caravan park where they were staying. Two men in their late twenties from Melbourne, they drove a white 1968 HK Holden which they referred to as the K. In the weeks that we picked fruit, these two older men would be like brothers to us; giving us a lift to and back from the fruit block each day, explaining the quicker ways to pick fruit, loaning us one of their eskies for our food and beer and joining us for beers in the Irymple Pub some nights. We pitched our two-man tent in the red dust of the caravan park, wiping bull ants out of the way with our thongs. Each of us took turns to sleep with our head facing the tent flap. I often woke in this position to bull ants crawling over my face and Jack's snoring. The heat from the tent drove me outside at dawn to sit on the esky and ponder my situation. It was a long drive back to Panmure but the Irymple Hotel was a short walk away and it would become our home away from home over the coming weeks. Jack and Steve were arguing with each other and they clearly had had enough of spending time in the tent. Most nights we ate at the pub and returned to our tent where we sat around talking or arguing while polishing off a slab. Each night the park was alive to shouts, laughter, drinking and crying. By the end of the third week of grape picking, Jack, Steve and I were being given credit on our wages from the publican. We barely had enough money to scrape together for the train ride back to Melbourne and then Warrnambool. In the time I was away, I missed Theresa's wedding at Panmure, the first wedding in our family. Broke and far from home, I spent the night of her wedding sitting on a bar stool at the Irymple Hotel trying to forget about the decision I had made.

The following year, Jack and I decided that we would have another go at fruit picking and this time we would pick properly and not drink our earnings away. Both of us were keen to make money and slug away at it so that we might make a profit on our hard labour. I had organized for the orange HQ I bought from Mick to be spray-painted maroon. I put some wide tyres on it and tried to hot up the six cylinder the best that I could, without knowing much about cars. The drive up through the Wimmera and Mallee was long and arduous. Jack didn't have his licence and so I drove all the way through St Arnaud, Birchip, Lascelles, Speed, Tempey and Ouyen to Mildura. The wheat silos of the small Mallee towns were visible for miles and the further we drove into the wheat country the reality set in that we were so far away from home that we couldn't return. At some stages the railway line ran parallel to the road and quite a few of the towns had a rail line running up the guts of the main street. The flatness of the wheat paddocks set around us like concrete. There were few cars on the road; just the occasional farmer's ute or a Kingswood towing a caravan. We found our way to a fruit block between Irymple and Mildura. The blockie owned two fruit blocks and there was some wealth about his new brick house immersed in a lush garden circling a lawn and shaded by a willow tree. Twenty metres from the house were the grapevines, red sand and rusted iron of the packing sheds.

The pickers' quarters were basic. A tin shed with a concrete floor broken up into smaller rooms with two single beds in each room. There was a row of showers, where the hot water ran out after one shower, and some plastic chairs were arranged under a tin verandah. Jack and I had a room to ourselves. The beds were stiff and there was a strong smell of hard water and dirt about the place. Prickles such as three corner jacks were everywhere outside and one of our first jobs each night after picking was to pull out the jacks from shoes and thongs as the pain of standing on a jack in bare feet was excruciating. Determined not to repeat our picking efforts from the year before, Jack and I picked for long hours; beginning each day at six-thirty and toiling away until two pm when the heat of the day kicked in. Most days we took a three hour break and returned to the vines at five to pick until seven pm. We shopped in Mildura once a week for supplies and usually went to the pub on a Saturday night. With this mostly disciplined approach to life we were able to make $1600.00 each in four weeks.

Other pickers varied in character. Traditionally, fruit pickers were itinerant workers from working class backgrounds or uni students supplementing their incomes during uni holidays. A common viewpoint from Mildura locals was that fruit pickers meant trouble and that they were not to be trusted. The mobility of the workers contributed to this impression. A picker could move from block to block or out of the district on a whim. In the 1980s, before fruit picking was taxed and tax file numbers were introduced, most fruit pickers were paid by cheque or cash. No doubt exploitation of fruit pickers occurred but Jack and I were lucky that we chanced upon a trustworthy blockie. Most nights we sat on the plastic chairs outside the tin shack smoking, drinking and talking.

Saturday nights I drove into town where inevitably I drove and Jack drank, or on occasions we both did. Striking up friendships with other pickers was easy in a crowded pub with all the men around you either wearing singlets and shorts or tee shirts and shorts. Office workers stayed away from the pubs that we drank in. The first two beers barely hit the sides of our throats as we drank to escape the heat and the prospect of more buckets of grapes the next day. Jack was more social than I, and he was always looking around to see who he could talk to. One night we ran into Nev, an older man with floppy brown hair and a thick moustache. He was from Bowen in Queensland and was picking on a fruit block across the Murray in New South Wales. He laughed a lot, shared ciggies with us and drank with us from pub to pub. He was in his fifties, had been married and so paid close attention to any teenage girl we came across. It was one of those nights where I ended up driving Jack and Nev across Mildura looking for a party, but ultimately we ended up driving down to the banks of the Murray to drink and be dickheads. Jack and Nev laughed and screamed their heads off to the darkness of the river while I sat on the bonnet of the HQ smoking and wondering how I was going to get Jack home to our block. We drank our cans and I pointed the HQ back towards the lights of Deakin Avenue. I remember turning around at one point to see Nev in the back seat smoking a ciggie and laughing. The next minute he was vomiting out the window with the vomit being swept back behind us in the slipstream of the car. It was one of those moments that seemed to encapsulate my life at that point in time. I let Nev out at the corner of the next block for he seemed to know how he was going to get home. He wiped his mouth, waved to us, and staggered back across the footpath into the glare of a Sports Girl shop front. We never caught up with him again. He was just one of many pickers floating around Mildura at night, men who were potentially trouble, looking for people to drink with.

A trio of pickers who were sharing a room at our tin shack were in fact typical of the wild characters I met in Mildura. Jack and I could never quite work out the sleeping arrangements as the male was a wiry, tattooed man of forty who seemed to be in a relationship with a woman in her thirties and yet there was a younger woman in her twenties also sharing their room. The women rarely said much as the man talked non-stop; mostly bullshit stories of his past such as taking pot shots with his rifle at the balls on a bowling green close to his house. An air of suspicion pervaded the trio. If either women spoke, it was mainly the older woman, simply agreeing with what the man said. Despite his bravado and talk, he was a fast picker and the three of them easily out-picked Jack and I until we hit our straps in the final weeks of picking. The man had a habit of leaving a long-neck bottle of beer at the end of each grape vine so that he could pick his way to the reward throughout the day. He would be drinking by ten in the morning. Sometimes the women would join him as well. Once a bottle was finished, he picked up his picker's knife and worked his way to the bottle at the end of the next row. Some days he had a break from the drinking and I often wondered what kind of life the two women had listening to the man's opinions throughout each day. There was something hardened about these people; their skin more leathery than from working outdoors in the sun. They were some of the first people I met who carried the weight of their larger experiences. They were wilder than the world I had grown up in. After the harvest was over, Jack and I were driving to our next job when we heard a police announcement over the radio of a man and two women wanted for questioning and that members of the public were not to approach them. The descriptions fitted the trio we had been working with. Both of us laughed and shook our heads in relief. Everything we sensed about the trio was dodgy and the radio merely confirmed what some locals feared from fruit pickers.

Paringi

The following year, I returned to Mildura to try my hand at fruit picking again and maybe earn enough so that I could follow the fruit picking season to Queensland. I was naïve enough to think that this was a reality with my grey ute fitted with a home made canopy tarp that I could sleep in if needed. I found work at a fruit block at Paringi, east of Mildura, which consisted of rows and rows of grapevines sprawling down a slope and an orchard of orange, mandarin and lemon trees growing on higher ground. Clusters of avocado trees grew around the vines and near the citrus so that when I finished each day's work at five, I could walk through the block picking the fruit that I liked for dessert that night. My living quarters were an old round caravan on stumps beside a picker's shed with two rooms and a bathroom. Hot water came via lighting the hot water service with wood each night. The van was fine for one with a small double-bed and kitchen. I had brought a small black and white TV with me from Panmure, imagining the many different places I might be in to watch it.

The van was positioned near a boundary of the block, quite a distance from the owner, Martyn's house. Although this was the first time I had really spent time on my own, I was quite happy cooking for myself, watching *Minder* on a Friday night and sleeping amidst the wind and storms that rocked the van sideways. Although the wage wasn't high, I was able to save quite a bit of money by the fact that I wasn't spending it. I drove into Mildura on a Friday night for the weekly shopping and treated myself with KFC so that I wouldn't have to cook that night. It is difficult to remember what I was reading at that time other than *The Sunraysia Daily* and *Rolling Stone* magazine. I didn't have any teachers or readers to guide me with what to read. I picked up authors' names from Mick and Annie when I spoke to them on the phone, but it hadn't occurred to me to join the Mildura library.

In retrospect, just being alone, working hard in the block each day, collapsing on the bed, my muscles aching from physical work was good for me. I had routines of cooking, washing and cleaning that kept me busy from too much time thinking about family and the life I had left behind at Panmure. Sometimes I called Mum and Dad from a phone box outside a caravan park up the road, and their voices and lives, so familiar to me brought back my childhood in an instant. The tone of Mum's voice opened up the spaces of the house to me. I could imagine them sitting around the open fire in the kitchen or picture Mum sitting on the telephone stool in the lounge room. Mum talked about the latest football score, who was playing against who the next week while Dad described some of the work that he and Jack, who had left school to work on the farm, were doing. I had separated myself from them and was living a life that in some ways appealed to me. Yet I wasn't sharing it with anybody. I didn't have anybody to talk to or bounce ideas off. Sometimes I stepped out of the phone box, looked at my grey ute and wondered what I had. I drove back to the fruit block and thought of the night ahead in the van. I kept thinking of the night they would be having on the farm compared to the night I had watching the news on the black and white TV. I wasn't convinced I was living in the right place, yet I needed to earn more money if I was to move on. The owners, Martyn and his family and his father Bob, were just happy to have a worker who stayed on the job and who turned up regularly each morning.

One of the busiest times on the block was the harvesting of mandarins, oranges and lemons. Each type of fruit needed to be picked by hand from the tree, lowered into a picking bag which was then emptied into the picking bin. Martyn's rate was twenty-five dollars for a full bin, and on a good day, I could fill three bins of mandarins, oranges or lemons. The trees were tall and the foliage thick. A curved metal ladder was used to pick around the tree and by leaning my weight into the ladder I could reach into the depths of the tree to retrieve the fruit from the inner branches. The smell of mandarins and oranges enriched the picking day, and although I could, I didn't eat too much of the fruit as I picked. Picking lemons was the most challenging as the thorns from the lemon branches became spikes that cut at my wrists, arms, face and legs. I wore long sleeve shirts for protection and cut-off socks over my wrists, but still I was lacerated. The orange tree orchard was over ten rows deep and it took several weeks to harvest the fruit. Occasionally, other pickers were employed on a casual basis, but the most regular of these casual pickers was Gerald.

Gerald had been working as a seasonal picker at Martyn's block for several years. He rode his Honda 125 over three days down from Mackay in Queensland to spend two months at Martyn's block picking oranges, mandarins and lemons from the trees. He was inordinately quick as a picker and while he worked alone, he could easily pick the same quantity of fruit as two people might be able to. He had black thick-rimmed glasses and greasy dark hair. Not dissimilar to Dick Smith in appearance, a comparison also emphasized by the fact that Gerald was almost always in a khaki shirt, shorts and boots. He may have been a bit put out by my arrival on the block as no longer was he the main picker bringing in the harvest for Martyn. But he didn't mention this point, nor did he wonder how long I was going to remain on the block. He stayed in the picker's hut at the rear of my van, and although we were living close to each other for several months, our social interaction was confined to a few words about the harvest from the safety of our ladders.

Gerald was not without his idiosyncrasies. His decision to ride a Honda 125 from Queensland to Victoria over three days clearly suggested he was happy spending time on his own. He was a seasoned picker, who in effect, was his own boss. He worked alone happily, and as far as I knew he wasn't married. One afternoon when I was having trouble lighting the hot water service for a shower, he called out to me from his hut to give some advice. I opened the door and there was Gerald in bed with all his clothes on at 5:30. While it was a cool night, it wasn't really a night to be rugged up. There was something lonely about seeing him in bed with all his picker's clothes on plus a thick jumper. I thought that this is Gerald's way of coping with the loneliness that each of us grappled with at different stages of each day. I didn't see a book and he didn't bother about asking Martyn to supply him with a TV. On the other hand, I passed the time at night watching local TV and the ABC on my portable black and white, reading newspapers and sometimes standing outside the van smoking and staring into the starlit night.

Perhaps, Gerald's most noticeable trait was his logorrhea, or excessive talking to himself which occurred while he was picking fruit. The first time that I heard someone talking when I was up a ladder reaching into a lemon tree, I assumed that a family of pickers had arrived to help out with the harvest. I climbed down from my ladder and walked between the rows of lemon and orange trees and the only person I could see was Gerald. He was some distance away and I could hear his arms flaying at a tree as he quickly filled his fruit basket. I stepped closer, intrigued now, and stood listening. The talking started up again and sure enough it was Gerald's unmistakable nasally voice. I stood two rows away from him catching my breath, trying to make out what he was saying. He mentioned people's names, it sounded like a conversation:

> 'Mary told me that I shouldn't, I shouldn't do that but you know I told her that was when yesterday, yesterday those people came and when I was a boy, oh well when I was a boy we used to play these games, and then I said to Mary...'

It was partially jumbled speech, sometimes clearer than others. I smiled and walked back to my ladder thinking how weird the world was.

In time I became used to Gerald's talking and perhaps more gradually, he became used to my presence picking in the row next to him, aware that I could hear what he was saying. He generally stopped or paused if I was in earshot and would then resume his self-talk when he was further away from me. I mentioned Gerald's habit to Martyn, and he shook his head and smiled.

'I know. It sounds as if he's nuts, but he's the most decent picker I've had. He arrives by bike each year, works solidly and then returns to Queensland. Without him, I'd never get the fruit in.' I was learning a lot about people. Gerald was one of the strangest, yet most normal persons I had met in awhile. There didn't seem to be a dishonest bone in him. Compared to many people who might say one thing and think or do the other, I always knew where I stood with Gerald, despite the fact that he talked to himself constantly.

Later that year, Mick arrived on the fruit block to help out with replacing the strainer posts of each vine and harvesting the citrus crop. He had been living the life of a punk in St Kilda, going out to the Seaview Ballroom, living in cheap rentals and spending his money on records and clothes. He was looking for work but was feeling trapped by the St Kilda scene of drugs, parties and music. I invited him up to the block to help alleviate my homesickness but also to give him a chance to work hard and save some money – money he wasn't seeing in St Kilda.

When I picked him up from the Mildura train station I was surprised by how thin he was. His skin had that pasty, inner city pallor, and his hair seemed dry and brittle from all the times he had dyed it. Thankfully, he had kept it a simple dark colour, as I didn't want him to cause any worry or concern to Martyn and Bob. Digging the holes for the grape vine strainer posts was some of the hardest work Mick or I had had to do. While a post-hole digger was used to dig a hole to a depth of three or more feet, the loose clay and dirt in each hole left behind by the digger had to be scraped out by shovel. It was back-breaking work as we bent down to lift the clay out, check the depth of the hole, dig some more until the hole was deep and clean enough for a post to be lowered into it. Both of us trimmed and toned up during this work and after a few weeks, Mick began to look healthy again.

The caravan could accommodate four people but it had been comfortable for one. I had to make room for Mick so each night we lowered the kitchen table until it was level with the vinyl couches and Mick slept on the table for a bed. It was another routine that we became used to; another thing we simply had to do. Similar to our Friday night trips to the shopping centre for a six pack and KFC, our days were driven by routine and small celebrations. Mick had brought some of his music from Melbourne up with him and once again my mind was being opened up to the latest alternative music. He had the first Violent Femmes album on tape. Sometimes we checked out bands touring Mildura such as The Angels and Uncanny X Men at the Bridge Hotel in Mildura. Any touring act that came to Mildura was worth seeing. Like many country towns, Saturday nights in Mildura involved cover bands, country and western outfits and jukebox discos.

Once again, Mick was shaking up my thoughts and ideas of what I wanted to do with my life. I had been working on the block for four months and knew that my time was coming to an end. I had seen the life of a seasoned fruit picker with Gerald and realized that despite his peculiarities, it was not the life that I wanted. Perhaps Gerald was one of the outcomes for a person who works alone labouring away picking fruit at their own pace – you start to develop your own language and talk to yourself. One day Martyn approached me when I was picking oranges and asked if I wanted to stay on at the block and become a manager. I would manage the harvesting of the crops and general maintenance of the vines and fruit trees. Naturally there would be an increase in pay. After Martyn walked away, I was shaking. I had been thinking for days how best I might be able to leave the block, how I might break it to Martyn that I wanted to move on. Now he had trumped the ideas I had been keeping to myself.

Within a week I was driving my ute away from Paringi and south back to Warrnambool. Mick's stories of pubs and music in St Kilda had woken something in me. I wanted to try living in the city and mixing with people who weren't so motivated by footy, getting pissed every weekend or causing havoc on footy trips. If I remained working on the fruit block this was the life that was in front of me. I could be independent, rent a house and develop a life around the Bambill footy club where I had been playing, but these people were not my people. I would be displaced in this landscape, as much as Mick was when he arrived in Mildura with his St Kilda skin. Martyn and his family, as decent as they were, were not my people and I would always be an outsider trying to fit in. I wasn't sure if by moving to the city I would discover who my people were, yet at twenty I craved more than what Paringi or Mildura could offer. I wanted a sense of excitement to my days and not feel that in order to belong, I would have to follow what the decent people around me were doing. I didn't make it to Queensland and so my dream of picking fruit around Australia remained just that. I really didn't know what I wanted to do as I drove away from Paringi, yet I knew that in order to make a decision, I needed to drive.

Killing Beefy

'What do you want to move to Melbourne for?' Jack asked.

'Why not? More things to do there than here,' I replied.

'Suit yourself,' he smiled and lit a Winfield. 'you wouldn't get me in the city for nothing. Shit of a place.' He laughed and looked over at Dad, who had a radio strap slung around his neck. He was tuning into a race that was about to come up.

Dad nodded and shook his index finger, as if asking for quiet.

Jack continued.

'I mean, what are you gonna do once you're there and everything?'

'Dunno, get a job. Mick will help me out."

"SHHH quiet, you buggers!'

We both smile at Dad and say nothing. I motion with my fingers for Jack to pass over a ciggie. I haven't smoked since I was fifteen, when I had a few at the footy, behind some cypress trees. They made me feel crook and I've never really gone back to them.

I light up and it doesn't taste too bad.

Mum comes into the kitchen, glances at Jack and I smoking around the table and walks away. I can tell she's not impressed.

The race finishes.

Dad looks over at me.

'Brendan, I thought you had more brains. Those things will kill you.'

'Didn't you smoke for ten years when you were working at Nestles?

'Yes, but,' he replies, 'but, I give them away.' And if you're smart, you'll give them away too, son.'

'Bloody idiot,' Jack mutters to nobody in particular. I exhale and look out the kitchen window to the dairy.

'So what else has changed since I've been away. Where's Beefy?'

'You've been eating her.'

'What!"

I look at Jack and he's pissing himself.

'What do you mean, I've been eating her?'

At this point, Mum returns to the kitchen and overhears the conversation.

'Beefy, oh yes, that was sad', she says. 'You kids used to ride her, didn't you?'

'We killed her', Dad says. 'She wasn't giving much milk and we needed some meat in the freezer. I got a bloke up the road to butcher her and then we cut her up and put her in the freezer bags in the freezer.'

Mum stands by the table with a tea towel in her hand.

'It's what you do Brendan. It's what you have to do on a farm. You of all people should know that.' She walks back to the laundry.

Dad sits with his arms folded and smiling at me from the head of the table.

I shake my head. My face is flushed. I push my chair back to walk outside.

'Beefy. Imagine killing Beefy', I mutter to myself. In the playroom beside the kitchen, there are toys and a child's toy pram scattered across the chipboard floor. Old toys from our childhood that Mum has recycled for the grandkids. I look in at the abacus set, prams, plastic fruit, plastic kitchen setting, the mess. The room has a lived-in feel, but it could be from another century.

One rainy afternoon, I loaded up the grey Kingswood ute with my worldly possessions, draped a green tarp that Dad used for covering superphosphate over the wardrobe, dressing table and other belongings that I had, tied it all down and drove off into torrential rain. While I was tying down the ropes, Dad walked over from the machinery shed to wish me luck for the drive and the move. He turned half away from me and slipped a folded fifty into my hand. 'You might be needing this.' I was surprised by his concern, his awareness that I might be in need of money. Fifty bucks wasn't a great deal, but it was the idea of it that made me remember the gesture.

With ten children to worry about, it must have been hard for Mum and Dad to not favour one of us over the other, and to maintain a connection with the unique foibles and passions of each son or daughter. Dad has always been a man of few words when it has come to demonstrating affection and no doubt it is an attitude that I have inherited, for better or worse. I drove down our gravel lane past the line of sagging boobiallas toward Vickers Road and looked in the rear vision mirror at Mum and Dad standing by the garage waving. Well, I won't be seeing them for a while, I thought to myself. I still felt as though I had failed on my around Australia trip by only getting as far as Paringi in NSW. This time I wanted to show them what I might become. They'd said goodbye to me numerous times before, but this time I knew I wouldn't be returning in a hurry.

On that six hour trek south from Paringi to Panmure I was racking my brain with what I might do when I moved to Melbourne. The landscape of the Mallee and Wimmera was horizontal and the chipped back roads maintained a true level as I passed through Ouyen, Hopetoun, Minyip, Stawell, Mortlake and into the home country. Yet driving through a stable, flat country wasn't helping me to make a decision about where I should call home. Home was the country that began south of Mortlake and continued in a wide arc around to Koroit and Port Fairy in the west and to Camperdown in the east. These were the places of slanting wind and weeks of misty rain I had grown up with. Places I knew intimately; so much so that I could dream them and carry a nightmare image of each place in my head. I didn't want to live in this home country. I didn't want to be a farmer. In my mind, the city sat on the horizon like a giant glow worm pulsating and flashing its neon in day light. I was somewhere between Ararat and Panmure when I decided I wanted to become a radio announcer.

I didn't have a clear view of where I was going literally, as I drove into slanting rain all the way to Melbourne. But I had a room in an Elwood flat, and an address to go by. By the time I pulled into Shelley Street, the wardrobe and dressing table were stained green from the dye of the superphosphate tarp. The colours and smells of the country remained with me.

Baptised

The flat in Shelley Street was on the upper floor of a two storey 60s style orange brick block. I had never lived in a flat before and it took some getting used to the fact that I couldn't simply walk out the door and touch the earth with my feet. There was a view to the south through the leaves of plane trees and to the further reaches of the sky over Port Phillip Bay. There were a lot of other two and three storey blocks of flats nearby, many with art-deco or fifties style retro flourishes. Some had curved balconies and were painted cream, yellow and various shades of brown. Some still were given names such as Braemar, Sherbourne and Windermere. I had only known of farms being given names; those made–up or Aboriginal names that could be seen at the start of long gravel drive ways, such as Merino Downs, Barunah Plains or Menindigo. Each of those farms had been associated with money and sometimes a squatter's heritage. Where did the names of the flats of Elwood originate from? In those first weeks of living in the flat, I stood on the balcony overlooking Shelley Street, watching office workers walk home and wondered how I could I ever fit in.

My first real experience of inner city living occurred when I went to see Public Image Limited or PIL at the Seaview Ballroom in Fitzroy Street, St Kilda. Mick had been a regular at The Ballroom since he moved to Melbourne some years before. He had seen countless bands, he wore the ripped jeans, fishnet tops and dyed hair that was popular then. On the other hand, I wore a leopard print tee shirt, jeans and an attitude that I hoped was punk enough to get me through the Ballroom's door. I had never been to a punk gig before and even though Mick and his friends had prepped me, all I had to compare to PIL was seeing The Angels at The Bridge Hotel in Mildura.

Although The Sex Pistols had died a sorry death, their legacy lived on in the minds of many angry young punks who wore the leathers, ripped jeans and multiple piercings. Punk bands were still playing in pubs as other Melbourne bands began to move towards New Wave and alternative sounds. Mick was playing drums in a band called Great Caesar's Ghost. They weren't really punk, more Garage New Wave. At one of their few gigs, the lead singer poured a jug of beer over his head and began to abuse the crowd. That was the kind of social interaction that occurred between bands and fans then. I still have memories of dancing to 'Never Mind the Bollocks' in our bedroom on the farm in the 1970s. I can still remember the adrenalin rush of watching them perform Anarchy in the UK on Countdown. PIL at The Seaview Ballroom was the gig to be at; after all, Johnny Rotten would be playing.

I followed Mick and his friends up the marble steps of the entrance, bought a can of beer at the bar and then continued upstairs to the old ballroom where the band was to play. Fifteen minutes before the band came on, the room was a seething mass of people pushing and swaying to the support bands. Punks wearing mohawks and orange-spiked hair were skulling cans of beer and flinging the empties over the crowd's heads. I stood my ground in the middle but I was being squeezed by punks from all sides. I could smell their sweat, see them gob out into the crowd, I could smell some of their breaths. A small stage was crammed up one end of the room. The house music looped a recent PIL hit: *This is What you Want, This is What you Get*. The crowd surged forward. The air was thick with the smells of sweat, beer, cigarette smoke and chewing gum. The floor was bouncing beneath my shoes. I wasn't sure what was going to happen next. It seemed that the crowd was capable of anything. If a fight broke out, I'd have to get involved. There was no escape. The music became louder and I could feel a crescendo building. Johnny Rotten walked on stage to loud cheers and whistles. He was wearing a long white shirt. He glared at the audience with his large blue eyes and snarled – 'so this is the home of Melbourne punk!' The band moved into 'The Order of Death',

Rotten sneered and the chaos began. People began throwing half full cans of beer around the room and taking aim at the stage. At one point, Rotten snarled at the crowd and threatened to stop playing if they didn't stop throwing cans of beer at him.

People spat, pogoed and roared at each other. I was killing myself laughing at the energy and madness of the room. I was being pushed and swayed by a crowd and there wasn't any way I could move out of the room. I *felt* like a buoy in a surging sea, a car on two wheels threatening to roll over. I'd lost Mick and I was alone; trapped in a mass of sweating bodies, wholly appropriate when PIL played the Sex Pistols song 'Bodies'. I felt like an animal. They played one other Sex Pistol song; 'Anarchy in the UK'. This was the song that everybody shook their fists to. It was the song that had galvanized a generation after seeing it on 'Countdown' in 1976. It was the song that epitomized the night for me; raw energy, a signature riff and a dose of political anger. PIL had brought anarchy to the Seaview Ballroom and my body was throbbing. Afterwards I was searching through the crowd to tell Mick what I had experienced. It felt as if I had played a game of footy. My legs were twice their weight and I could barely lift my shoes from the floor. It had been a gig that I was to remember and keep coming back to as an experience that had shifted something within me. Under the halo of PIL, I had been baptized into Melbourne nightlife.

Like walking down a paddock

Growing up in the country gave me a sense of space that I took for granted. Each day I could walk out the back door of our farmhouse and run my eye over paddocks, a line of bush, slight, gradual hills and cypress trees. The sky was vast and the weather patterns from the west filled our days so regularly that I could forecast the weather by looking at the clouds. Much of this psychic and visual space became narrowed and cramped when I moved to the city. Instead of waking up to the moan of wind and the cawing of crows, I woke up to traffic and the rattle of trams. Instead of a slow, gradual start to a farm day after the morning's milking there was the urgency of people rushing to work and of the day being hurried away. It took me awhile to locate where I was in the city and where I could possibly go. This sense of not belonging and not knowing has no doubt affected other people from the country when they first move to the city to live.

Apart from driving around the streets or riding trams to familiarize myself with the city, I took to walking as a way of getting to know a place that I lived in. It was something that I did with each of the share houses that I moved into across Melbourne. After dumping my stuff into the often small bedroom, I headed out to the footpaths to read the houses, significant buildings, or find the nearest tram stop. I was on the lookout for quirkiness or unusual gardens, something that suggested to me a story about the people who lived in the area. I traced the patterns of back streets, how they lead to main streets, how one way lead to a side street where I might discover a house that belonged in both another country and century. Forever a creature of routine, I walked the streets of the suburb I had moved into for several weeks until the street names and houses had become embedded in my memory. When I lived in North Caulfield, I walked around Caulfield Park, looking at the large houses, the lives settled behind high fences, people running and exercising in the park. It was a world foreign to me and yet I was learning to live with it. A neighbour, an old Greek man, walked up and down our street each afternoon before dinner. Sometimes he stopped to talk to people, but often he just waddled up and down the short dead-end street, hands clasped behind his back, lost in his thoughts. Walking for him, was some kind of vigil before night descended. At the corner of Balaclava Road and Hawthorn Road, a tram can turn four ways according to the different route it may be on. In time, I was able to walk in different directions across the suburbs when I wanted to but at first I had to walk a straight line to the tram stop, milk bar, the main shopping strip. Walking, for me, was not only a way of knowing where I was living, it was how I began to be placed in a city where the sounds of trams echoing along wide flat streets became the sounds of a river guiding me to where I needed to be.

When I lived in Elwood I liked to walk along the canal path to gain a sense of where I was. Blue stone paths lined the edge of the canal which in those days was often foul-smelling and low in water. Shopping trolleys and plastic bags littered the canal's banks. The canal was the closest Elwood had to a river and the water in the canal seemed to rarely move. Yet it was the space around the canal that drew me to the water. There were reflections of clouds in the water and the open space between buildings gave room to the sky and allowed my mind to breathe. Walking along the canal path towards The Broadway always helped me to open my eyes, lift my moods. It was almost like walking down a paddock.

The Espy, Prince of Wales, The Venue and Seaview Ballroom were the places to go and see bands in St Kilda, and to be seen at. There were house and flat parties on a weekend, often begun after a session at the Prince of Wales where people would be invited back for drinks that went into the dawn hours. Even though I worked in a timber yard during the day, I dressed in black op shop jackets and jeans and loud shirts at night and pounded the footpaths of The Broadway in both directions to save money and to be able to drink. Many of the people I knew didn't have a car or the money to be able to afford one. They got by on student allowances or the dole and had enough money to pay the rent, buy groceries and have a few beers. Walking home after a late night out was a common thing to do. I walked down Barkly Street past the old Aquarium, the sex shops, and cafes towards The Village Belle hotel with the hope of having one more beer for the longer walk home to Elwood. The walk home along the footpath of The Broadway was a staggering walk at the beginning, but after half an hour in the cold night air, my senses regained their alertness and I was sober by the time I reached our flat in Shelley Street. The pubs in St Kilda gave me a sense of where my generation was at but it was the footpaths of Elwood that helped me to get to wherever I was going.

One Easter weekend, I remained in the Elwood flat while my flat mates travelled back to the western district for Easter. I had a promise of a party on the weekend that I wanted to go to, rather than seeing my family but the party fell through and so I spent much of the weekend alone. It was the first extended break I had spent alone in the city. Some of that time I remember being consumed by self-pity and my lack of friends. However, I did go out for walks to Point Ormond and along the beach at Elwood, no doubt cutting a forlorn figure like the many other forlorn figures walking along the beach in black clothes. It was a weekend where I was again forced to confront who I was and what I was doing. Why was I sitting in an Elwood flat watching TV alone? This wasn't the view that I had imagined from Paringi. The social life that I had expected to validate what I was doing just wasn't happening. At the time I was reading Jack Kerouac, The Beats, William Burroughs and Allen Ginsberg. I was drawn to their romanticized visions of the outsider, of the people who live on the fringes of city life and who are either poets, musicians or artists. I was listening to Nick Cave, Paul Kelly's 'Post' and Midnight Oil's '10-1' album. Love-sick narratives and political raves were where I was at. At this point, I was avoiding Bob

Dylan because I thought he was too obvious. Somewhere I had been put onto *Dante's Inferno* and thought that I should read it. I had bought the first volume, *Hell*, some time earlier, and so on that Easter weekend, I sat down to read it. The trilogy is set over the Easter weekend, beginning with Hell on Good Friday, Purgatory on Easter Saturday and culminating in Paradiso or Heaven on Easter Sunday. While the narrative is an account of a character who could be Dante being led down into the circles of hell by the poet Virgil, I wasn't thinking of descending into my own version of hell. Yet my mood flattened while I moved between the kitchen and lounge, making myself toasted sandwiches, sitting on the couch watching the afternoon soften around me. I didn't finish reading *Hell* that weekend, although I could easily relate to the visceral imagery and the religious symbols from my Catholic upbringing. Since I had moved to the city, it seemed that I had kept myself busy socially so that I wouldn't have had to spend too much time by myself. I was caught up with the idea that I needed a firm social set in order to be in the world. Even though people responded to me better when I was with friends or others, I couldn't see that in order to be happy with myself, I had to spend time with myself. And yet it was difficult trying to fit into life in a city without a firm idea of who my friends were.

Some years later, I was still walking home late from pubs and nightclubs. Mostly, this was out of necessity because I had spent what money I had on beers. I developed a habit of lingering in bars until closing time, often with friends, sometimes alone, waiting to find the right time to walk up to a girl, often watching other more confident blokes chat up the girl I had been eyeing off. On some occasions, I chose to walk home through the night to my flat in Elwood. After 3am, it felt as though I had the city to myself as I trudged over Princes Bridge towards the shadowy footpaths of St Kilda Road. While cars and taxis streamed out of the city, I walked along in my thin-soled shoes, black jacket and Levis thinking about the night I just had, girls

I failed to talk to, all the while maintaining a momentum of gathering up the streets, walking out of frustration, sometimes out of exhilaration. Despite having no money for a taxi, nor any friends going my way, I walked through the images in my head; the scraps of poems I had been thinking about, my family in the country and the paddocks I would be returning to every six or seven weeks. By the time I reached the purple eye on top of the Cadbury Schweppes building near St Kilda Junction, my feet were aching. The walks sobered me up and gave me pains in my shins. And yet, the rewards for these late night walks came when dawn started to break over the dull bitumen of the streets. Buildings rose out of darkness, men on the pedestrian signals lost their glow, sometimes I saw sleepy-eyed drivers making off to work. The beginning of a new day always lifted the night shadows with hope. I was rejuvenated, tired and with the right amount of detachment from my surroundings that helped me to see the world anew. In later years, I have come to know this time as sparkling time; when the interplay of light breaking through trees, bird sounds and the freshness of the air motivates me to, sometimes, chance upon insights to the world around me. Often I am slow to pick up on ideas or what people say. Sometimes it is only at dawn do I realize the world for what it is. After crossing the expanse of St Kilda Junction, and noting other dark-clad figures strolling the streets, I made my way up Barkly Street, familiar haunts energising me. I felt at home with the 1950s style flats, the John Lennon Bar on the corner of Inkerman Street, the run down op shops and cafes were all where I belonged. I had walked from the city, six kilometres, the hard way, the way I knew life from farming. Along the way, I walked off the beers and managed to clear my head with thoughts of stories, people, sometimes a line of poetry I kept repeating until it became embedded, a part of the new morning. In some ways, walking home from the city was like spending time in my study, writing poems in my head and of finally getting a few things done.

Learning to write, learning to read

The novels of Jack Kerouac and writings of beat poets such as Allen Ginsberg tapped into my disaffection with life in Melbourne. Like many other twenty-something men, I was entranced by the stories of open roads, drinking, parties and a heightened way of experiencing life. It was the year of the Australian Bicentenary and I wanted nothing to do with Tall Ships or Captain Cook. At the time, life could be lived cheaply in the inner-city suburbs of Melbourne. It was possible to rent a room in a share house for thirty dollars a week, live on the dole or work part-time by choice. This meant that artists, musicians, writers and students could hang out at pubs such as the Prince of Wales and The Seaview Ballroom in St Kilda, gate-crash each others' parties, drink, take a lot of drugs, and for sustenance, live under the shadow of The Birthday Party. During this period, I worked in timber yards and a Laminex distribution centre driving trucks and delivering laminex to the northern suburbs of Melbourne. By night, I was wearing black jackets, loud 60's style shirts and drinking at parties as if I was a Beat writer. Despite my earnestness, there was a lot of pretension to my view of writers and the idea that this might be a way to meet girls. I was adopting the look of a writer and I hadn't written anything.

The divisions between my working life and my social life widened. I found it hard to accept the ideas of some of the working class people I worked beside. I wanted more than simply working to save money, and having left the country, I thought that I should leave the idea of a work ethic behind. Yet my experiences of growing up in the country didn't always gel with the inner-city types I was meeting in pubs and at parties. Many people with their dyed hair, safety pins in noses and ripped jeans didn't know where Panmure was, and so for awhile I stopped mentioning it. Many of the artists and musicians I met were from inner-city Melbourne, often from private school backgrounds; there seemed to be little in common besides the beer and our attitudes. I found it hard talking to girls about working in timber yards, let alone dairy cows. I began keeping a diary of my days and frustrations. Since leaving school at the end of year eleven, I had barely written anything. At first it felt strange to be writing something that wasn't related to my work. The writing was messy and the sentences were unformed or rambling, as in the style of Kerouac. It was a type of vomit diary where everything went in, regardless of what I was thinking.

Self-indulgent, unduly influenced by the Beats, the diary became my main outlet for writing and for recording my frustrations with life. No doubt this approach is not new; so many of us have kept diaries when we were younger and justifiably burnt them when we were older. I didn't know any other males who kept diaries and so I didn't make a habit of telling people that I wrote in one. The only other person I knew who kept a diary was my elder sister Annie, and she had always been the sister who read a lot. Years later, I discovered that Dad had been keeping work diaries for some years. The diaries are typical of a farmer's day and the entries are brief: 'Allan Beattie died. Sowed rape back paddock. 168 points.' While these pocket diaries didn't allow Dad to expand upon his thoughts of the day, they are fascinating for the way they record the elements of his working days. Towards the end of her life, one of Dad's sister's Rose, maintained a diary that appeared to sum up each year of her life in a single entry. The first entry to the diaries is fascinating for its brevity and for what it reveals.

1940, Ryans still living at Moyne. War still on.

This was the family farm that Dad grew up on, at Moyne in western Victoria, a short distance from Koroit. Rose had worked on the railways for much of her life, at first at Camperdown and then for a number of years in the canteens at Spencer Street in Melbourne. She lived for many years with her husband Phil in Glen Waverly.

1972: April 11, Tuesday. Phil and I went to town, bought home a new car. $4859:00, got $300:00 off for cash.

Both Rose and Phil had grown up in the Depression and so their attitude towards money was to save and not spend. One of Rose's touching entries was a brief description of Phil's death.

2012 July 25 Wednesday, 9:15 am, Phil's 88th birthday, Audrey came over, had lunch after sat in lounge talking, seeing Audrey off we both went out to see her off. Phil said I am going in, too cold. When I came in, he came out of the bathroom, asked for a chair, took a puff of the inhaler, dropped his head, fell back, eyes rolled. I rang an ambulance, they came almost straight away. They worked on him but was too late. Father Pat came and anointed him and the doctor also came.

Maintaining a diary of their days may not have been so strange for Dad's family when the written word was the main way that people could record their lives, however brief the accounts were, and perhaps were expected to be. The brief laconic note on a life was often seen as secondary to the life lived. And yet I knew that when I kept a diary, it was still not a fashionable thing to do.

Meanwhile, I worked, drank a lot, became depressed with my life, wrote in the diary and repeated the pattern until it became a habit. After a year of keeping the diary and reading over it, I could see that the sentences were not only clear but that paragraphs were forming. It had been the routine of writing, of returning to the page that enabled me to articulate what I had been thinking, even though nobody else read it. Gradually the writing took over as a form of expression. I began copying quotes and passages from writers, for inspiration and also for the style and rhythm of their sentences. Poems began to emerge in notebooks but they were unformed ramblings of my thoughts. I was writing about people around me; neighbours, housemates, work colleagues. I didn't tell people what I was doing, least of all my family. Yet I was experiencing the cathartic thrill of getting an idea down, a rant or a description of a tram ride. Self-expression it might have been, but it became the outlet I needed for not fitting in, not being happy with who I was or was trying to become. There were no answers with what I wrote, yet the diaries became a path for me to move away from labouring jobs and into an awareness of an inner life. It would take me four or five years before I wrote my first decent poem. That was only after much reading of other poets, awkward and vague drafts, and the common sense suggestions from some writing teachers. I had no plan for what I wanted to write yet I knew the elation of having written something down, however insignificant.

My ticket out of the suburban blues was studying at Swinburne University. I had applied to enroll in an Arts course but because I hadn't completed year twelve, I was accepted into an Arts preparatory course. In this course were people who had either left school early like myself, had been thrown out of school or their grades were not high enough for a general Arts course. It was an intensive six months of studying English, sociology and history subjects. I loved it, especially being exposed to old Australian films, a sociology subject where I completed a research project on gentrification in St Kilda and having a chance to read a wider range of authors courtesy of the university library. Finally, I had the opportunity to acquire books without having to buy them from second hand bookshops. Apart from borrowing books needed to help with my studies I gravitated towards the literature section; the 823s in the Dewey decimal code, a code that I would haunt for years. I borrowed Dylan Thomas' poetry and hopelessly tried to imitate his long, forceful lines in my own writing. I was drawn to the romantic sweep of his poetry, his writing about village life and the great villanelle, 'Do Not Go Gentle Into That Good Night' tapped into the familial emotion that I'd known about through Mass at Panmure. One afternoon, when I was browsing in the library I came across a copy of Michael Dransfield's 'Drug Poems' which had fallen out of the shelf. I looked at the black and white cover of a bearded Dransfield gazing out at the reader. Who would title a book of poetry, Drug Poems? I hadn't heard of him before so I borrowed the book and read it feverishly on the tram home up Glenferrie Road to Caulfield.

I was struck by Dransfield's layout and design of his poems as much as the heavy drug content of the poems. Here was a poet who wasn't using punctuation, who set his lines across the page and used a loose slangy syntax to describe a world I knew a little of. It was a far cry from Dylan Thomas. A poem such as 'Bum's Rush' caught my attention with its imagery of Norse demons, eskimos and human lemmings disappearing 'where the ice is thinnest'. I set about looking for more Dransfield in the second hand bookshops that I knew and it may have been at this time in 1988 that I first came across Kris Hemensley's poetry bookshop, Collected Works and found a copy of Dransfield's 'Collected Poems' published by UQP. The black and white etching of Dransfield on the cover looking side-on at the reader and wearing a high collar seemed to distance him from the voice within the poetry collection. There were a lot of poems in the collection and there seemed to be serious claims being made for Dransfield in the introduction by Rodney Hall. I remember catching a tram down to St Kilda and walking along the beach to Albert Park where I sat down on the sand and read the whole book. I wanted to be alone with the city behind me as I read through the range of Dransfield's poems. Poems such as 'The City Theory' and 'Geography' tapped into my sense of feeling claustrophobic in the city and my longing for romantic love. Dransfield mentioned a range of writers and artists such as Byron, Stephen Mallarme, Rachmaninoff and Wyeth – writers, musicians and artists that I wanted to seek out. At the time, Dransfield seemed to be the epitome of this romantic ideal of a poet that I had coursing through my head. Instead of American role models such as Bukowski and the Beat writers, now I had an Australian writer who I could project my sense of alienation onto.

Dransfield's poems also opened the door for me to other Australian poets. Through the Swinburne library and good second hand bookshops such as the Academic and General and Grattan Street bookshops in Carlton, I began reading other Australian poets from the same period of Dransfield- the 'poets of 68' gang: Robert Adamson, John Tranter, John Forbes and Charles Buckmaster. Here was an Australian poetry, of mostly men, that seemed to operate outside the hype and politics of Australia's Bicentennial year. Again like Dransfield, there were lower case words, a lack of punctuation, poems ranging across the page and dense block-like poems. All of a sudden my concept of what poetry could be was being opened up and rearranged, despite my own writing being stuck in a world of tortured syntax and didactic romanticism.

Later, when I was accepted into the Diploma of Creative Writing at RMIT I had the confidence and perhaps naivety of a beginner writer – necessary attributes at the time as I crossed Victoria Street and walked uphill beside the red brick monolith that was building 51 of RMIT. I had little idea of what I was in for, yet I thought that finally I had found a course that was suited to my lofty writing ideals. There were people from all walks of life in the course and most students were in their twenties and thirties with a handful of more mature students, Alexis Wright being one of them. The short story and poetry workshops were daunting at first when we had to listen to each other's writing and make connections with the content of a poem to the person reading it aloud. There were many surprises in what people read out. There was lot of disguised personal material about break-ups, some drug use as well as poetic reflections on life with a capital P. I liked the structure and expectation of having to present something each week to class be it a story or a poem and either have it praised or critiqued, sometimes heavy-handedly. At the time, I was reading a lot of Dirty realist writing – Raymond Carver, Richard Ford and Jayne Anne Phillips. I was trying to fashion my own stories out of working class characters but many of the stories remained unfinished. The late Judy Duffy, one of the founders of the course, was enthusiastic and encouraging of all student writing and in her novel writing class I laboured away at a novel that explored some of my fruit picking experiences from Mildura. Each day, Judy and Antoni Jach who taught short story writing would mention writers that I hadn't heard of and suggest to all of us that we should be reading them. This word of mouth way of introducing us to wider literary references was invaluable to me. I had more than enough reading to do, I just needed to find out what I wanted to say in my writing.

Two other teachers that taught me that year left a lasting impression on the development of my writing. Judith Rodriguez came to the course as a recognised poet and teacher. While she had her particular likes in poets she was eclectic in her interests and was encouraging of all student writing. Judith made us slow down the reading of our poems and she critiqued the poems slowly, sometimes line by line with the class to discover what each of us might be writing. Through Judith, I discovered more women poets than I had been exposed to – Adrienne Rich, Ania Walwicz and Jennifer Rankin whose poems I would read repeatedly over the years. At the end of the semester, Judith presented an award to myself and another student whose poems she considered the most outstanding of the semester. I was amazed that she saw something of promise in the poems that I was writing, which were mainly observations of city life and characters that I had met. Yet this was the type of writing that I wanted to pursue – life that was around me, rather than the lives of writers in books.

Judith left the course at the end of semester one to take up a teaching appointment at Deakin University's Toorak campus where Gerald Murnane was teaching. Her replacement was the poet John Forbes, who had recently moved down from Sydney. John was the opposite of Judith in many ways and his sometimes abrupt or direct nature rattled some students who were looking for more sympathetic or encouraging criticism. I warmed to his style and his knowledge and interest in poetry. He entered the room reeking of cigarettes and often wore a blue BLF worker's jacket to suggest his union or working class affiliations. A large man with short wavy hair and glasses, his physique commanded a presence in the class room, yet he spoke with consideration when discussing a poem he had chosen to share. While he introduced the class to poets such as Frank O'Hara, John Ashbery, Gig Ryan, Laurie Duggan and others he also shared poems by John Manifold and Randall Jarrell. When I told him that I had been reading Kerouac, Ginsberg and Bukowski, John replied that your writing will be influenced by who you read and that maybe you should give the Beats a rest. He could be particularly cutting if he found a student's work to be pretentious, unclear or deliberately poetic. Sometimes he simply said, that part of your poem is shit. However, he always sought to focus on which parts of the poem worked and what could be improved upon. He often said that if you can do anything but write then you should, which was a funny thing to say in a writing course. But he was trying to weed out the students who were not particularly serious about writing, students who wrote because they thought it would be interesting for them to write, or because other teachers and friends told them that they could write. He was generous with his time and often met students for drinks after class in the nearby John Curtin Hotel in Lygon Street or occasionally in the more popular pubs in Fitzroy. One night there was a gathering of students in a Fitzroy pub where the celebrations stretched from late afternoon until late into the night. There was a lot of singing towards the end of the night and I can still remember John belting out 'Dead Flowers' by the Stones to an audience of cheering students. He read us his own poems and discussed the formation of some of them and the drafts that they went through. In doing so, John showed us that while he was a published poet, he always needed to connect with an audience, and that poetry was writing that didn't belong inside the universities, but in pubs and cafes wherever people met.

While I was studying at RMIT, I was living in a share house on Beaconsfield Parade in Albert Park, one of the last share houses to be rented on the Parade that is now dominated by expensive townhouses and apartment blocks. While I lived in the share house, I often walked across to the beach to watch the clouds; it was almost looking at an expanse of paddocks. The RMIT course was offering me plenty of inspiration and like-minded friends but so much of my time was spent drinking and playing pool – living the romantic writer life that seems to afflict so many inner city writing types. In fact I was living with another writer, Andrew Murray, who had moved down from Sydney where he had been a journalist with the 'Sydney Morning Herald'. Andrew's mission was to complete a novel that he was part way through. He spoke with a slight English accent and smiled a lot when he spoke which gave him some authority in conversation. He was a charmer to women and fell for any single women he saw or who came to visit a friend in the house. One time a female friend of a housemate moved in to replace the housemate while she was overseas for three months. On the night after the female friend moved in, Andrew was shagging her in his bedroom. The much younger woman, who was the spitting image of Audrey Hepburn, seemed to be impressed by Andrew's lines and world-weary knowledge. They remained a couple until she hopped it three months later.

While I embraced the look of Nick Cave – faded black jeans, op shop jackets and beer, Andrew aimed sartorially higher by smoking Gauloises, listening to jazz and Tom Waits and regaling the household with how great his novel was going. Neither Andrew nor I spoke much about our writing interests and as much as I was willing to show him my writing, he never showed me any excerpts from his novel. Still, he had the ambition to be an important writer and thought that it was only a matter of time before his novel was published. On the other hand, I was struggling to keep up with my writing projects and coming from a viewpoint where to write each day was to put down words on a page and see if they made a sentence. I had few ambitions about where writing might take me, yet I enjoyed some parts of it – when I discovered that I could write something that I could still read the following week. In retrospect, Andrew showed me many of the traps in calling yourself a writer before you have found a reason to write. He had the style and affectation of a writer, so common amongst inner-city men, he was articulate, funny at times, and he knew how to tell a story with a cigarette between his fingers. And yet I never did see any pages of the novel he was working on.

Despite the encouragement I received at RMIT, I was still not a published writer. Like Andrew Murray, I thought of myself as a writer, as many people do, but I hadn't discovered what it was I could write about. Some years later, when I was living in Manchester, I was asked by a friend of a friend who was interested in the fact that I called myself a writer, what it was that I wrote about. I replied in a vague way; inner city lives, the city, interesting people. I remember him scoffing at me and repeating, *yes but what is it that you want to write about? What do you know? Who are you going to write for?* I was put out at the time because I thought he was being literal, yet his questions remained with me as challenges and it would take me some years before I could confidently say, this is what I write about.

Toads

The first job that I landed in Melbourne through responding to an ad in 'The Age' was working as a timber hand at Boston Timber in Port Melbourne. I had never been to Port Melbourne before and knew little of its working-class history. The timber yard was an education for me in many ways. The working conditions were often dangerous, loud and involved plenty of heavy lifting. Customer orders of cut timber were lifted by strap and crane over stacks of 8x2s, 8x1s and so on. Nobody wore orange vests or hard hats and I had to be constantly on the lookout for stacks of timber swinging through the air, sometimes at head height. Like the factory job at Kraft, the timber yard was another place where I punched a time card into a time clock when I arrived for work and at the end of the day when I left. The stamped numbers of 8:25, 8:21 and 5.01 or 5.03 recorded my days as did folded notes in a pay packet record each week. Three hundred and fifty to 400 dollars a week was a reasonable wage in 1985 for a single male paying low rent. Much of my wage was spent going out to see bands each weekend. Most days I bought my lunch and walked a short distance to a strip of shops where I bought a hamburger and a sav in batter.

The workers in the timber yard hailed from an assortment of backgrounds. There were a few men, both young and old, from Croatia and other Eastern European countries. Some of the older men didn't speak much on account of their faltering English, but they had the strength that was needed in a tight situation. They would arrive for work with their lunch in school bags, or a Gladstone bag, read the newspaper and watch Shane and I play table tennis in the work lunch room. Shane was a machinist on an apprenticeship. He was also from Croatia with unruly, thick red hair and a cheerful competitive streak when it came to table tennis. He usually had the upper hand on me, but I did manage to improve my game of table tennis at the timber yard while the older Croatian men sat on wooden chairs watching us until the siren to return to work was heard.

Due to the physical nature of the work, the timber yard also attracted itinerant workers, some of whom had experience in timber mills around Jamieson in northern Victoria, Yarra Glen, and some who appeared to bluff their way through a job interview. There was also a high turnover of workers, either on the bandsaw or as forklift drivers in the outer timber yard. While the timber yard had affiliations with the Painters and Dockers union, union membership was discouraged by management. The basic line was if staff worked hard and orders were kept up with, then the rewards would flow. While drinking after work occurred regularly on a Friday, sometimes management invited the timber workers to have a drink at a Port Melbourne or South Melbourne hotel. On these occasions, the bars were noisy and smoky, crowded with older men in stubbie shorts and blue singlets while other men in neat open-necked shirts and slacks shouted beers and renewed acquaintances with the wharfies and Painters and Dockers. There were older men sitting on stools smoking at the bar while their voices crackled and spat with a voice box. There was one double leg amputee who sat near the bar in his wheel chair scowling at whoever was near him. After work, these bars were largely a male domain and had seemingly remained unchanged from the 1960s. Female drinkers were mostly associated with men or work groups. There weren't the groups of women that are seen today enjoying drinks in hotel bars and lounges. Consequently, any woman who walked through the bar to get a drink was checked out, commented on or dismissed by the desire to return to a beer. One day, our timber yard manager, introduced me to an older man with a huge beer gut and a thick moustache, and later whispered that he was the man to see if you wanted somebody knocked off.

Much of my time at the timber yard was spent on the band saw, either as the sawyer operating the machine and being responsible for slicing the long flitches of timber or tailing out.

A person tailing out walked backwards away from the bandsaw holding a cut length of timber upright. The tailer-out would often send a length of timber sliding back to the sawyer to be cut into a thinner size. A common story going around the timber yard was that one day a length of timber became stuck in the bandsaw but was then discharged at great speed, sending the person tailing out flying backwards into the wall of the timber yard with a length of timber embedded in his stomach. Many of the experienced timber workers were missing fore-fingers or thumbs from taking short cuts with a rip saw or band saw. I absorbed the stories as part of the air that I breathed in Port Melbourne, wary of their truths and exaggerations.

The sawyer had to balance a 30-40 foot flitch of timber which might be up to 20 inches in width on a steel-wheeled trolley and guide it in a straight line into the bandsaw that buzzed and jiggered up and down in a frenetic manner. A certain amount of skill and physical strength was needed to be a sawyer. Earphones were essential and in those days, timber yard workers often went about their business with a cigarette dangling from their mouth. For some men if they had a rollie dangling from their mouth it helped them to concentrate or be able to lift a heavy piece of timber. One morning I found a worker having a bong behind a stack of timber flitches in the outside yard. He couldn't see anything wrong with it and gave me a dirty look when I took him to see the timber yard manager. When I was working at the timber yard, I was smoking up to a pack of cigarettes a day, including smoking when I was guiding lengths of timber through the bandsaw.

The bandsaw blade had to be replaced each day for sharpening in the saw sharpener's workshop. There were two older men who sharpened the bandsaws by placing the shining metal in a vice and then hand filing the teeth of the saw. Each machinist worked on the bandsaws in a methodical manner, filing each tooth until it was razor sharp. Their workshop was immaculate with all the tools having a place on the wall or on a bench. The wonderful aromas of grease, metal filings and the acrid odour of metal being cut greeted me each time I stepped into their workshop. Whenever there was a quiet time in the yard, I liked to talk to the two older men, one of whom wore blue overalls and the other who wore thick-rimmed black glasses and who seemed to always have a cigarette in his mouth. Both men were full of homespun wisdom, stories and advice for a layabout man in his twenties. They knew how inexperienced I was in the timber yard and were prepared to teach me what they knew about bandsaws and timber. I soaked up their knowledge while stirring them back whenever I could.

One day, one of the men was fixing a problem with the bandsaw while I was operating it. I was maneuvering a flitch of timber from the stack beside where I was cutting. I had to pull the flitch from its stack and bounce it down onto the trolley and then guide the flitch towards the bandsaw. This was a job I performed each day and so mostly I managed to bounce the flitches down toward the bandsaw with some agility and rhythm. However, the saw sharpener had not left the bandsaw area when I began to bounce the flitch onto the trolley. The flitch bounced off the trolley and fell onto the trolley rails and against the older man's ankles. His cry of pain told me that this was serious and so with the help of other workers I pulled the flitch from his ankles, turned off the bandsaw and helped him to safety. It turned out that one ankle was badly smashed and he had to take time off work. Perhaps he shouldn't have been where he was when I was operating the bandsaw. Perhaps I should have waited for him to leave the area before I bounced the flitch onto the trolley. The end result was that he never returned to work in the timber yard again. He was in his early sixties, his ankle was so badly injured that he could only hobble around some months after the accident. I felt terrible for what I had done to him and his working life. There were no fines for the company and I am not sure how much he was compensated. It's an accident that I have thought about a lot and have replayed different versions of it in my mind afterwards. How easily I had damaged a person's life. How reckless could I have been?

The consequences of not completing year twelve and be able to work in a profession were continuing to affect me. After two years at the timber yard, I was becoming tired of the physical strain the job was taking on me. The social status of the job also was a concern for me as it didn't seem to help when I was trying to meet girls at parties in St Kilda. Many of them I was meeting at the Espy and The Prince of Wales were from Melbourne's eastern suburbs, others were from private schools. While I could connect with some girls through a mutual love of music and sympathise with attitudes such as trying to avoid having to get a job, when it came to talking about my work in the timber yard, the girls didn't show any interest. Who could they expect to meet through a person who worked in a timber yard?

After I had decided that I wanted to leave the timber yard, I began looking forward to the day that I wouldn't have to drive down to Port Melbourne past the drab warehouses and factories that employed so many people. There is rarely anything pretty about an industrial work area; heavy traffic, trucks, macho men, an absence of trees and grass, the prospect of mundane or repetitive work. I was also moving away from the built and social environment of Port Melbourne in a number of other ways. The pubs of St Kilda and Prahran had exposed me to artists, attractive middle-class girls and university. Studying at university seemed to be a much more preferable life to carrying heavy loads of timber around a timber yard. On my last day at the yard, I moved a stack of timber flitches away from a wall in a holding bay and spray painted in black paint a range of criticisms and quotes onto the wall. I am not sure why I became motivated to graffiti the wall of the timber yard but I remember feeling a sense of anger at the life I had been leading and a sense of elation that I was soon to leave this environment. I remember I spray painted lines such as *Never get married, Yuppie-scum,*

You're all capitalists, Save the proletariat etc. In my time working at the timber yard, I had been largely a typical employee and had never become involved in any trouble with the management or other employees. I was leaving messages for the management to discover after I had left the company. It was a strange or bizarre way of communicating my anger or political feelings as after I had spray painted the messages onto the wall, I moved the stack of flitches back to conceal the graffiti. It would take the next forklift driver a number of weeks to discover, after which the managers would be scratching their heads to work out who had spray painted the messages. In another way, it was one of my first public acts of writing, and of trying to work out my political ideals or allegiances.

I left the timber yard and found another job as a truck driver delivering laminex to kitchen designers and joinery companies across the northern suburbs. That was what you could do in the 1980s – leave one job, have a few weeks rest and then shortly after find another. I found all of my labouring driving jobs through the newspaper. There were still many unemployed people, but as long as I had a car licence and I was young I was always going to stand a chance of finding work. Much of my early years of living in Melbourne had been spent in St Kilda and Caulfield – suburbs south of the Yarra. I had only ventured into Fitzroy and Carlton at night and didn't know that side of the city well. The Yarra river divides Melbourne in many ways and historically the rougher working class suburbs of Fitzroy, Collingwood, Richmond, Carlton were all on the northern side. The south with St Kilda and its beaches is a suburb of old mansions, and as a place to visit on weekends was seen as softer, a suburb for the wealthy and middle class. My country origins hadn't prepared me for the loyalties that some people showed for the southern or northern sides of the Yarra. Some people rarely crossed the river. The inner north also had Melbourne University, cheap terrace houses and sometimes more politically motivated young people. People living cheaply in St Kilda were often on the dole and played in bands. While the wealth of the inner city suburbs has changed a lot, the Yarra as a dividing line remains as do the clogged arteries of Punt Road, the congested mainline that connects the south to the north of inner-city Melbourne.

Driving a three tonne delivery van around the suburbs of Melbourne meant that I was often on my own throughout the day. I relished the independence this gave me and to be able to drive into areas of Melbourne I hadn't been to before. Each day there were twenty-five to thirty drop offs of laminex sheeting, MDM board and laminex coated board. At times it was physically demanding work unloading the laminex board but I was mostly kept fit hopping in and out of the truck and sometimes running to drop off the laminex sheeting. The daily route I went on took me into the far-flung northern suburbs of Broadmeadows and Thomastown and then looped over to the western suburbs of Sunshine and Deer Park before finally climbing over the Westgate Bridge to the depot in South Melbourne. I had never driven up Sydney Road before or to the end of St George's Road. To avoid traffic lights, I took back roads through the dense housing of Preston, Thornbury and Reservoir. The traffic was always intense on the busy roads such as Plenty Road and Settlement Road. Trucks belched dirty fumes and made a racket taking off from the lights. Sitting in a truck I could see the driving habits and risks car drivers took to overtake trucks. Men in hotted-up Falcons and Holdens planted the foot as they took off from the lights. Drivers overtook each other in hair-raising situations just to be in front. Once I reached Mahoney's Road in Thomastown, I too could put the foot down as I always had only two or three more drops in Sunshine before finishing for the day. Sometimes the carpenters and joiners chatted to me as they signed for their orders. They were decent men, often Italian, Greek or Lebanese running either family businesses or working for a medium sized kitchen company. They were people I could relate to, understand and share jokes with. Yet I had a chip on my shoulder about the working class which I largely kept to myself, partially derived from my wanting to escape from it.

While I was delivering laminex around the northern suburbs of Melbourne I was continuing to explore the writing of The Beats and Charles Bukowski. Through Jack Kerouac, I read Allen Ginsberg's 'Howl', William Burrough's 'Naked Lunch', John Clellon Holmes' 'Go' and various other Beat writers. I had a romantic ideal of parties, women and not having to work. No doubt many other aspiring writers have been afflicted by this ideal but in the 1980s I carried it like a badge on my chest. I think Mick introduced me to Bukowski through his own reading of American literature. Mick also read a lot; writers such as Nelson Algren, Henry Miller and writers who were mentioned by Nick Cave and other musicians, writers whose names were passed around like code at St Kilda parties. When I told Mick I was reading some of Bukowski's poetry he smiled and enthused about the books such as 'Post Office' that he had read. Although Mick and I weren't competing with who had read the latest great book, like the influence his musical tastes had on me when I was growing up, I was very much guided by the authors that he mentioned.

While I was aware of Bukowski's attitudes towards women in his poetry, I was still enthralled by his use of simple language, his lack of punctuation and the romantic visions of drinking and a hard life. It was a life that I was aspiring to lead at night in my trips to The Espy and The Prince of Wales. At the time, I couldn't see how misogynist and sexist his writing was and it seems typical now that then, most of my reading was written by macho men. Norman Mailer's 'The Naked and The Dead' introduced me to other war novels such as 'From Here to Eternity' and 'The Thin Red Line' by James Jones. The Beat writers and publishers largely excluded women writers from the period due to the society's conventional ideals of women and of female writers. It wasn't until Carolyn Cassady's 'Off The Road' was published much later that a less biased version of the period could be read. Naturally I tried to incorporate some of Bukowski's attitude and writing style into my own and I carried notebooks around with me as if I was an oracle to describe the world that I saw and imagined.

Gradually my time at the laminex company became more of a drag and an ordeal. Negotiating traffic jams and long distances through the suburbs became repetitive and dull. I listened to the radio to lighten the day and kept a notebook of my scribblings beside me in the cabin of the truck. When I had time at the lights I would madly write down what was around me:

> Trucks roll by, exhaust brake on truck hisses bringing it to a stop. High street Thomastown, men moving witch's hats, cars turning every way, traffic is incessant.

At night, I might go home and write about the day in a diary I kept or try to fashion my truck driving words into a poem. Other days, I drove in a sweat as the truck lacked air-conditioning. Perspiration dripped from my forehead and arms and as I wrote, my arms glistened with the sweat and urgency of what I was trying to describe. I was often critical of the world around me – the men in their hotted up cars, the pebble dash buildings of Preston and Thomastown I was passing through, the constant traffic. Sometimes I was caught at the train lines over Sydney Road and waited for minutes watching older women shuffling along the street or men standing on a corner watching the traffic. This was not the world that I had been reading about in 'The Beats and Bukowski'. It was a humdrum world of women pushing shopping jeeps, families waiting at the lights, road workers smoking while they looked into a cavity by the side of the road. One day I heard Bob Dylan's 'Desolation Row' played on PBS in its entirety. Suddenly, here was a song that seemed to capture my criticisms of society and the phoniness of people. I couldn't believe it when I heard it for the first time. It had the length of a story and the associations of a poem. Bob Dylan's literary references to Ezra Pound and TS Eliot confirmed for me that the poetry and literature that I was reading could be brought into the everyday. Yet it would be some years before I bought my first Dylan album.

Some time later, I returned to working in timber yards, at Wilson's timber yard in Port Melbourne. I made up orders for tradesmen and was occasionally allowed to use the band saw to create orders from flitches of oregon. Again the timber yard was a case study for change in the workforce. Some of the employees were older men who loved the grog, working on a part time basis helping to compile orders and carry out odd jobs around the yard. One of these jobs was to cut up unused lengths of timber into smaller lengths so that they could be used either in orders or as firewood for people. One such man, Bob, was in his late forties. He had the classic 'Norm' body – slouched shoulders, beer gut, red face, pumpkin nose and cheeks lined with broken capillaries. His seventeen year old son often stopped by the yard to see Bob and he was a mirror image of Bob, even at seventeen. Another of these men, Jack, operated the rip saw. Jack had the DTs, so much so that his fingers shook as he pushed lengths of timber past the spinning blade. Jack's face was also creased by alcohol. He rarely maintained eye contact with me. He seemed to be embarrassed by his blood-shot left eye with its drooping eye-lid. His nose was like a road under repair – soft and mushy. He always wore a black tee shirt and faded jeans and hopped about the rip saw and yard like an excited rabbit. The yard foreman, Wayne, was an ex-teacher in his early forties who smiled a lot and showed me the ropes in the yard. Wayne was the person I went to about workers' rights and the attitude of the boss. Nobody at the yard was in a union. Wayne and I often talked about work environments and class differences highlighted by the Wilson family employing many down and out working-class men. I remember Wayne also telling me how unhappy he was with his own personal life. He looked at me and said 'all I want to do is to understand my mother'. I was a bit freaked out but then again I'm never surprised by what a man will say to another man at work. Sometimes people will admit to all manner of things about themselves in a work place, probably because there's no family member nearby to give them that dirty, silencing look.

Edward Wilson, the manager of the yard was a shy, reticent man with red cheeks and a 1950s short back and sides haircut. Most days he remained in his office located within the hardware business that adjoined the timber yard. Whenever Wilson walked out to the stacks of oregon and pine, we knew something was up. He wore open-necked shirts, clean pants and polished shoes; casual work clothes that still set him apart from the rough and tumble of the timber yard. The yard had been passed down to Wilson by his father. According to Wayne, Wilson never had to lift a finger. 'That bugger has never had to question himself. All he has to do is wait until his old man keels over.' In some ways, Wilson reminded me of some farmers I had grown up with. Men who inherited the farm from their fathers or had to wait until their fathers died before they could take over the farm. Men who had a hunted look about themselves. Men who never seemed quite satisfied with who they had become.

Wilson also had a habit of taking long lunches and usually strode carefully down Bay Street from one of the many pubs in Port Melbourne and into his office around two pm with a bloated face. In the 1980s, business lunches often went until early to late afternoon. One day after his long lunch, Wilson called me into his office. I'd been skiving from work on a semi-regular basis, mostly Mondays and Fridays. While I usually rang in to say that I was sick, one week I didn't bother turning up at all. I'd been having a good time with a girlfriend and her house mates who fed me and let me stay at their share house in Collingwood. The day that I returned to work from the week off, Wilson didn't even bother calling me in. I thought that just maybe I'd pulled a week's work from him and still could be paid. Several days later, I stepped into his office that was crowded with stacks of manilla folders, a filing cabinet and an over-sized mahogany desk. What I remember about the conversation was that Wilson's face was flushed and he didn't seem too angry about me missing days from work. He did ask what he should do with me. I replied, if you want to sack me, then sack me. He nodded and that was it. I had sacked myself. I walked from his office feeling light-headed and pleased with myself.

Despite my slack behaviour at the timber yard and fully deserving to be sacked, I felt sorry for Wilson that he had to get half pissed to sack me. In my mind, I was gone from the yard months before. Working in a timber yard had nothing to do with playing pool in Fitzroy pubs, chasing girls and gate crashing share house parties. But I couldn't tell Wilson that. He was from a different side of life to me; of privilege, ease and guaranteed expectations. He was like Dylan's Mr Jones – *something is happening and you don't know what it is*. We were from different generations who had no idea of each other. Nor did we try to understand each other. In my twenties, I excelled at being a dickhead.

With a regular income coming my way through work at the Melbourne University book shop, my plans for travelling overseas took on an urgency. The rhythms and repetitions of the working week only seemed to propel my wishes to do something with the money. As soon as I was able to, I booked a one way ticket to London via a stopover in Thailand. I had also sat the Silver Top taxi licence test in February. I worked weekends out of the Silver Top depot in Carlton and weekdays at the book shop. Working seven days a week didn't leave me with much time to spend the money I was making.

At first, I drove taxis on Friday nights in and around the city, but the stress of picking up drunk or dodgy passengers became too much of a risk. I preferred driving the streets looking for passengers or responding to radio calls for work rather than working from a taxi rank. The taxi shifts were either, 5am until 5pm during the day, or 5pm until 5am overnight. Night work meant a greater chance of passengers doing a runner, which happened to me a few times after I had driven passengers into the far-flung eastern suburbs. Other times I was either yelled at or sworn at. In one incident, a drunk passenger in the back seat leant forward to pull a cord around my neck and pretend to his laughing mates that he was going to strangle me. Another time, a drunk passenger made me stop the taxi in the city where he got out of the back seat, thumped on the driver's side door while yelling at me to get out of the taxi so that he could drive himself home. Drunks, I'd had enough of them.

Driving taxis during the day on weekends didn't provide a lot of money. On average I cleared $130.00 cash a day for the twelve hour shift but some days it was less. The main benefit of driving cabs on the weekend was that it stopped me from spending money in pubs and eating out. Growing up on a farm had provided me with plenty of experience in getting up early for work. Saturday mornings, I woke at 4:30, had a bite to eat and rode my bike through the dark streets of Fitzroy to the taxi depot in Carlton. Some mornings it was bitterly cold or raining which meant hanging up my wet weather gear at the depot, before sliding into the roominess and brown vinyl of a late 80s Ford Falcon for the day shift.

I was lucky enough to be driving taxis in the early 1990s before the computerized booking system came in, before the mandatory uniform regulations for taxi drivers, but also before any type of security shield or guard was installed in cabs. I cruised through the city, around the inner city suburbs of Collingwood, Carlton, Fitzroy, Richmond and down to St Kilda. I was rarely without a passenger for more than half an hour and because I was often driving around I was able to see the city from different angles, for what it was worth. The passengers I picked up often made the difference between each weekend day. There were the elderly needing a lift to the shops or family houses; elderly women tipped, men less so. One morning I was in South Yarra and I answered a call to collect a passenger from an apartment. Once I beeped, a man in his thirties came down to the cab. It was 5:30 on a Saturday morning. He was wearing a suit jacket and open necked shirt. Money dripped from him. He wore a gold bracelet, raybans and a gold chain around his neck. He wanted the airport and all the way he didn't stop talking, asking me about taxi driving, my thoughts on the world, footy, politics, occasionally sharing little details about his life. He was funny, sarcastic and I was enjoying the banter on the quiet roads out to the airport. A businessmen, I assumed his Queensland destination was not a family holiday. Once we reached the airport he gave me a grin and shook my hand. I knew I wouldn't see him again. As by routine, I scanned the seat and floor of the cab after he had hopped out. Some cash had fallen onto the floor. One hundred and twenty five dollars. By the time I looked up, he was gone and the airport taxi attendant was moving me on. It was the kind of tip that made taxi driving on a Saturday worthwhile.

Saturday morning shifts often started by driving clubbers and late night party-goers home to the suburbs. The majority of the passengers dozed or stared out the window as I barrelled along Whitehorse Road or swung around corners and roundabouts in the back streets of Glen Iris and Ashburton. I never pulled up at taxi ranks in the eastern suburbs as the wait would be too long. Driving back toward the city, tram lines gleaming under streetlights, the forms of houses and trees taking shape as the light began to lift, I felt out of step with the rhythms of people's lives. I was the driver ferrying them home from late nights or driving them to appointments on a Saturday morning. One afternoon I spotted the poet, John Forbes, who had taught me at RMIT, in his faded BLF jacket leaving a Collingwood TAB on Smith Street. I gave him a wave and he rushed across the street to ask if I could drive him to a bank and then back to the TAB. I laughed at his request but drove him to the bank. He seemed a bit worked up and I knew what any amount of money meant to him. Each of my jobs blended into the next job so that there was little difference between Saturday morning and Saturday afternoon. Radio telecasts of the day's footy matches from the MCG or wherever kept some part of my mind distracted. Sunday afternoons were often dead and I had to hunt around known places such as the St Kilda Esplanade market for a job, or hope to get lucky with a job out to the airport. By the end of the shift on a Sunday afternoon, I was exhausted and often rode my bike home to North Fitzroy with the faces of the passengers I picked up oscillating through my head. A six pack and a kebab from the kebab shop on Brunswick Street usually helped me to wipe the working day from existence.

Songs of longing and drama

My sister Kathryn had moved to Melbourne and was completing her Honours year in art at RMIT. Her flat was full of art books, paintings and a back room was converted into a painting studio. Upstairs was another artist, Eliza Lee Gunn, a talented painter who later passed away at an early age from cancer. I warmed to Eliza's direct and engaging character and she often asked me questions such as – what is it that you write about? How is the poetry going? Questions that I didn't really have an answer for as the poetry that I was writing was largely unformed and confined to notebooks. Yet for someone who was self-conscious about this writing thing that they were doing, I appreciated the space that Eliza gave for me to try and talk about writing. I had always been drawn to the world of painters – the mess in their studios, the plans for paintings, works in progress and their ideas that seemed to be outside the humdrum world of working for a wage. Sometimes I called into the studios of other friends and sat around drinking and talking throughout afternoons. Studio spaces were always welcoming spaces as were the artists I met from all walks of life. Some nights, Kathryn, Mick and I walked down to St Kilda to see a band at the Espy or The Prince of Wales. Standing around watching the Triffids and The Go Betweens, listening to their songs of love lost and open country spaces was often the therapy I needed. I'd look around at the people dancing, swaying or nodding their heads to Grant McClennan's earnestness and forget about what personal woes I might have had. These and other bands such as Paul Kelly sang about the people and the country that I lived in. I'd think of Panmure and the people I had moved away from, and those people that I was glad to be away from. Songs of longing and drama such as 'Wide Open Road', 'Holy Water' and 'In The Pines' from the Triffids helped me to imagine country spaces amongst the crowds of the Espy's lounge bar. As much as I preferred the parties and social life of living in a city, my obligations to family gatherings in the country were rarely missed.

Periodically, I left the city for the country. Usually it was at Easter, once or twice throughout the year and at Christmas. When my ute was operating, I drove down the Princes Highway, either with Annie or Kathryn or on my own. Sometimes we took the train and arriving at Spencer Street station on a Friday night or Saturday morning, I always found a sense of communion with other ex-country people catching the train home to see their parents. These people were easily recognizable. They were often dressed in black or alternative clothes and carried an air of resentment and pride about themselves. These were the people from the country who either worked, studied or were on the dole and who couldn't afford a car. Like myself in my Nick Cave jacket, faded black jeans and patched up boots, they stood out from other country people heading back home in their windcheaters, baggy jeans and runners. Sometimes I shared a train compartment with them but nobody spoke. We had our books and magazines to burrow into. Only older people seemed to be willing to strike up a conversation; a conversation invariably based on who we knew in common. I'd watch the alternative looking women and men step off the train and be greeted by mothers dressed in Sloppy Joes and jeans and recognize my own mother in them. Their sons and daughters would step back laughing with their parents exclaiming at their clothes and the colour of their hair. These were the people who had left the country in a hurry for university or work and who had no intention of returning. These people who didn't fit in with their dyed hair and sharp looks, these people who had left the country for the city they had read about in novels, these people who didn't want to work in an abattoir, drink with the same people at the same pub or sing along to 'Bye Bye Miss American Pie', these people who had no desire to return to the country, yet knew its roads and weatherboard houses intimately as the moments in a relationship gone stale, these people who could smell the country in the way people spoke, these people who relaxed with the sound of tyres kissing a gravel road, yet tensed at the mention of old school friends, a football club, these people who kept their return ticket closely guarded as the secrets they knew they would have to one day confront, these people I knew. I knew these people.

As soon as I had returned to the farm at Panmure, I was undergoing a period of readjustment; the smells from the dairy, the quiet, clean air, sounds of crows, the bright stretching distances of the paddocks. Mum and Dad would share all the news as we sat around the red laminex table in the kitchen. I would look around the room to see what objects had disappeared from view. The copper reproduction of The Last Supper was still on the wall as was the embroidered map of Ireland. A new dog, Larry, a blue heeler mongrel, was sitting in the dust by the back door. Things had changed on the farm with Jack working on it and planning to take it over one day. Football was still determining Mum and Dad's lives and if there was a game being played at the Panmure oval I often went down to have a look as well. Although I recognized people around the club and chatted briefly, my life and spirit was elsewhere. When I spoke about my life in Melbourne, the conversations tended to be brief as old friends found it hard to relate to bands and parties in St Kilda. Inevitably, there were arguments and clashes with Mum and Dad over politics and my view of the world. One of the most difficult lessons to learn about returning to your parents after time away is that your parents rarely change their viewpoints or way of life. While I had undergone change almost on a daily basis in Melbourne, Mum and Dad continued to live their lives on the farm according to the rituals that I had grown up with. Dad came into the kitchen after milking in the morning to eat his breakfast while reading 'The Warrnambool Standard.' Mum's day was determined by the loads of washing she had to do, as well as any cleaning she could do around the house. They both supported the Liberal party and thought

Malcolm Fraser, who had Western District blood in him, and therefore was to be supported, was a voice from the country in the city. My support for Labor and the Arts seemed to clash with many of their views. I remember many occasions where after an argument I stormed off and walked down the paddocks disappointed by my parents. As much as I loved them, I couldn't share their viewpoints on religion, Aborigines, the environment or Dad's economic arguments. When I returned from the city to the country I always hoped that the visits to the farm would be restful occasions. Sometimes by Sunday night, I was looking forward to the train home.

Walk like a cow

In his essay, 'Walking', Henry David Thoreau exclaims to the reader, 'you must walk like a camel, which is said to be the only beast that ruminates when walking'. Thoreau was lauding the benefits of reflecting while walking around the wilds of Concord, and no doubt he would have also approved of the ruminating qualities of the cow as it walks. After a cow has left the dairy, it will often pause on the track to the paddock, as if contemplating the night ahead, and stand there, chewing its cud, watching other cows file toward the night paddock. Growing up on a dairy farm at Panmure, walking, for me, was a daily work activity. I walked to get the cows in for milking, waded through flooded drains chasing cows and newborn calves, and stumbled over the furrows of ploughed paddocks picking up stones. Each of those walks brought me closer to knowing and understanding the paddocks I took for granted each day.

Memory walks

My memories of walking through paddocks to get cows in are some of the strongest memories I have. This may have something to do with being able to be on my own, to claim some space away from my brothers and sisters. It may also have something to do with the everyday richness such memories evoke: walking in rubber boots through knee high grass, on the lookout for snakes, and stumbling over lumps in the dirt that the cows had made with their hooves. Barry Lopez suggests that 'one learns a landscape by perceiving the relationships in it'. My knowledge of the landscape I grew up in has been developed through working the land, talking about it, dreaming of paddocks at night, and through writing about it.

When Mum and Dad arrived at Vickers Road in 1966, many of the paddocks were overgrown with tussocks and thistles. There were stones scattered everywhere, many also just below the earth's surface. The stones had to be cleared from the paddocks so that the paddocks could be 'sewn' for rape or clover. Mick and I spent many weekends and summer holidays picking up stones. We walked from stone to stone, chucking them on the carry-all attached to the tractor. It was a way of getting to know the paddock: its terrain and the rich dirt smells of a recently harrowed paddock. We left the paddock only when a pyramid of stone had been constructed on the carry-all. I sat on the tractor wheel guard, watching with trepidation, as the tractor wheels bounced lightly down the track. It was monotonous work in the heat of summer. Walking around paddocks, picking up stones two or three at a time, feeling the weight of the stones in our hands, and then cutting the tips of our fingers on the big ones that wouldn't be moved.

Working the land takes you into its intricate corners, places you can't see from the road, places which occasionally change with a new track to the dairy, but which often retain the memory of certain experiences. I remember walking behind a herd of heifers at an out-paddock which we leased from a local farmer. The heifers were approximately 14 months old, flighty, inquisitive and stirred up by the experience of being taken out of their paddock. As I shooed them up a laneway, they came across the carcass of a dead calf. Noses down, the heifers sniffed at the bones and circled around the carcass. Each heifer had to sniff the carcass before moving on. I could only watch and ask my own questions about what the heifers were thinking. Something primal was emanating between the calf's bones and the cows. Now my memory of that experience has become haunted by that patch of grass on the laneway.

In the paddock beside our farmhouse is the Maternity Paddock, where cows that are ready to calve are separated from the herd so that my brother Jack can check on them regularly. At night he might walk around the paddock with his spotlight looking for cows with their backs arched and moaning, or cows that are 'down' with milk fever or unable to deliver a large A.I. calf on their own. On my return trips to the farm, the memories of pulling calves from cows or of finding dead calves smeared across the grass are awakened. The key may be a row of tussocks, a swampy recess where the dam used to be, or the caked mud around a drain that I used to wade through. These return trips are also a way of helping me get in touch with the land. It is as if by walking the paddocks again, I can enter the land and return to what the land holds for me. Yet, these walks have become a kind of pilgrimage that I am wary of. I am reluctant to become nostalgic through my memory of childhood or of the farm that I grew up on. After all, it is cleared land with the main purpose being to breed dairy cattle from it. However, something shifts inside of me when I first see the paddocks after time away. Some emotional welling-up behind the eyes occurs when I see the cypress trees with one side shaved by the wind bordering the cattle track.

I return at different times of the year: when the mud is a foot deep around the dairy and the jonquils are wavering along the roadside; when the paddocks are shut up for silage in early spring, or when rows of round bales announce the close of the year and memories of carting in square bales on Christmas day. There have been changes to the farm that I grew up on, and it is these changes that stop me when I am walking around the farm now. The herringbone dairy has been replaced by a rotary dairy. There are sewage pits used to irrigate paddocks, more native plantations, more water troughs, smaller paddocks so that the cows can eat them out more efficiently. While it can seem as if I am seeing the farm for the first time, there is also the burden of memory that reminds me of where the windmill used to be. While every place on the farm appears to be held by memory, the loss inherent in these memories is palpable as I stand in the back paddock looking at the trees along the bush track, Mt Warrnambool in the near distance, and across to the right, the boundary fence bordering Monk's farm. Memory takes me into the paddocks, and it is the present that takes me out of them.

But it seems that it is through memories that I have been creating my own relationships within the landscape. Perhaps the act of walking through the paddocks each time I return home strengthens these relationships. Perhaps it is through the images recalled in poems that I have been able to realise a relationship between winter and cape weed slowly covering the carcass of a bull.

Walking through the hoof prints of cows seems to locate me. The hoof prints remind me of how recently the cows have walked into a particular paddock, whether the cows are pregnant or not, or if the paddock has poor drainage. In my memories of these walks, the paddocks are positioned close up, as if I can smell the mud around the gateway rising up to the lip of my rubber boots. As I walk, my eye sweeps over the paddocks and rises to the clouds collecting overhead. This is how I used to be able to tell the time: close observation of clouds and light. Just as the cows became used to the routine of being brought to the dairy for milking each day, so I became used to the weather fronts sweeping in from the west, ibis' fluttering around the overflow drain from the dairy, light dimming as the chill began to rise off the paddocks in the afternoon. I read the paddocks by signs: familiar plantations of cypress trees, a dead gum tree stranded in a paddock, the sound of traffic two miles away on the highway, and the finality of the boundary fence. Each of these signs seems to contain the present and past within them.

Walking within boundaries

While the boundary fence is a practical structure for keeping cows within a farmer's property, and for marking the dividing line between his and the neighbour's paddocks, on a psychological level the boundary fence can form an emotional enclosure to the farmer looking out over paddocks. Unlike the change enclosure brought to the villages of England in the 19thC, where the construction of fences and land clearing contributed to many farmers losing their land, the boundary fences on my parents' farm have become enclosures to our family's emotional experiences. Within those boundaries, our daily lives were played out. I grew up respecting that the land on the other side of the fence belonged to either Moloneys or Monks. And yet, as children will often do, my brothers and sisters frequently stepped through the boundary fence that was sheltered by a strip of bush. An old four-wheel drive track wound through the bush that separated our farm from the neighbours. My brothers and sisters and I walked along this bush track, exploring its shadowy recesses, willing ourselves to go further as we knew we were entering foreign territory – land that belonged to the neighbours. These walks amongst the ferns, fallen trees, rabbit burrows and furtive noises in the undergrowth were our adventures beyond the boundary fence where the paddocks felt different. Walking along the track had taken us away from the emotional hold of the farm and into something else.

I grew up looking over paddocks to fences that could be climbed through. As a boy, I often walked through the paddocks just to reach the boundary fence, put my hand on the top barbed wire strand, and look back at the path I had trampled through knee-high rye grass. Perhaps 'good fences do make good neighbours', but only if we have grown up with them.

The boundary fence is also a form of enclosure to a farmer's detailed knowledge of paddocks; what year the paddock was last ploughed, how well the cows do when feeding on that paddock. When people visit our family farm, out of habit, I point out to them the farm boundaries. Perhaps this is a form of boasting about how much land we own, not a lot in comparison to other farmers. It is also a reminder that within these boundaries experience has transformed my relationship to the paddocks. The paddock beside our dairy will always be remembered as the paddock where I almost stepped on a red-bellied black snake stretched out and asleep in long grass. The boundary fences are more than demarcation lines for farmers brooding over ancient feuds; they are physical structures that cows and farming families have become used to.

After the Ash Wednesday bushfires swept through our farm in 1983, many of the fences were destroyed. Cows wandered between farms until the boundary fences could be restored. Volunteers from across Victoria helped our family rebuild these fences. In the first few weeks after the fire, when the days were quieter due to the absence of birds, lines of treated pine posts formed eerie silhouettes against the blackened paddocks. Wire was nailed to the posts, and the new boundary fences began to suggest stability, growth, and a return to order so vital after a bushfire. Once the fences were standing, the possibility of recovery appeared to be real. Now, each boundary fence on the farm represents that period of time when we were without fences. The fences enclose my experiences in a way that memory fails to.

The ridges of old fence lines linger as the ruins of earlier years and different farming methods. Old ridges, formed by grass growing where cows cannot reach them, are exposed by new fence lines. The old ridges remain as lines of dirt ghosting the centre of a new paddock. When I walk the paddocks, I carry the old fence line in my head so that when I look over the paddock, I see two fence lines, old and new, adding another layer to twenty acres.

Working walks

When I return to the farm, I walk around trying to become reacquainted with the feel of the paddocks. This comes back to me through memories, through work, through experiences, through thinking about them. It is the one constant within my life: the feel of each paddock as I walk through it. This is the paddock with the solitary big tree in it. That is the paddock where the river used to flood, and leave us with the cloying smell of mud for weeks afterward. While a certain amount of nostalgia is involved in these walks around the farm, walking the paddocks has also become for me a means of defeating loss, of overcoming it, and returning to a place I know.

Walking around the paddocks, I am reminded of how much farm work has framed my way of looking at the paddocks. Much of my walking on the farm was spent walking behind cows. Chasing after cows and calves, walking into a head wind, rain biting at my cheeks, the stud on the collar of the oilskin flapping at my chin, walking head down like a cow, determined, stubbornly refusing to yield to weather. Often there was nowhere to shelter. The worst it could get was when the calf was too weak to walk. The cow might move ahead in response to my presence, knowing it had to move toward the dairy. On numerous occasions, I carried weak Jersey calves through mud and rain toward the dry concrete of the calf shed beside the dairy. These walks through the waterlogged paddocks were desperate walks. Often the mud around the gateway to the dairy was a foot deep. My footsteps were ungainly and awkward. No sooner had I reached the concrete of the dairy, that I dropped my bundle and the calf fell like a half full bag of potatoes onto the concrete. After it got its breath back, the calf would clamber to its feet and trot toward the udder of its mother bawling nearby.

Walking after cows and calves is a working walk. You are forced to stumble along behind the cow and calf, adopting the calf's pace, its clumsy tentative steps, and the circles it finds itself in as it attempts to walk beside its mother's flank. Apart from the frustration involved in herding cows and calves toward the dairy, what I remember most of these occasions is that I was often rushing to get the job done before footy. All I could think about was the goals I might kick, or which girls might bother to turn up to watch us play. Meanwhile the cows stepped heavily through the mud, weighted low like galleons on a dirty sea, a constant murmur emanating from their mouths as they looked around to see where their calf was. A surrogate member of this temporary family, (the calf would either be weaned or sold in three days time), I brought up the rear, shooing them along, impatient, clambering through the mud.

While a cow walks in a straight line, not moving from side to side, it also walks a deviating line. This line seems to be closely linked to two elements a cow encounters each day: the geography of a paddock and habit. Due to their physical size, cows will walk across a hill rather than down the steepest incline. Being a herd animal, a cow will mostly follow other cows along the track they walked the day before. Their cow tracks meander around bumps and ridges in the dirt, and so, the tracks suggest the intimate knowledge the cows have of each paddock. Each day the cows walk along these tracks, perhaps for security, most likely because the tracks have a more practical basis. When viewed from a distance the cow tracks describe the routine of a cow's day. One track will lead straight to a water trough. Another track will fork off toward shelter on the boundary fence, while other tracks converge like veins around a heart at the paddock's gate.

Getting the cows in on foot demands that you allow more time for the job. Walking through paddocks in rubber boots also means that you scuff your boots in the grass as you walk. I was always told that I dragged my feet as a child. No doubt, this was related to my habit of walking around in daydreams, or as Dad used to say, walking around with your eyes closed. Scuffing your boots as you walk through grass, forces connections between yourself and the dirt. You sink into the muddy patches around gateways. You feel the land as you walk on it. The lumps and holes cows make as they trudge through drains become a part of your own slippery physical terrain. Walking through their hoof prints, I come closer to walking like a cow.

The walk of a cow

If habit determines the domesticity of a cow, it is rhythm that gives a cow its unique gait. As a cow walks, her head bobs, and her back legs seem to bear the weight of her stomach as her hips sway from side to side, milk arcing across the dirt. Walking behind a herd of 300 cows instills a reflective quiet in you as your eye runs along the cows' nodding heads and ridges of their backs. For a short period, you are unified in purpose with the cows – to walk toward the dairy. Whether it be at dawn when the 'sky is beginning to bruise', or late afternoon, when the light is softened by a front moving in from the west, walking behind the cows is a meditative experience. Your mind wanders to the paddocks, the spaces around you. It is almost a dreaming state where you are caught in the midst of ritual – repeating what you did the day before, and so taking for granted the rhythms of your walk. Knowing they are about to be milked, the cows simply amble down the track paying little attention to the yelps of cattle dogs.

The hierarchy of cows can be clearly seen when the herd is walking toward the dairy. It is a mix of personality types not dissimilar to the seating arrangements of students in a classroom. The cows that give a lot of milk are usually near the front, while the young heifers and big Friesians who throw their weight around can be found at the rear of the herd. Occasionally, a Friesian might ram a small Jersey into a fence. Cows that are bullin' (on heat) will jump on each other's backs in anticipation of the event. Bullin' cows can upset a herd with their high temperatures and unsettled nature, and they are usually separated and milked first.

Apart from these occasional skirmishes, a dairy herd will mope along at its natural rhythm, ruminating like Thoreau's camel. Walking behind the cows, I often found myself adopting a similar rhythm to the way they walked; plodding along in my rubber boots, kicking at stones, happy to have this time to myself. This might be an image of the simple, rural life, yet these quiet, reflective moments were often contrasted by the busyness of farming – milking, feeding thirty calves before dark, checking on pregnant cows with a spotlight in the maternity paddock. Walking behind the cows I was always walking towards our farmhouse, the machinery shed, the washing on the five clothes' lines, and of course the dairy. As I walked towards home, I thought about this place where I lived; how strange it was in its familiarity. It was almost indescribable; this glum acceptance of where I lived, and an almost downbeat appreciation of whatever was right or wrong about the place, formed out of these moments of routine. The track the cows walked was built from local scoria, cambered for drainage, yet I still know its potholes as intimately as the cows that formed tracks around them. Dad always told my brothers and I never to hurry the cows down the track, it will upset them, put them off their milking. It is a practice Jack still carries out, although these days he idles behind the cows on his quad bike.

While it is not possible to know what a cow is thinking of as it walks, the slow, ambling rhythm of her walk, the chewing of her cud all suggest a contemplative way of experiencing the world. Perhaps a cow is a model for us in contemplation. Clearly, walking has many purposes for us; it can take us out into the world, it can take us within ourselves, it can be the process from where memories begin. It is also a way of experiencing the world without rushing, or driving as many of us do these days. Walking encourages us to look in detail at the world, and often to ruminate on how things work. At night, I dream of paddocks. Sometimes I fly over them, other times I am wading through the swampy overflow of dams after winter rains. The strongest form of intimacy I have with land is through memory. Separated from the farm I grew up on, I walk the paddocks in my head, at work, when I am walking our dog. These saunterings through the paddocks help to locate me and are a way of putting my feet in the hoof prints of cows.

Cows in India

The first time I saw cows in India
I wanted to round them up.

Yard them, milk them, close the gate
on a paddock, watch them nod along a cattle track.

Instead they wandered down alleys
up steps, along ghats, singular as saddhus.

They ate what was given – scraps, leftovers,
plastic, cardboard, even slurping their tongues

into huge woks of curries as they shambled
onward, forever onwards. Although,

I have seen a Brahman meditate in the middle
of cyclists, rickshaws, buses and beggars. Unlike

Holstein Friesians, the Indian cow is neither jumpy
or ear-tagged. They possess a quiet that is mundane

as flicking a fly with an ear. I've seen them dead
at roundabouts, have had to back away

from the trembling eye of a water buffalo.
I travelled to India, not looking for answers

just fences, gates, that farm
the cows in India lacked.

Locals even painted their horns blue,
hung flowers round their necks.

The first time I saw cows in India
I wanted to round them up.

When I was travelling through India, I learnt to appreciate the wisdom of the expression, to walk like a cow. With over one billion people, India is a country where the city streets and thoroughfares are crowded by rivers of people surging forward. Part of the shock for many travelers is how to cope with the noise and crowds as they attempt to cross the streets. Away from the main roads of the large cities, there appears to be few road rules; each person to themselves. Dusty and polluted roads are seething with trucks, buses, motorbikes, auto-rickshaws, carts powered by V8 engines, cyclists, the occasional camel, pedestrians and cows. When I first arrived in Delhi and attempted to cross the roads, I stood beside the gutter marveling at the chaos that was passing before me. Men wearing dhotis or checked shirts and flannel pants walked beside the traffic unperturbed by the noise of horns, the rumble of engines and petrol fumes. There was a timeless quality to the chaos, as if it had always been like this. Each day was a maddening traffic day where to cross the road became almost a life and death risk I knew I would have to take. Occasionally a Brahman cow rose from the side of the road and slowly plodded forward into the path of oncoming traffic. I looked on in horror at the wall of cars and trucks bearing down on the ghostly beast and then watched amazed as they swerved, blasted their horns or steered around the animal sacred to India. Often the cow would pause in the middle of a congested road, chew its cud, and glance around before slowly continuing on with its journey. The cow's expedition across the road was often followed by women in saris and children eager to cross to the other side. Just as the cow was accepted into the traffic's throng, so too were people; cars, cyclists and auto-rickshaws steering around them. Slowly it dawned upon me that if I was ever going to cross to the other side of the road outside Delhi train station, I would have to walk like a cow, slowly in a straight line, my movements predictable and recognizable to drivers who would simply realign their paths around me. And yet, having grown up on a farm walking behind cows on their way to the dairy, I was more than comfortable with the slow deliberate gait of the Brahman. In some ways, it has been how I have been walking ever since.

In those first days of arriving in India, I was very conscious of other travelers. Men and women wore beads, jewelry, striped or loose pants, faded vests, shawls and sandals. The hippie look was very much the accepted look. I felt out of place in my jeans, runners and shirts and it took me awhile to find something that was loose and comfortable but not too way out to be considered hippie. However, clothing was only one part of the perceived Western look. There was also the attitude of experience common to people who had been traveling through India for some time. It was cool to have travel stories, to have seen Rishikesh, Manali, Hampi, Pushkar, Anjuna and the host of other villages and beaches that set the experienced traveler apart from novices such as myself. The pinnacle of cool was to buy an Enfield motorbike and take your chances on the Indian roads, travelling from freak village to freak village.

In time, I made my way to some of the freak villages and one time outside a café in Pushkar I watched the social hierarchy of cool in action. There had been a group of travelers staying in Pushkar, some of whom rode Enfields. There were perhaps fifteen to twenty in the group sitting at chairs and tables outside a café. A woman who seemed to be a friend of one of the other women in the group began asking people if they wanted a coffee. At first, she asked the people sitting beside her, and insisted on paying for the coffees herself. She was English and dressed in comfortable cotton clothes, not quite seasoned India but approaching it. After her friends replied that they would love a coffee, she proceeded to ask all those around her if they would like a coffee. People turned to reply, sure if you don't mind. The woman answered, 'Great, I'll get them.' I watched as she went from table to table, to the men lounging beside their Enfields, to other women in a group who nodded their acceptance, all the while the English woman insisting she would buy the coffees. In time, the coffees arrived, were drunk and then the group, took off on their Enfields, women riding pillion behind their pony-tailed men, other members of the group walked down the dusty road chatting and laughing. The English woman returned to sit with a female friend and waved to them all as they left. I watched this whole scene with dismay. Part of me thought that she was uncool to even try to be friends with those people. Friendships can't be bought. I couldn't help empathizing with her attempts to ingratiate herself so openly with the cool travelers. However, she looked too straight and unsure of herself, exhibiting all the signs of a novice traveller to ever be accepted into the 'cool' group. It was not that the coffee would have cost much, it was more that she was prepared to be so open and hospitable to travelers who were accustomed to taking what they wanted on their terms and then moving on.

Although I had heard about the cows of India before I set foot in the country, the experience of seeing grey Brahmans plodding down crowded alleys was something else. From my experiences of milking cows on a dairy farm in western Victoria, I was used to seeing cows in paddocks with fences around them. The Friesians and Jersey cows that we milked on the farm were ear-tagged for identification and joined with the semen from an A.I. bull out of an Artifical Insemination catalogue. The cows on our farm led a docile, ordered existence. They plodded to and from the dairy twice a day, gave birth to calves from two years old, and had calves dragged from them so that the cows could continue producing high butterfat milk. By the age of seven or eight, the cows were sold to the local knackery where their bodies would be broken down into pet food. The order that we imposed on their lives appeared to be cruel and unforgiving at times, for all along, the cows were part of a business plan to make money for the farm. If a cow managed to step through a fence onto a roadside verge to feed on grass, she was quickly rounded up. The only time that I saw cows wandering freely across paddocks on our farm was after the Ash Wednesday bushfires when most of the fences had been burnt and some of our cows and the neighbour's cows were mixed up for a few days. It was a disorder that I struggled to cope with at the time. Yet here I was in India walking beside cows wandering the streets and alleys, chewing on vegetables that people had thrown to them. They didn't seem bothered about anything. Sometimes the cows sat in the middle of roads and roundabouts with the traffic raging around them. The sight of the ghostly Brahmans and occasional Jerseys not only symbolized the sacredness and spirituality of Indian life, it also suggested a different way of looking at the world. Why couldn't cows be let loose to wander the streets? Perhaps, I too could wander like a cow around India.

My interest in religion and cows coalesced in the holy city of Varanasi. I managed to find ideal accommodation staying on a small houseboat that was moored to the bank. The boat had little more than a wooden floor to sleep on, a roof where I often sat reading Pablo Neruda's *Memoir* and watched the colourful and bizarre life in front of me. The holy ghats which lead down to the Ganges are both sacred places for Hindus to make offerings, to cremate their dead at Manikarnika ghat while also being a welcome space for the locals and tourists to escape the crowded alleys and street stalls of the city. Each morning, a procession of Hindus walk down to the river to bathe, do yoga and make offerings while the dusty light of the Ganges gradually becomes sharper. Along the terraced steps of the ghats women and men grunt through the day washing and wringing out saris which are then left to dry on the steps in the dust and heat. Others collect and lay out rows of cow dung to dry on the steps so that it can be later used as fuel for cooking. Sadhus sit on vantage points overlooking the river, meditating, smoking chillums of hash and occasionally befriending tourists. While each day was similar, I never knew what to expect. One night I was walking back to my houseboat and passed a man sitting cross-legged on a ghat with a rug laid out before him. On the rug were five human skulls in a row. I stopped to check if they were real and he assured me they were from a nearby cemetery. I asked him why did he have five and he looked at me, puzzled by such a question and replied, 'Who cares? Maybe tomorrow I get two more and have seven. Do you want your fortune told?'

From the cows in India, I learnt that it was possible to travel the country without becoming caught up with the places I should visit, the clothes I should be wearing and the people I should be hanging out with. It took me a long time to realise this. It was also through travelling amongst the crowds of India alone that I learnt to accept my own space and company. Of course, it is different travelling alone as a male in India than to a woman travelling alone, yet perhaps some of the insights single travellers have in India are similar. When I first saw cows sauntering along the roads in Delhi, I felt a sense of nostalgic pride. Here were animals that I understood. Yet the sense of order I had acquired from growing up on a dairy farm was being shaken by the very cows I thought I knew; cows who were allowed to roam freely, cows who didn't have to be milked twice a day for a living, cows who were allowed to be themselves. It was a different way of looking at a cow.

The open-cut mine

It is 250 kilometres from Melbourne to Warrnambool, a distance Nanna travelled with her daughter Grace in the back of a hearse, a distance that took over two hours to drive, yet it was a distance that I could bridge in the blink of an eye from a lounge table in East St Kilda. The force of the country was something that I couldn't ignore. It returned in the weekly phone calls to Mum and Dad. It returned in the phone calls to Mick, Annie and Kathryn from our respective rented homes in Melbourne. All we had to do was ask each other, 'have you spoken to Mum and Dad this week?' for the guilts and paddocks of the country to return. Even though I lived in a share house with people who grew up in the suburbs, the country hovered like a shadow on the edge of conversations as I explained where I had come from and what my parents did. Whenever talk moved to the country, the paddocks of the Western District sewed themselves together like a quilt in my head. This was the otherland that many of us carry, of other places, of ancestral places, of places we might like to move to, places that can weigh on us as a burden and places some of us spend a life escaping from. Whenever I returned to Panmure, it was as if I was returning to an open-cut mine of memories, attitudes, feelings and a sense of being that I thought didn't need so much air. It all came back to me – the undimmed, downbeat beauty of the paddocks and cypress trees as well as the sense of myself as an outsider needing to escape many of the attitudes of locals. Sometimes it helped by returning to the farm with a friend and to take on the role of a tour guide, to show someone how I was affected by the land around me.

One weekend I borrowed a car and drove down the Princes Highway with an old friend, Karen. She had spent some of her formative years growing up in Warrnambool, and had actually been knocked down by a truck there when she was five. Karen had been sent flying across the road and onto the nature strip;

miraculously she wasn't badly hurt. For Karen, Warrnambool was a site of childhood memories, a place of the sea, wind, and the open, sunny spaces of childhood. I, on the other hand, had a darker view of the town where I was bullied at school and where traditional Catholic attitudes clashed with my liberalised view of the world. We drove around the sights of Warrnambool – Thunder Point, Lady Bay Beach, out to Koroit, Tower Hill and Port Fairy. Karen came from a political background, of student politics, feminism and also a large Catholic family. She could easily relate to the busyness of our family on the farm and she was curious about the indigenous history of places such as Tower Hill and Port Fairy. Only when I was talking to people from outside the district such as Karen could I discuss issues such as indigenous massacres, whether Aborigines witnessed volcanoes, and the darker history of white settlement in the area. Within my own family, such topics were sometimes off-limits, or if they were discussed descended into outrage and shouting. My parents had views of Aborigines that seemed to be part of a wider collective view in the western district of how much aborigines worked and what handouts they were receiving. Karen on the other hand, wanted to know about Von Guerard's painting of Tower Hill and of the Murdering Gully massacre at Glenormiston where the Whyte Brothers had attacked groups of defenceless Aborigines camped beside a water hole. Each of these places opened up something within me as I was drawn to the landscape of Tower Hill and Koroit through my childhood associations with the places. This was the knowledge that came effortlessly to me. When I was in the country, I could talk about it at length, and not only through memories, but through cows, football, the back roads between towns as well as its history of massacres and of stealing land. 'All the negative stuff,' we joked. It seemed that only by speaking with a friend who was living outside the district that I could examine some of the unpalatable truths that were avoided within my own family and the district.

I can only imagine what life for an Aboriginal person might have been like if they were living in the Warrnambool district during the 1970s. Despite the strength and family bonds that existed at the former Framlingham Aboriginal Mission, which is located twenty kilometres from Warrnambool, for former elder, Banjo Clarke and other members of his extended family, Warrnambool possessed many elements of a racist town. Banjo referred to such incidents in his book, *Wisdom Man*, when at times there were car loads of 'whitefellas' driving out from Warrnambool to Framlingham, yelling, 'Let's kill the blacks'. And yet Banjo's book is a life-affirming memoir of his love of Framlingham bush, his knowledge of Aboriginal culture, native animals and the love he had for his family. Banjo was very much a man who sought unity between Aboriginal people and non-Aboriginal people. He was liked and loved by people both within Framlingham, beyond the district and closer to home. Panmure is approximately fifteen kilometres from Framlingham and so Banjo and the Clarke family were well-known names when I was growing up. There were Clarkes who played for the Panmure football club and people that I knew who worked at Coleman's quarry on the Warramyea Road with Banjo. One of Banjo's cousins rented our farmhouse on the 'farm across the road' for a period of time. Yet despite Banjo's friendly and forgiving view on life, it did not necessarily mean life was peaceful for him.

In the 1970s, Warrnambool had one pub that was known as where indigenous people drank. The Victoria Hotel, or Vic, used to be located on the corner of Liebig and Kepler streets in Warrnambool. It was a pub where I had my first raspberry on a high stool beside Dad who was talking with his farmer friends. Naturally, many different types of people drank at The Vic yet fear and gossip were enough to keep others away and within their own sub-cultures. The genteel of Warrnambool drank at The Warrnambool hotel, uni students drank at the Cri, or Criterion hotel and anyone who wanted to see a band, crowded into the Lady Bay hotel, along with the surfies. The same type of fear and prejudice seeped through me whenever I ran into the Lombardo brothers. The Lombardos were from Aboriginal and Italian backgrounds and they terrorized boys at schools, fought in gangs at the Premier Speedway Hot Rods and in any pubs they could get into. The older Lombardo boys had sharpie haircuts, wore short striped cardigans, high-heeled shoes, and tight jeans. When they walked along the streets of Warrnambool, they spread themselves across the footpaths shuffling along, smoking and bumping into anybody who got in their way. Whenever I saw them from a distance, I crossed the road and tried not to look as petrified as I was. While my fear of the Lombardos may have had some justification at times, I didn't know them personally, nor did I know many Aborigines, apart from the footballers I met and Banjo Clarke. It was this distance and ignorance of Aboriginal lives that I absorbed from my upbringing and education, which I never really challenged within myself until I left the district. I had to leave the district to find out about the Stolen Generation as well as to recognise that racism towards indigenous people was not confined to Warrnambool. When I picked fruit in Mildura, I saw the state of some homes where Aboriginal people lived at Dareton across the Murray river from Mildura. I saw the exclusive clubs and bars that wouldn't allow Aboriginal people to enter. In the country, it seemed that it was easier to exclude an indigenous person than it was to welcome them. No doubt attitudes towards Aborigines have changed in Warrnambool and much of Australia since those days, although the memories of Geoff Clarke and what he did on the football field and off it may be remembered by many people in Warrnambool for some time. Not that one Aboriginal person can represent an ancient culture. There are many more Aboriginal people who have enriched everyone's lives in the district, Archie Roach, who lived for some time at Framlingham, being one.

I walked with Karen around our farm, following Mt Emu Creek around to the bluestone ford that bridges the river as part of a back track that connects with the township of Panmure. The river had recently been in flood. Tussocks matted with mud lay at angles from where the weight of the floodwaters had left them. Branches and posts were snagged part way up the redgums. Moss and reeds coated a fence line that receded into the still swollen waters. I took some photos of the river and tried to explain to Karen what memories I had of it flooding in the past. We returned towards the old weatherboard farmhouse on the hill, passing a dam that had been turned into a rubbish dump with rusted corrugated iron and stubbies scattered amongst the weeds. Karen asked me about my experiences of the Ash Wednesday bushfires after I told her that we were walking through the fallow paddock that I had rushed the cows onto that day. Each time I talked about the fires, it was as though I was revisiting something personal that few people knew about. Just as Karen's accident with the truck had come close to defining her life, it gradually dawned on me in the paddock with Karen, that in order to gain some distance from my memories of the fire and its effects, I would have to return to the fires and stand in these paddocks again.

I loved returning to the farm, the family house, the yellow kitchen walls, the open fire in the kitchen, the grandfather clock on the mantle piece and the view out the kitchen window to cows filing up the track towards the day or night paddocks. The house and farm were a haven of memories, of formative experiences, a place where I could be myself without trying to be. However, some days I simply needed space to myself and to walk out into the paddocks, away from people, away from the city that was in the distance like a slowly approaching rain-shadow. Only when I was in the paddocks could I see the paddocks for what they were. Only when I was walking up the cattle track that divides the paddocks on the home farm could I have a sense that these paddocks were timeless. The land had been here long before me as Gunditjamara land and it will continue to be here long after I have died. Walking the paddocks took me closer to who I thought I was and where I thought I had come from.

A writing practice that I have developed over the years involves returning to our family farm and walking the paddocks to renew my understanding and emotional connection to them. After stepping into one of our cattle tracks and walking towards a back paddock, memories begin to arise and soon I am transplanted into another time and place. Images of walking behind the cows, of chasing after a calf merge with the present view of the paddocks which might be dry and bleached if it is summer, or lush with muddy patches around gateways. Often, I am caught between the past and the present, and it is in this liminal state of being that lines for poems present themselves. I always carry a notebook with me to jot down ideas or words that come to me in the paddocks. Naturally, I take photos on my phone, but it is in the act of being in the paddocks that the outside world ceases to be, and that I can really look and take note of what I see; what has changed, which trees are collapsing, how the view of the broad river flats affects me. It is like a supercharged observation because the force of memories and close knowledge of the farm is driving how I see the paddocks, cows and trees. Following is one of my early poems that I wrote after taking notes while walking the paddocks. Some of the lines in the poem were written in my notebook as I stood in the paddock, so I refer to this poem as being written in the paddocks.

Milk fever

ibis' picking in mud
heifers crowding around to sniff my jeans

a fence post being banged in paddocks away
beneath the pine trees, a dead cow

her stomach torn apart by dogs and foxes
wind arguing with a eucalypt plantation

my father whistling from the check-out
to collect ten kids in Target

he feeds the springers pellets before they calve
last year six cows were lost to milk fever

these paddock spaces are pockets of memory
Mt Warrnambool caught in the drizzle

a cow decaying amongst mossy rocks
a dog's instinct for killing snakes

shopping on a Wednesday with 20 cents
my nerves shot by the hum of an electric fence

the isolation of the back-river flats
dark water stroked by reeds

the white plank fence that sagged around the house
barbed wire fences bowed by falling trees

wood from the wheelbarrow outside the back door
mum pregnant, on her knees, mopping the floor

dead crows and sheep skins draped over the chook shed walls
dust clouds pulling eyes to the car coming down the road

wind rising from the hole in the floor beside my bed
where the machinery shed was, where the diesel tank was

walking along the bush track
I was on edge between boundary fences

stumbling through hoof prints,
reassured by shotgun cartridges

my first drink in a hotel was a raspberry
on a high stool beside my father

I saw neighbours grinning out of the dark
shadows approaching the frosted glass

the view of paddocks and Occupation Lane
are the same, it's where I'm looking from that's changed

A paddock

Throughout 1996, I returned to RMIT to complete the Diploma of Professional Writing while working part time at a market research company in St Kilda. Like many other arts graduates and writer types, data entry was where I washed up. I spent whole days entering lines of numbers from market research surveys into the computer and sneaking breaks while the manager was not looking, to furtively read some poetry or a page from a novel I was carrying around with me. I had a window view of a car park, a hedge and beyond that the Junction Oval end of Fitzroy Street, St Kilda. Some days I went out of my mind with boredom, but I was living close to the bread line and I depended upon the $15:00 per hour that I was being paid to cover rent and bills. I had moved again, this time to a share house in Southey Street, Elwood and felt a bit old to be doing so. The two women I shared with were also in their early 30s. However, ours was a friendship that didn't last long as both women moved out within a month of each other. It may have been my lack of cooking, cleaning or the fact that I spent so much time in my room trying to write. Despite the hassle of advertising for new housemates, I enjoyed the retro feel of the red brick cottage; its blue lounge walls, Turkish carpet down the hall and the odour of incense wafting to you as you opened the front door. Most days when I had classes, I rode my mountain bike into the city, along St Kilda road, dodging car doors and maniac drivers. By the time I made it to the top end of Swanston Street and RMIT I was hot and sweaty but also exhilarated. I was trying to write a screenplay about a murder in the country and I thought I knew what I was doing.

I don't remember much of my first screen writing class, however, Alison – a fellow student – and I bumped into each other after the class at a second hand bookshop near Grattan Street in Carlton. The screen writing tutor, the late Bill Green, must have suggested some books we needed to read and like the diligent students that we were, Alison and I were in the bookshop scouring the shelves for the titles. Apparently, she had spotted me earlier in the day, on the tram into town wearing my hippie Indian vest and reading a book. She has told me since that it was a curious mix of individual fashion and reading that caught her attention, even more so when I turned up later in the screenwriting class. In the bookshop, Alison seized upon these coincidences and asked, 'Are you stalking me?' Surprised and taken aback by the direct question, I wasn't sure if she was joking or not. 'No, of course not'. Alison smiled and awkwardly, we began to talk about Bill Green and the books we were looking for.

For much of the year, Alison and I shared a friendship with another student from the course, Sam. We met at pubs and cafes to discuss our various writing projects, all the while imagining publication would only be a matter of time. One Sunday, Alison drove me out in her 1967 Ford Falcon to an exhibition at Heide Art Gallery. Sam was meant to come but she had to cancel at the last minute. I hadn't really spent a whole day with Alison before, even though we had been friends for most of the year. I found it easy to talk to her. She was direct, straight-forward, had a quirky sense of humour, and a love of religious icons and floating pens. She seemed to be her own person. We walked down to the creek, past the metal cow sculptures that I took offence to personally and thought an insult to real cows and stood in the shadows of some red gums and oaks watching the river eddy past us. The passage of water soon had us talking about our pasts – hers living in Broken Hill and my experiences in camping out at Lake Mungo. Mutual interests rippled between us and soon I was talking about Mt Emu Creek and its presence in my life. Unknown to me at the time, Alison was breaking up with her boyfriend. Yet on that day, I saw the excursion as just something to do between friends. Not having a car, meant that I was always keen to go for a drive anywhere beyond the inner city. However,

I was intrigued by the ease with which both of us could give ourselves to the moment, of looking at the creek and talking about life, regardless of the world both of us knew on the other side of Heidelberg Road.

One week later, Alison and I arranged to meet at my house and watch the Melbourne Cup with champagne. It was a warm sunny morning and I walked down to The Village Belle hotel in St Kilda to place a bet on the Cup before the crowds descended. I didn't know anything about the runners in the Cup and so like many people I was betting blind. However, a short time after I had placed my bet, the TAB computer system crashed and nobody could place a bet anywhere. People kept on assuming the computers would be brought back to life. I walked back to Southey Street to find Alison sitting in the lounge. We shared some champagne and dips before returning to St Kilda where Acland Street was abuzz with day-trippers and people walking around trying to find somewhere to place a bet. We walked through the crowds toward the shadowy part of Acland Street, past the McDonalds and up the hill past the old blocks of flats that Mick was living in when I first moved to the city in 1984, past the old church that was home to Theatre Works and down the hill to The Prince of Wales on Fitzroy Street.

The front bar was subdued with only a few drinkers present. We ordered beers and started talking. Alison's father was an Anglican Arch-Deacon in Geelong, and her mother, a mid-wife at Geelong's St John of God Hospital. Alison's religious background seemed to motivate her political ideas and together with her days studying occupational therapy at Lincoln Institute, and her involvement with the student newspaper she developed a passion for social justice causes. She grew up watching her father celebrate church services while she helped prepare the church for weddings by sweeping up confetti afterwards. Her experiences with religious ceremony and rituals was similar to mine, yet the differences between the Anglican and Catholic churches became points to debate. Alison was justifiably proud of her father's involvement in the Anglican church while I was ambivalent about my own experiences of being made to go to Mass. The fact that Alison's father, Hugh, was an Arch-Deacon unnerved me at first because the Catholic priests that I grew up with seemed unapproachable, distant and yet were given the utmost respect by their Catholic congregation. However, as I later came to know him, Hugh did exude a commanding presence and he was a most kind and considerate man, willing to let his daughter take a chance with a wayward son of a farmer.

Unlike my own family who were seemingly rooted to the paddocks on our farm, Alison's family had to move around Victoria and Tasmania every few years when her father was posted to a new parish. This constant moving as a child produced an adaptability and a restlessness in herself. She had grown up accustomed to change, of making new friends at school and of leaving friends behind, while I had grown up on a farm where often the only change was in the passing of clouds overhead. But my experiences of working on the farm had also produced a desire to travel, to meet different people and to experience life beyond my family's limits. In this sense, Alison and I seemed to be united as we were on the day by beer, drinking pot for pot throughout the afternoon and into the evening. Bar staff came and went and as the evening began, a country swing band started playing. We danced and sang to 'Ring of Fire' along with the gays, druggies, old punks and Fitzroy Street types who wandered in to have a look. At the front bar of The Prince you could be anyone you wanted to be, except suburban. It felt easy to stand beside Alison and shout in her ear while watching the disparate crowd kick on. Here was a woman who knew who she was, and where we were going, as we both staggered home up the Acland Street hill.

In 1997 we moved into a weatherboard cottage in Abbotsford. It was the first time I had lived with a partner, and had a partner who agreed to live with me. We signed the lease on a small double-fronted weatherboard in Abbotsford that looked out onto houses a car width away. The street was so narrow that cars had to pull over into a park or reverse up the street to allow oncoming cars to pass. The back yard consisted of a wonky trellis supporting an unruly grapevine, a shed made from pressed tin and an outhouse. A bluestone alleyway that once would have been used by the ice man and the night man ran along the rear of the property. On one side, our neighbours were Greek and on the other side the man's surname was Ryan. On Saturdays, we could hear the roar of the crowd from the MCG. Most days we were serenaded by the hum of Hoddle Street. Despite the galley kitchen and the sloping hallway, the house felt right. We were both excited to be starting something new.

Early in the year, Alison drove me down to Panmure in her Falcon so that she could finally meet my parents, in fact the whole family. My younger sister Rebecca was celebrating her 21st at the football clubrooms, the same clubrooms I had watched the fight break out before the unveiling of the premiership flag in 1980. Two barrels had been organized, Mick was the DJ, my brothers Jack and Kieran were behind the bar. With ten children in our family, it was never hard to organize an event or party. No doubt Alison forgot names on the night as she checked out our family, and was in turn appraised. It was not only an introduction to the Ryans that she was copping, but also local footy culture and country ways she hadn't encountered before. The men tended to stand near the bar while women and children either danced or sat by the sidelines. The gender divide fell into place like brickwork. Many of the people I had grown up with had either left the district or were elsewhere. Some had put on weight, were red in the cheeks from too much meat, others that I still knew were older, settled in their marriages and offered me a look of half-recognition. That's what it felt like on the night – I was the city person who knew the local history but who talked of a life that couldn't be contained within a football club room. Yet dancing to 'Come On Eileen' with Alison and the family afforded both of us the credibility we couldn't buy. Rebecca's favourite song gave us an excuse to let our guard down, to not expect anything but a laugh for the next three minutes. No doubt, my parents were impressed by the stylish woman I had managed to bring home to the clubrooms.

Although I had lived in share houses for over ten years around Melbourne and had become used to living with a variety of people, it was still a leap of faith for Alison to share a house with me. House cleanliness had never been my forte and bathroom hygiene often let me down. Drips beneath the toilet, hairs in the vanity, layers of dust covering the tiles – all these had to go. House cleanliness in a five person share house was often a lost battleground where one or two housemates might clean regularly while others just maintained a semblance of order in their bedrooms. It didn't take me long to see that this philosophy wouldn't work with Alison, nor would my inability to contribute more to the running of the house. Alison was a full-time professional working in mental health and so contributing to the bulk of the rent. I was working casually at a data entry firm in St Kilda. Some weeks I entered numbers into a computer full-time, other weeks, depending on the work schedule I worked two days per week. The long, stop-start bus ride up Hoddle Street twice a day did my head in. I preserved my sanity by reading, mostly poetry, such as Seamus Heaney, Philip Hodgins, Ted Berrigan and a host of other American poets. I didn't want to stay in data entry yet without the money I couldn't afford to leave. However, now that I was in a relationship that had lasted longer than my previous relationships, it was tempting to assume that if change didn't occur, life could simply roll along. I lived in a house with a beautiful woman. I had someone to eat out with. I had someone to come home to. A better job would come up sooner or later.

My way of coping with a depressing work life was to devote any spare time to writing and reading. Both Alison and I were lucky to have a room each in which to write and at night and on weekends I would spend hours reading and working on poems for what I hoped might be my first poetry collection with Five Islands Press in Wollongong. Alison was writing a novel and while our writing projects were different in form, we had plenty to talk and discuss about books, ideas and favourite writers.

The room in which I wrote had a window that looked out onto a faded paling fence and a wily jasmine bush which when it blossomed, filled the room with its sweet scent. I was reading a lot of Wordsworth at the time, going in for the English Romantic pastorals and the fervour of Coleridge and Keats. Perhaps my close-up view of the fence contributed to my inward view of the world. In contrast, Alison's writing room looked out onto a small verandah and the street. Although the street was mostly devoid of traffic, our Greek neighbours walked up and down to chat to other neighbours, while others strolled by pushing prams, walking dogs and giving Alison a sense of life as she wrote. Alison's cousin, Roz, lived nearby and together the two women strengthened their friendship with daily catch-ups and phone calls which also embedded Alison's sense of place within her family. Both Alison and Roz were outgoing, driven by a passion for social justice, and lovers of music. On the other hand, I was becoming increasingly absorbed by poetry and writers, which I knew was starting to affect my world view. It was also starting to affect the way that Alison felt I was expressing myself to her. She found it hard at times to accept my lack of actions or words to show my love for her. While I had thought that if I cooked, cleaned up the house and was around for her it might be enough, but over several talks I learnt that Alison wanted more from a partner. I had never wanted to be the silent male, unable to express his feelings. I had thought that writing poetry might demonstrate that I could show my feelings, yet my poetry was often written for myself, even when it was inspired by Alison such as the birthday poems I wrote for her – they were still poems that I wrote and had to be happy with. I had grown up in the country with a plenitude of silent, laconic males. While Dad was far from silent, often verbally praising Mum for the work she did around the house, her cooking and dealing with ten children, he rarely showed physical affection towards her. Perhaps it was because there were too many children in the way. Occasionally, he grabbed Mum in an affectionate headlock and danced around the kitchen with her, or ruffled her hair as he might ruffle a child's hair in passing. When Mum and Dad returned from the weekend away with Marriage Encounter in the 1970s, we were all slightly embarrassed by them going for a walk down the road holding hands. Hugs and physical affection had not been practised openly in our family, which might partially explain my lack of open affection to Alison. Perhaps I was just like the men with creased necks who spoke out the corner of their mouths and devoted their daily lives to cows and the paddocks. I had hoped that when I moved to the city, the inwardness of such men, their inability to say how they felt or to think about how a woman might see the world, would magically fade from my DNA and I would be the worldly male I aspired to be. I guess Alison wasn't fooled either by the trappings of writing poetry. She would never be a Dorothy typing up William Wordsworth's poems. She gave me valuable feedback on the poems that I wrote, particularly the beginnings and endings, but she wasn't impressed with the poetry world, which seemed to consist of many men who either lacked social confidence or who wanted to chat her up. Alison wanted me to surprise her with hugs and ideas, that the poems I was looking for couldn't provide. In short, she wanted me to be someone I'd thought I already was. Through our regular walks through the Collingwod Children's Farm to Dights Falls or crossing Dog Turd Bridge over the Yarra and into Studley Park or down past the abandoned clothing warehouses toward Victoria Street for Vietnamese, it gradually dawned on me that living with a person meant giving that person something besides talking about your own life. It meant letting that person into your inner life and vice versa, creating a new space, a paddock for the two of you to walk out into together.

John Forbes in Carlton

After I returned from overseas I caught up with John Forbes at a reading at La Mama where he and Alan Wearne sat in the front row of the small theatre cheering on Emma Lew. I had read some of her poems published in the journal *Otis Rush* and thought that her poems were mysterious and sharp, reminiscent of Gig Ryan's poetry. She read to an appreciative crowd and in the break John told me that he was accepting poets to tutor. Since returning from overseas I had been trying to find some direction in my life. I was working part-time and living in a share house in East St Kilda. I hadn't written much while I was overseas for two years, yet I felt that I had a lot of material within me to write about. I was also nervous about what John might think of my poems, as he wasn't exactly a lover of poems about the country. His own poems were urban, cool, mocking and loaded with clever associations. What would he say about my poems of India and overseas?

John lived in a weatherboard house in Station Street, just off Princes Street in Carlton. The house had a share house feel; messy, books stacked in the hallway, a lack of food in the kitchen. John nearly always wore a black tee shirt, jeans and he smoked throughout the tutorials. He looked at my poems and wasn't completely dismissive, yet I knew that he was reading over the poems for the money. I gave him a folder of thirty poems which I asked him to read over and then give me some feedback in future tutorials. He liked the poems set in the country, poems like 'Farm' and 'Stitching Autumn' where he could see what I was doing but he thought more recent poems about Fitzroy and India were verging on being poetical. He read through each poem, line by line, pointing out what worked and what was pretentious. He never missed a lazy word.

The tutorial sessions with John continued intermittently throughout 1994-96. I saw him every two weeks, sometimes on a monthly basis, and then I might not see him for three months, or until I had some more poems to show him. He had one of the quickest minds I knew, loaded with history, cultural references, American poetry, Australian poetry, music and Catholicism. Most of the time I was trying to keep up with him. Sometimes I just smiled and muttered to show him that I understood. Some days I walked away from his house disillusioned with what I was writing and disappointed that John hadn't told me what I had to do in order to write better. Sometimes he showed me his own poems that he was working on, poems such as 'Humidity' and 'Roman Poem' which I could only admire and wonder how he wrote them. Whether we were discussing mine or his own poems, John was expansive, generous and imbued with stories about failed Australian poets or people he had met on writing workshops who failed to produce anything. He rarely discussed his poetry friends. I read about them in their poems to John and occasionally vice versa. Talking with John was like talking with a strange uncle who had a world of experience that he occasionally tapped into, but who kept me at a distance. One day, after I arrived and we were exchanging stories of our weeks, John mentioned that he had spent the night with a woman. He looked pretty pleased for himself and I was amused by the fact that he said, 'After all this time, it's good to know that I can still do it.' At the time, I was in an ongoing relationship with Alison, and thought it both funny and sad, that John referred to sleeping with a woman the way I might have when I was in my twenties. I thought that for someone so smart and well-read, some parts of his life hadn't developed. In comparison, I was glad that I was in a relationship where I was learning, changing and considering another person's life apart from my own. I never thought of John with a girlfriend and in fact he was known by some poets as God on a bike, in reference to the bike he rode around Carlton and his standing in the Australian poetry community. Perhaps it was his combative nature that kept women wary. Perhaps it was single-minded dedication to writing poetry.

What I learnt from John about precision of words, line length, ideas and playfulness took me years to digest. When I caught a tram away from his house in Carlton, my mind would be ringing with his words, and at times it was as if I was seeing the world anew. He continued to like my poems about the country saying that they had an authority of tone while he tore apart poems that leaned on wrong choice of words, or poems that asked for more than they were worth. One afternoon, we had to walk around to Princes Street to a florist to change a fifty dollar note so that I could pay John. I had recently picked up an old Australian poetry anthology that had his poem 'Antipodean Heads' in it. As we walked we began discussing punk and early eighties music as John had recognized a line from another poet as reminding him of an old Wreckless Eric lyric. I had only heard of Wreckless Eric and didn't know his music. John began singing one of his songs and then began shouting the words at me with his face bared while he jumped up and down in a rage of passion. Meanwhile, the peak hour traffic was building up along Princes Street. I was slightly embarrassed by John's dancing and wondered what the drivers would be thinking. Here was a fortyish year old man wearing glasses with a zipped-up vinyl jacket jumping up and own, flailing his arms. Here was the unpredictability of the moment. I laughed and shook my head. While John could be sensible and articulate there was also a manic clown streak in him. If he hadn't become a poet, I don't know what else he could have been.

In 1995, I self-published a book of poetry titled *Bare Me Days*. Different to most poetry books, it came out in a limited edition of fourteen copies. The covers of the book were bound in paperbark, straight from the trees of East St Kilda. Some books had rough bark covers, others had smooth salmon covers. The poems were printed on sandstone recycle paper with Japanese Enrushyi end papers. Each book retailed for fifty dollars, a lot of money at the time, and money I could use to pay my debts to various friends.

I asked John to come down to the Village Belle Hotel in St Kilda to launch the book. He turned up late, spoke in favour of the book, citing the poem 'Waves' as the best poem he had read about taking a trip. After the launch, John read some of his own poems, which I wanted him to, as he was reading to a mostly non-literate St Kilda audience. The small crowd appreciated his poems but as is the custom, didn't buy his books that he had brought along. I gave John twenty bucks for coming down south of the river and after a beer or two he hightailed it back on the orange 246 bus up Punt Road to Collingwood.

Towards the end of 1996, I contacted John to see if he would read over a manuscript of poems that I wanted to send off to a publisher. Some of the poems were old, others more recent but I was afflicted with the worry of having them around my neck like Coleridge's albatross. I had to get rid of them. I hadn't seen John for three months at that time and he had aged quite a bit; greying around the temples, his face pock-marked and saggy. Customarily he was wearing a tee shirt and jeans and he reminded me of an overgrown student. The Station Street house was much tidier than before with a large oak table dominating the kitchen. Boxes of books still lined the hallway. I glanced at the books as was my habit and recognized *The Odyssey* and other Greek texts. John seemed distracted and was constantly looking for a cigarette. He had a three month residency coming up at Loughborough University in England, the prospect of which seemed to be unsettling him. I had publishers in mind for my book but I was realistic about the manuscript's chances. He said any publisher you can get to publish your work is a good thing. I gave him two weeks to read the manuscript, and met him a fortnight later at his house in Station Street. As I arrived at his house, John was being dropped off by a friend from 'The Age Book of the Year Awards'. Eric Beach had won the poetry section for his book *Weeping for Babylon* and John seemed to be half-pissed when I saw him. We sat down at his kitchen table, he pushed away some dishes, and through successive cigarettes

John slowly began to warm up to the poems that he had read. He didn't think I should submit the manuscript yet as there was some 'dreck' amongst the poems that worked. He was particularly tough on my descriptive city poems and on my 'poetic' poems.

A lot of the lines that he liked were from my personal life, the farm and relationships. He reminded me to follow my instincts and write in a way that nobody else does. 'Never hide what you really want to say in your poems. Bring it all out.' At one stage, we had a disagreement about a poem titled 'Going To Going To'. He thought so what of the poem and that the subject matter didn't really surprise him. I replied well, it's really a young person's poem, which John took the wrong way and told me to fuck off. He was very sensitive about his age and of appearing old. I explained that what I really meant was that I was young when I wrote the poem and so the poem has some of the weakness of youth in it. John proceeded to tell me about a woman in her late twenties who he was besotted with and who was coming to see him for poetry tutorials. He then recounted how he had been a success at university, had received a grant to complete a PHD, which was never completed, and threw himself into books and reading. Now, late in life, he seemed to regret the imbalance this pursuit of the intellect had on his knowledge of people. He said he didn't know people – knew nothing about them, and now wanted to make up for this imbalance in understanding people. To me, it felt weird to hear this from John, yet it seemed to explain for me why some people found him edgy and hard to get to know. Yet I was grateful for his criticisms and remarks, harsh as they may have been. I knew I would be getting value out of them for months to come.

In late January 1998, I called around to John's house in Station Street to give him a copy of my new chapbook, *Mungo Poems*, published by Chris Grierson's Soup publications. It was a small collection of poems, 14 pages, largely based around the long narrative poem, 'Lake Mungo', which I had written after camping beside the dry lake the year before. The other long narrative poem, written in the style of 'Farm', was 'Dry Cow Dawn', an evocation of farm rituals, cows and an interweaving between memory and farm light. The cover featured charcoal drawings of the Mungo lunettes by my sister, Kathryn. I hadn't seen John for a while and he didn't look well. He struggled to see me when I appeared at his front door and when I gave him a copy of the chapbook he held the pages close to his face so that he could read over it. His glasses were elsewhere. He spoke about his next book, which would become *Damaged Glamour* that was due for release in July, and of flying over to Cambridge for a poetry conference at Easter. I had just been to a week-long poetry conference run by Five Islands Press at Wollongong and we talked about the merits of conferences and residencies for a while. He remembered going to a poetry conference at Goolwa in the 1970s and an intense hippie named Tristram who stayed in his room and wrote 10,000 words of a novel. We talked about Melbourne and Sydney poetry scenes and he suggested Sydney poets are more friendly than Melbourne poets – 'In Melbourne, you have to second-guess everyone.' He was concerned about his appearance, believing his hunched back stopped him from being attractive to women. John was so into books and writing that his physical appearance would always be of secondary concern to him. He couldn't find his bike helmet and I followed him around the house talking while he looked for it. We said our goodbyes on the footpath. He was riding his black racing bike up to North Fitzroy and said thanks for calling around. 'Give me a ring some time'. I walked away towards Brunswick Street, relieved that I had seen John and chuckling to myself at some of the things he said. His personal life didn't seem to be going so well yet I sensed that it was poetry that would get him through.

Two days later, I was on holiday at Philip Island with friends when I saw the brief article in *The Age* – Aussie Poet dies of heart attack. I couldn't believe it and I stumbled around in shock for some time. The fact that I had only seen John two days before made his death appear so much more shocking and unbelievable. One day we were sitting around his wooden kitchen table discussing poetry and two days later I would not have the opportunity to ever do that again. It seemed so unfair that he died at an age before being given some of the dues for his writing. John was a man who had given his life to writing poetry, perhaps naively believing in the maxim – if you look after your poetry, life will look after you.

From the first time I had met John at RMIT in 1989, my friendship with him had been a teacher/student friendship which I was quite happy to have. In many ways, I was lucky to have the one-on-one tutorials with him after I returned from overseas in 1994. Without his teaching and blunt instructions, I could have ventured into the territory of a 'hippie poet' – someone who thought that they were much better at writing poetry than they actually were. I was deeply saddened by the circumstances of his life and of how a person who had committed so much of their life to writing and thinking about poetry could die so suddenly, broke and unable to sustain a long term relationship. Despite all this, the lessons and help that John gave me have continued to resonate down the years. In 1999, a year after his death, I was on holiday in Paris and, like many tourists, I ventured to the bookshop, Shakespeare and Co. On the door was a poster for *The Iowa Review* from the U.S listing several poems by John Forbes in its winter issue. Finally, justice was being done.

John's death both saddened and galvanized me. His early death reminded me that it was possible to be a well-respected poet and still have life's circumstances rob you of due recognition. Not that recognition is the only reason poets write. It is more that John undoubtedly had more poems to write and he wasn't able to. His death reminded me that I needed to hurry up and have my first proper book of poetry published, otherwise I might miss out and this whole idea of writing could just be a fantasy. At the beginning of 1998, I didn't have enough poems for a collection, yet with the poems I had written about Ash Wednesday, I sensed a body of work could be emerging.

Later that year, I attended The Wollongong Poetry workshop run by Ron Pretty and Five Islands Press at Wollongong University. The workshop was a revelation for me in many ways. Not only did I meet other early-to-beginning poets from around the country, I was also exposed to the teaching of poets such as Kevin Brophy, Ron Pretty, Joanne Burns and Carol and Richard Frost from the U.S. I loved the workshops; the reading aloud of poems, the varied poems from poets and the advice each of the poetry tutors gave us. At last I was surrounded by like-minded people who spoke openly about writing poetry, other poets that I had read, and of taking writing poetry seriously. In one session with Carol Frost, she was talking about the American Poet, Frank O'Hara. She made reference to his poem, 'Why I am not a Painter', a poem that I knew. While she spoke, a light bulb moment occurred and I thought, I've got to write a poem called 'Why I am not a farmer'. The minute I thought of that title, I immediately thought, no, I couldn't, yet the idea wouldn't go away. After the session, I returned to my room and thought well, I will just make some notes about the idea. A whole range of negative ideas and images about farming poured out of me. I wrote a page and my heart was racing. I couldn't write a poem like this could I?

Sometime after John's death I went to a poetry workshop held at Alan Wearne's flat in South Yarra. I had been to some of his workshops previously, but not on a regular basis. In the workshops, various poets such as Emma Lew, Jan Stumbles, Clare Gaskin and others read their poems and received modest criticism until Alan held forth and often dissected the poem line by line. I never quite knew what Alan would say as his face often belied his feelings or he would smile and exclaim, 'I see what you mean, but,' after which he would often uncannily add, 'I think you might need to read some Louis MacNiece or Carlos Drummond De Andrade.' Alan was generous with the books that he lent and he was often accurate in his criticisms. Praise was hard won, yet when he enjoyed the near-finished draft of *Why I am not a Farmer* I was relieved, that just maybe I was writing about the Western District in a way that hadn't been done before.

A town called malice

The songs that greeted me as I stumbled down the hall on a Saturday morning often affected my day. Sometimes it was the mood generated by the song, the memories that a song could dredge up for me, or a song that I hadn't heard in a long time suddenly reminded me of how good it had been. I rarely listened to commercial radio, mainly 3RRR and 3PBS, the public radio stations of Melbourne. One morning, RRR was playing 'A Town Called Malice' by The Jam. Once again, I was hooked by its upbeat rhythms, the infectious keyboard and the clamouring urgency of Paul Weller's voice. It was the song that urged you to become involved in life, to dance in the confined space of our galley kitchen in Abbotsford. It was also a song that took me back to the bedroom that I shared with Mick where I first heard The Jam and it was a song that infected my day with a dose of political anger. In short it was a coach's address to go out and take the day on!

With the lyrics about bored housewives and small town England echoing in my head, I walked up toward the Dan O'Connell in North Carlton later that day to read in their open section. The Dan was just one of a number of pubs that held poetry readings; others being The Evelyn and The Perseverance hotels in Fitzroy. The audience migrated between the three pubs as did some poets who might read at two pubs in an afternoon. Poets such as Ken Smeaton, Kerry Scuffins, Grant McCracken, Kerry Loughrey, John Ashton, Rex Buckingham and Patrick Alexander sometimes read to adoring crowds. Sometimes the noise in the bar was so loud that poets had to yell, which was never hard for some poets. Other times, a feature poet might be reading to an audience of four, each of them more interested in reading their own poem in the open section. I was always amazed at the confidence some poets had in reading their poems aloud, particularly when I thought their poems needed a lot more work.

I was always incredibly nervous when I read, and I often took swigs from a small bottle of whiskey outside the pubs so that I had the confidence to walk inside, strike up a conversation with strangers at a table and read the poems I had been labouring over all week. When I read poems about Ash Wednesday or the country, people listened, but I often felt out of place amongst their poems of inner city life, intense introspection or drinking. It was almost as though I was a farmer reading his poems to an urban audience who knew little about farming. There were a lot of poems about drinking and it was often a blokey atmosphere at The Dan where women were cheered loudly for their poems and then sometimes chatted up at the bar. After I finished my reading, I'd hightail it out of The Dan. I needed the fresh air of the street and to be away from the second-guessing nervous poetry conversations. I was happiest out walking, of returning to the anonymous state of observing, and of watching the city bubble around me.

Periodically, I met up with Murph for a drink and a discussion of the legacies that the Western District had bequeathed us. Murph grew up near Ellerslie, about twenty minutes drive from Panmure. He had the blonde haired look of a surfie yet he spoke with the provocations of a person who had read history and politics. I was drawn to his knarky view on life, his sense of humour and his embedded family values. Our drinking sessions were often long and entertaining and invariably we met up at The Public Bar in North Melbourne which was a no-frills bar with footy on a wide-screen catering to backpackers and drinkers until 7am. We drank stubby for stubby looking out onto Victoria Street and the Markets. It wasn't a grand view, in many ways it was grimy, polluted and built-up, with the only beauty being the sunsets over the terraces of North Melbourne in summer. But with Murph my view was elsewhere – to the west and the entertaining stories he told with his broad grin and eyes darting around the bar for someone he might recognize. At the time, he was working as a tour guide for rich tourists, driving them around the Great Ocean Road and up into the Yarra Valley wineries. His descriptions of the well-heeled tourists getting tanked and leaving a mess on his buses were cutting as was his scorn for the politicians of the day. Together we laughed at John Howard in his ridiculous akubra hat, scorned his treatment of Aborigines and of lying to Australians about refugees throwing a child into the ocean in order to be rescued. In this sense we were probably like many other people out for a drink at The Public Bar, however the other area that bound us and perhaps separated us from some of the private schooled drinkers standing around us, were our experiences of the Western District. Each of us had a cross of sorts to bear. Murph's experiences at St Pat's College in Ballarat had shown him what some boys would do to survive such an aggressively masculine environment. One of his friends from Noorat dumped Murph the week after they started at St Pats when the friend realized he would survive better if he was friends with the bully, rather than with Murph. Murph knew about the stories of abuse relating to Gerald Ridsdale, and at the time, such stories were still swept under the carpet by the Catholic church. I had never been able to forget about some of my own experiences at CBC in Warrnambool, and while neither Murph nor I were directly abused, we had seen what happened to boys who either didn't measure up as toughs in the school yard, or who had been abused by a Christian Brother. The longer we drank, the more detailed our discussions became on various people from our Western District. While we had both played football into our twenties, neither of us aped the football heroes that some country towns seem to revolve around. Both of us had seen what the adulation of footballers had done to some men and women. Like the codes and rules within the school grounds, a successful football career translated into acceptance within a country town, as long as the masculine boundaries of behaviour were adhered to. Yet the fall from grace for footballers could be swift such as the local footballer jailed for child abuse. While such codes have been challenged in more recent times, Murph and I knew that we had to leave behind the conservative politics and social conformity of our country towns if we were to survive. Our families were not wealthy pastoralists, or western district families who sent their children to board at Geelong Grammar. Our families were from dairy farms on back roads who sent their children to the local Catholic school, and whose parents watched their children hightail it to the city. Our towns were not quite towns of malice, yet there were enough days of ennui for Murph and I to realize the necessity of escape. As much as I felt at home as soon as I glimpsed Mt Elephant, Mt Noorat, Mt Warrnambool and Mt Emu Creek, the timeless appeal of the Western District landscape could only lure me. Our families drew us back along the Princes Highway to Ellerslie and Panmure yet neither Murph or I could live there. Like the Catholic church, the Western District was both a curse and a blessing; an otherland that both of us felt compelled to return to, and leave.

Blister country

The anger of living in the country
remains with you, becomes a hard stare
across a playground, a bar, a supermarket checkout.
Here, we look after our own.
Of talking business with men, problems with women.
Of being bashed in pub toilets
of being jeered at for wearing black
of fleeing each weekend, the town closing for the footy.
Saturday night, four men lined up at a urinal,
nobody speaks.

Stunted trees, lemon-tinged rye grass
lava blisters formed by pressure from below.
A moonscape of low-lying paddocks
the country nobody inhabits.
A wild place, I'll nurture, carry to the grave.
There's nothing flash in hummocks of rock
Old Crusher Road snaking through Harman's Valley,
and what became of the lava flow.

Here, wind is another language to rub against
buffeting faces, breaking capillaries across cheeks.
Where fence lines hum off-key,
a place so strange and compelling
a boy rides a motobike down the paddock to shoot himself.
The tension between rains prises the dirt apart,
crickets scurry.
Some kind of friction rises from within.

Afterword

Many times after milking in the morning or at night, I have looked out of the dairy to follow the line of milkers plodding up the cattle track towards their day or night paddock. Often there would be one or two cows standing on the track, just looking towards the paddocks. The cow might stand like this for five minutes, chewing its cud and then move on. I have often stood looking at a cow and wondered what was it thinking. Did it have thoughts? I was always drawn towards these thinkers or contemplaters looking out at the world. Something drew these cows to stop, stand and consider. And so it is, and has been, when I write that I find myself staring out the window, prompted by one thought which I invariably lose for the random study of the neighbour's prunus tree. Flannery O'Connor has said that a 'writer should never be afraid of staring, for it is when a person looks closely that things can be remembered or something can be revealed later'. Looking at the world closely is something that we do as children with all the innocence attached to that way of looking. But staring at a paddock or an urban street is also an act of contemplation, of considering or ruminating. The very act of remembering is an active process and no matter where I am in the world, I can easily run my mind over the paddocks on our farm. Nothing is missed. The paddocks seem to be imprinted within me yet from where I look the paddocks invariably change.

Writing this memoir of growing up on a dairy farm in the present climate only seems to emphasise the difference between the 1970s and 1980s and the year 2020. Climate change is affecting the world and in particular the dairying landscape in Australia. Many farmers are leaving the industry due to poor milk prices and costs for irrigation or fertilizer and grain feed needed to keep a dairy farm running. Plus the contribution that cows make to greenhouse gases through the release of methane, around 10% of Australia's greenhouse gas emissions according to the Department of Agriculture (2019), ensures that dairying may not be a long-term industry for some. Together with prolonged seasons of drought and the devastating bushfires in NSW and Victoria throughout 2019/2020, the ongoing effects of climate change in Australia may make dairy farming unviable and foolish to many. And yet, in the western district of Victoria drought does not appear to have the same prolonged effect that it does in NSW. Higher rainfall, richer soils and greater quantities of fertilizer spread over paddocks helps to create the impression that dairying can be a worthwhile industry in which to run a family farm.

Cows are creatures of habit; of being milked twice a day, a herd animal that follows other cows into a paddock, towards a trough or to shelter beneath trees in the middle of the day. Healthy cows can produce up to twenty litres of milk per day. Cows respond to affection, pats and the regular presence of milkers. Strangers can upset a cow in the dairy and lone cows introduced to a herd can be shunned by the more dominant or older cows. Perhaps I absorbed too much from cows so that now my affection towards them is generated by nostalgia. While I see the walk of a cow as a model for slow living and for reflecting upon life rather than reacting to it, I do admit that I am not a person who walks great distances. I enjoy bushwalking, walking our dog around the suburbs and going for solitary walks but I am not the intrepid walker that Robert MacFarlane writes about in his many books on walking. I walk when I am working on a poem, either before the first draft where ideas are rehearsed in my head or after I have completed a draft of a poem. On these walks, lines I have been troubled by often knit themselves together or I might decide to omit a stanza altogether. It is the act of walking as a creative act that frees up my thinking or as MacFarlane says 'walking as enabling sight and thought rather than retreat or escape'. For me, walking is connected with creativity, not with getting fit.

Since my first book, *Why I Am Not a Farmer*, was published in 2000 I have been lucky to have had six books of poetry published. While each book has been an achievement, sometimes a struggle to be published, there wasn't the same level of joy as when the first book was published. Regardless of it being a thin 32 page book from Five Islands Press, it was a book that validated my writing and the experiences of writing in bedrooms for the previous ten-fifteen years. For so long, I had sat at desks drafting and redrafting poems, had written scraps of poems that were never finished, had read numerous poetry collections and had wondered all along if I would ever see my poems in print. It had been a risk to write poetry, not only to see if I could write worthwhile poems, but also because there was very little money to be made from it. The very fact that a male from our family of ten children had a poetry collection published went against the grain of familial and local expectations. I had been a footballer and a labourer. I wasn't a farmer and I became a writer who wrote poetry. Very few people that I knew read poetry, least of all Dad, who initially thought it might be something I would do for awhile and then forget about – like when I wanted to become a radio DJ. However, with some of the poems in my first collection, *Why I Am Not a Farmer*, Dad could see his world reflected, and so the very nature of our family existence was on record, albeit from my perspective.

When we lived on the farm at Panmure, Mum and Dad often walked along Vickers Road towards the bridge over Mt Emu Creek to let their tea go down. Sometimes I watched them walk slowly up the hill from our front garden. They were two dark clothed figures gradually fading into the gravel of the road and the dusty bleached browns of the paddocks. What did they talk about? What moments did they share? For a period they would be gone completely and the road would be empty as it was most nights. Nobody but our neighbours, the Monks, or my parents drove along Vickers Road. In the soft light after tea, I watched cows nosing the grass and ambling in rows across a paddock. Their eating of grass, their production of milk was a twenty-four hour cycle. Before long, Mum and Dad were returning slowly down the hill toward the large drain that ran from our bull paddock through a culvert under the road. Their slow walking seemed to be in time with the country and with the cows.

Mum and Dad have since moved off the farm to retire, at first in the township of Panmure, and then to live in Warrnambool. My brother Jack manages the farm at Panmure with his own family and the farm has expanded through leasing arrangements to be nearly one thousand acres in size. No doubt the house has changed internally since we lived in it, but its exterior remains the same, as does much of the farm. Occasionally, I drive Dad out to the farm to look at the paddocks and at the farm that used to be his. I expect his heart lifts when we turn down Vickers Road and he looks at the green pick on the river flats, a herd of Friesians ruminating in the sun. From a stubborn dream he had as a boy, he has managed to own his own farm and leave it to one of his sons.

Predictably, there is a sense of loss or change when I walk the paddocks, and yet I can still see that boy of six walking around the track past the petrol tank. No longer do I have to walk the farm to see where I'm going. I know these hills and ridges. I know how to walk freely, like a cow.

www.ingramcontent.com/pod-product-compliance
Lightning Source LLC
Chambersburg PA
CBHW021432080526
44588CB00009B/502